Scriptin' with JavaScript and Ajax:

A Designer's Guide

CHARLES WYKE-SMITH

Scriptin' with JavaScript and Ajax: A Designer's Guide

Charles Wyke-Smith

New Riders
1249 Eighth Street
Berkeley, CA 94710
510/524-2178

Find us on the Web at www.newriders.com
To report errors, please send a note to errata@peachpit.com

New Riders is an imprint of Peachpit, a division of Pearson Education

Development Editor and Compositor: Beth Bast
Project Editor: Nancy Peterson
Technical Editor: Christian Heilmann
Production Coordinator: Hilal Sala
Copy Editor and Proofreader: Anne Marie Walker
Marketing Manager: Glenn Bisignani
Indexer: Joy Dean Lee
Cover Design: Aren Howell
Cover Production: Hilal Sala
Interior Design: Mimi Heft

Technical Note: This book was produced using Adobe InDesign. Code was developed in Adobe Dreamweaver. Graphics were designed in Adobe Fireworks and Adobe Photoshop. Screenshots were taken with SnapzProX by Ambrosia Software.

ISBN 13: 978-0-321-57260-8
ISBN 10: 0-321-57260-2

9 8 7 6 5 4 3 2 1

Printed and bound in the United States of America

For Beth

Acknowledgments

I want to first thank Nancy Ruenzell, Peachpit's publisher, for the opportunity to write another book on the New Rider's imprint, and Michael Nolan, Peachpit Acquisitions Editor, for encouraging me to complete the *...in'* trilogy.

Nancy Peterson, my Project Editor, has been a wise and gracious advisor while keeping me focused on the time deadline, which I have actually met. Our weekly conference calls have been a wonderful source of guidance and encouragement, and have greatly contributed to this book's direction and focus. To you, Nancy, my sincere thanks, and I hope we will meet in person sometime soon.

Thanks go to the editorial and production team at Peachpit: to production editor Hilal Sala for her attention to the myriad details getting the pages ready to go to press, to Anne Marie Walker for her copyediting and proofing, and to Joy Dean Lee for the indexing.

Several programmers have worked with me on this book. Michael Rosier assisted with the initial table of contents and some early code examples. Mark Turansky has been a valuable source of advice and ideas, and developed the framework examples in Chapter 6. Austin Markus of Ithus in San Francisco, who was the technical editor on my book *Codin' for the Web*, wrote the PHP and much of the jQuery for the Author Carousel example in Chapter 7.

My sincere thanks go to Chris Heilmann, International Development Evangelist for the Yahoo! Development Network and JavaScript genius. He has been invaluable as the technical editor of this book, and I am grateful to him for his detailed and always humorous feedback on the code. He also developed the YUI example in Chapter 7. I am glad that he is such a night owl because I have often been able to videoconference with him on Skype in the early hours in London where he lives to get advice when working late here in South Carolina. It has been a great experience working with Chris, and I thank him for the time he has given to this project.

Special thanks goes to Scott Fegette, Technical Product Manager for Dreamweaver at Adobe, for his ongoing support and encouragement.

A quick shout-out goes to David Sarnoff, Sean Rose, and Mike Harding, fellow musicians in my band Mental Note (www. mentalnoteband.com). Guys, being able to get out and play from time to time during the development of this book has helped keep me sane, and I appreciate your friendship and the time we spend making music.

Once again, a big hug and a kiss for my wife Beth, who has expanded her role from my previous books to Development Editor on this one, and who has advised me on every aspect of it. She has edited the drafts of the chapters, corrected my grammar, reedited my run-on sentences (yes, still doing that), and had me rework my explanations until I produced something she could understand. She has coordinated the deliveries of the numerous rounds of chapters with the Peachpit team, developed the diagrams from my sketches, and, not least, laid out the entire book in its final form in Adobe InDesign. Thanks to you, sweetie, we did it again!

To my lovely daughters, Jemma and Lucy, we once again have had less time together while I have been writing, and now it's time for our vacation. I love you so much, appreciate your patience while I have been shut in my office writing, and look forward to enjoying the rest of the summer with you both.

Finally, I want to thank you, my readers, for buying my books and for sharing your experiences using the techniques and ideas in them. I'm delighted to have finally completed this JavaScript book in response to all of you who have encouraged me to write it.

—Charles Wyke-Smith
Charleston, South Carolina, July 12, 2009

About the Author

Charles Wyke-Smith is the author of *Stylin' with CSS: A Designer's Guide* and *Codin' for the Web: A Designer's Guide to Developing Dynamic Web Sites.* Charles has been involved in print, multimedia and Web design for over twenty years. He founded PRINTZ Electronic Design in San Francisco in the mid-eighties, an early all-computerized design studio, and was a pioneer in interactive media development.

He has been creating Web sites since 1994 and has provided Web design and consulting service to companies including Wells-Fargo, Benefitfocus, ESPN Video Games, and University of California, San Francisco.

His work today focuses on online application development, with an emphasis on user experience, information architecture, and interface design.

An accomplished speaker and instructor, Charles has taught classes in multimedia interface design and has presented at many industry conference.

He lives with his wife, Beth, and two daughters in Charleston, South Carolina.

Contributors

Christian Heilmann is a geek and hacker by heart. He's been a professional Web developer for about eleven years and worked his way through several agencies up to Yahoo!, where he delivered Yahoo! Maps Europe and Yahoo! Answers.

He's written two books and contributed to three others on JavaScript, Web development, and accessibility. He managed teams in the U.S., India, and the U.K. to release dozens of online articles and hundreds of blog posts in the last few years.

He's been nominated Standards Champion of the Year 2008 by .net magazine in the UK. Currently he sports the job title International Developer Evangelist, spending his time going from conference to conference and university to university to train people on systems provided by Yahoo! and other Web companies.

Austin Markus is a Web application developer and principal of Ithus Digital in San Francisco.

He first got excited about computers and programming in the pre-Internet days, running a BBS out of his bedroom and marveling when people connected from around the country and the world. His early work included developing ActionScript demonstration applications for Macromedia and a Telex-to-Internet publishing system for the San Francisco Chronicle.

Today, he develops applications from e-commerce stores, to content management systems, to social networking applications.

Austin is a big believer in Open Source and has contributed modules to Drupal and jQuery among others. He thinks the next big thing will be pervasive computing and augmented reality. To this end, he is presently working on an application for the Android mobile platform to bridge the gap between the online and real world.

Contents

Introduction

Scriptin' with JavaScript and Ajax is the third in a series of books aimed at introducing designers and programmers to the process of developing browser-based interfaces. The first, *Stylin' with CSS*, focuses on the structure and styling of content, and the second, *Codin' for the Web*, focuses on the three-tier architecture of browser, middleware, and database that are the core components of almost every Web site.

The focus of this third book is JavaScript, and a JavaScript-based programming technique called Ajax that dramatically improves communication between the user's browser and the Web server. The goal of this book is to teach you how to use JavaScript and Ajax to develop sophisticated and responsive user interfaces for today's Web sites and online applications. Ajax has given a new purpose to JavaScript, and virtually all of today's successful sites and online applications use JavaScript and Ajax extensively.

About This Book

My objective in writing this book is to provide you with a solid understanding of how JavaScript is written and the possibilities it offers, and how to develop robust and compact code that runs reliably in all modern Web browsers. Through numerous examples that build on each other, you will develop the understanding and skills to use JavaScript to improve the user experience and performance of the Web sites you develop. All the examples can be readily added into your own pages, which is a great way to start using JavaScript. Along the way, I'll show you techniques, shortcuts, and pitfalls learned from the development of many projects.

As with my other books, the focus is on developing practical, professional, and, hopefully, profitable skills.

While this is a book about JavaScript, it has, by necessity, a broader scope. JavaScript cannot be used in isolation: Its purpose is to enhance a Web page with behaviors. It acts on a page's structure (the HTML markup) and its presentation (the CSS styling) to provide interactivity in what would otherwise be a static page. Through Ajax interactions, JavaScript can also request content from the server by communicating with the middleware that generates pages and manages communication with the database.

This means that HTML, CSS, and server middleware (I use PHP in this book) must all be considered when discussing JavaScript. Therefore, don't be surprised to find that many pages of this book illustrate HTML, CSS, and PHP code: This code is the context within which JavaScript operates. I provide detailed explanations of the purpose of such code, but you will benefit most from this book if you already have a good grounding in HTML, CSS, and PHP or another middleware language such as .NET or Java.

Also, let me state what this book is not. First, it is not a comprehensive coverage of JavaScript. While I show plenty of real-world examples using coding techniques that are far beyond the basics, I don't cover the most advanced topics such as prototypal inheritance and closures. However, after reading *Scriptin'*, such subjects will certainly be more understandable to you, and throughout, I provide many references to resources that can further grow your skills. Second, I don't provide details of every property and method of every object in the JavaScript language. There are many excellent reference books and online resources available that can provide you with that information, and I mention many of them in this book.

About JavaScript

JavaScript is the only programming language that runs in the browser, and you cannot build a modern Web application without it. Today's users expect forms to be validated as they fill them out, on-demand content delivery without waiting for new pages, and a general application-like look and feel to the interface. JavaScript is the key to meeting these expectations.

The lines between Web sites and online applications are becoming blurred: Is Facebook a Web site or an online application? It's accessed over the Web but its interface and its ability to update data without page refreshes give it characteristics of a desktop application. Certainly, I use the term Web site and online application rather interchangeably in this book—it may be becoming a meaningless distinction.

As part of its new role in powering interactive interfaces, JavaScript has recently been getting the kind of attention from browser developers that CSS received some years ago in an effort to standardize its implementation across all browsers. CSS is now much improved in this regard, but JavaScript still has many differences in the way it works across the various browsers. These differences are a throwback to the days of the "browser wars" where Netscape and

Microsoft spent the late 90s developing competing features in an effort to differentiate their virtually identical products.

JAVASCRIPT'S W3C AND MICROSOFT IMPLEMENTATION MODELS

A legacy of the browser wars is two different implementations of JavaScript. Microsoft browsers adhere to what I will refer to in this book as the Microsoft model, and other browsers, most notably Firefox, Safari, and Opera, follow a standard that I refer to in this book as the World Wide Web Consortium (W3C) model.

The most significant differences between the W3C and Microsoft models are in three crucial areas of JavaScript's implementation: the event object that records the location (which element) and the type (mouse click, key press, etc.) of user actions; the `XMLHttpRequest` object that manages Ajax requests; and the `load` event, which enables a page to be initialized with JavaScript-driven behaviors as soon as it arrives in the browser. In this book, I'll illustrate ways your code can detect whether the user's browser implements the W3C or Microsoft model and respond appropriately.

These browser differences, the often verbose nature of JavaScript code, and the demand for more sophisticated interactions in the user interface have driven the development of numerous JavaScript frameworks to address these issues. Frameworks, or libraries as they are often known, provide extensive prebuilt functionality for common tasks, sophisticated interface components, cross-browser compatibility, and, in many cases, virtually a new language that runs on top of JavaScript. Frameworks can dramatically reduce development time, and I'll show examples of several frameworks and their capabilities in the later chapters.

ACCESSIBILITY

For your Web site to reach the widest possible audience on the widest range of devices, JavaScript should be used only to enhance already functional Web pages. No site should entirely depend on JavaScript for its operation: This is an issue of accessibility that I discuss in Chapter 1. Unfortunately, many sites today are totally dependent on JavaScript for their operation. Such sites are unusable by those who cannot run JavaScript in their browsers, who are visually impaired and rely on screen readers, or who are physically incapable of the gestures that a JavaScript-driven site may require, such as using the mouse to drag and drop an element.

In this book, you will learn how to design Web sites that provide the best experience to users with JavaScript, and yet still provide an acceptable and functional experience for those users who, for whatever reason, cannot run JavaScript in their browsers or cannot interact with the more complex interface features JavaScript can provide. In Chapter 7, I show two projects that make extensive use of JavaScript and Ajax, yet both of these projects are still useable if JavaScript is not present.

Getting Ready to Use This Book

If you were to ask me, "How should I go about learning JavaScript from this book?," here's what I would say.

Start by just reading through the book. Find somewhere quiet when you have a couple of hours and skim through it. Don't worry about understanding everything the first time, just become familiar with the content of the book and the examples it contains. If you have a computer at hand so you can review the examples on the *Scriptin'* Web site as you read, so much the better.

Take time to study the code. Download the zip file of the code from www.scriptinwithajax.com and unzip it. Inside the folder called "code," you will find all the examples organized by chapter. It is very helpful as you review the examples in the book to have the associated code open in a code editor so you can see the wider context of the part of the code that I am discussing.

You can run the code on your own server. If you copy the entire code folder onto a Web server running PHP and type the URL of the code folder into the address bar of your browser, the `index.php` file in that folder will load and display links to all the examples.

After you are familiar with the code, take the examples and start incorporating them into your own projects. When you start to modify the code for your own purposes, your skills will develop quickly.

The code you write rarely works the first time, but with tools that give you visibility into what your code is doing, you can rapidly bridge the gap between what you think the code is doing and what it is actually happening. Reconciling these two states is called debugging.

To help you write and debug your code, I recommend you take the following steps to set up your computer.

1. Download the Firefox browser at www.getfirefox.com and install it. Firefox offers good development tools and is probably the most standards-compliant browser. Once you have your code working in Firefox, test it on other browsers and make any necessary adjustments.

2. Download and install two essential Firefox add-ons, also from www.getfirefox.com:

   The Web Developer toolbar. Search for this toolbar in the Add-On section of the site or go directly to https://addons.mozilla.org/en-US/firefox/addon/60. This toolbar allows you to turn JavaScript and CSS on and off as you work, validate your HTML and CSS as you write it, outline all the elements on the page to show their relationships, view a list of the ancestors of any element of the page, and much more. To me, its most indispensable feature is View Generated Source, which allows you to view markup that is dynamically generated by your JavaScript code as it runs.

   Firebug. Firebug provides JavaScript error reporting and allows you to insert breakpoints in the code so that at any point you can have the code stop running and see the state of all variables and objects in the JavaScript. I've mostly used alert dialogs in the examples when illustrating variable checking because it makes for nice simple screenshots, but Firebug is really a much better way to go once you are into serious development work. Check out www.digitalmediaminute.com/screencast/firebug-js for a good video tutorial on using Firebug.

I haven't attempted, and there isn't room, to show and explain every line of code of every example. Instead, I focus on the parts of the code that illustrate the topic I am discussing at that point. However, what I have done is ensure that all the concepts illustrated in the code have been explained at some point, and that the code is well commented so you can understand it.

Feedback Is Welcome

I know that despite my best efforts and the dedicated team of people who have worked on this book, it may contain errors and omissions that you, my dear readers, are so adept at finding and reporting to me. I will post any errata that are found, so please report these to me on the *Scriptin'* Web site. You are also welcome to write with comments, or to send me URLs of your work. I look forward to hearing from you.

Software-as-a-Service

I think it's clear that we are moving steadily to the point where "shrink-wrapped" software that is installed on the user's computer will all but disappear. It will surely be replaced by Rich Interface Applications (RIAs) where the interface runs in the browser and the Web server manages access to a variety of real-time data sources. This change in how software is conceived, designed, and delivered allows applications to constantly evolve rather than being released in discrete versions, and gives designers and developers nearly limitless scope when imagining and building new online experiences.

The already well-established Software-as-a-Service (SaaS) model, which makes possible such companies as Saleforce.com and Zoho. com, gives users on-demand, pay-as-you-go access to RIAs where they formally had to make expensive investments in monolithic desktop software programs. For the foreseeable future, these new RIAs will be powered by JavaScript, and I hope that *Scriptin'* will give you the knowledge, confidence, and inspiration to make your own contribution to this new and exciting era of the Web's evolution.

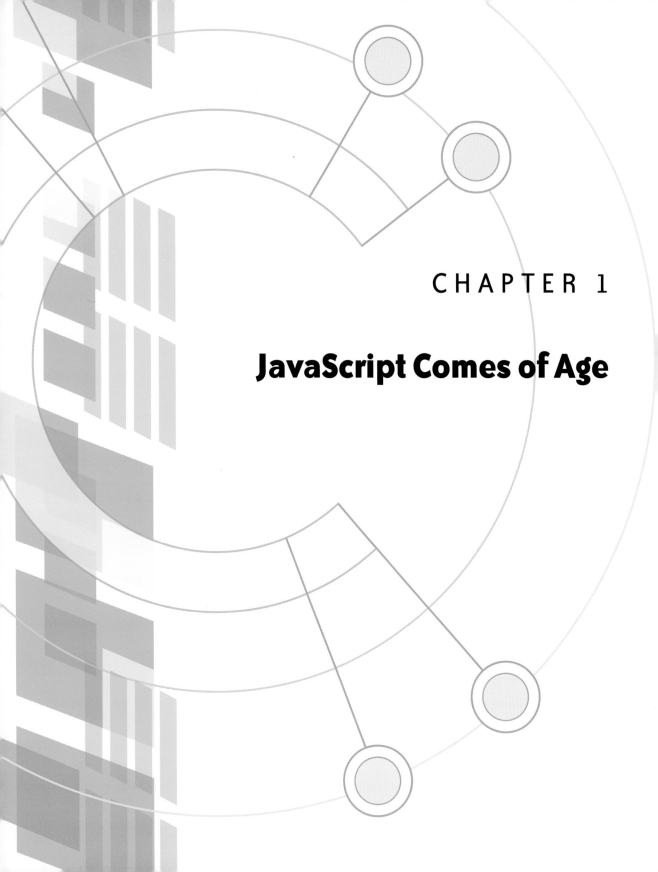

CHAPTER 1

JavaScript Comes of Age

MASTERING JAVASCRIPT is an essential skill for every Web designer. This wasn't always true, but JavaScript has taken on a new and important role in modern Web sites. For any interface designer or for any Web engineer who works with the presentation layer, it is now as important to know JavaScript as it is to know HTML and CSS.

While HTML has traditionally enabled you to create a structured Web page, and CSS enabled you to give it a pleasing visual appearance, a page created in this way has little or no visual response to user action, except perhaps for some links that highlight when rolled over or a simple CSS-driven drop-down menu. If a user sends data to the server by clicking a link or submitting a form, she must wait patiently for that data to be processed on the server and a new HTML page served back in response. This was the state of Web sites in the pre-Web 2.0 world and is a world in which many sites still live.

Web 2.0 is a somewhat overused term that is generously applied to everything that's new and not so new in today's world of Web, as this quote from Wikipedia indicates:

The term "Web 2.0" refers to a perceived second generation of web development and design, that aims to facilitate communication, secure information sharing, interoperability, and collaboration on the World Wide Web. Web 2.0 concepts have led to the development and evolution of web-based communities, hosted services, and applications; such as social-networking sites, video-sharing sites, wikis, blogs, and folksonomies.

Despite this kind of hyperbole, Web 2.0 offers an inspiring reality that all Web designers should gladly embrace.

From a purely design and technical perspective, the two key qualities that define this "second-generation of web development and design" are a fluid, interactive feel to the interface and the capability to request and receive data from the server "behind the scenes," and then present that data to the user without loading a new page.

In the hands of a talented and knowledgeable designer, these two interactions can transform a Web site into a Rich Interface Application (RIA). In an RIA, stylish and technically sophisticated interface components accept user input and then respond with new data seemingly instantly. A simple example is when a user mouses over a headline in a list of headlines, and almost instantly the description of that story is delivered from the server and added into the page below the headline. In the past, this effect could only be achieved by including the content of every story in the initial page, resulting in a massive page download. This capability to get data from the server and add it directly into the page is the result of a JavaScript-powered coding technique called Ajax. Because of Ajax, today's Web sites are morphing into what looks and feels like any regular "sovereign" application that runs on your computer.

Before Ajax and RIAs, all the processing power used in a Web site was on the server side. The browser simply collected the data to be sent to the server and rendered the pages with which the server responded. In contrast, the interface of an RIA runs on the client side in the browser, and can therefore make full use of the capabilities of the modern browser as an application platform and the ever-increasing horsepower of the user's computer.

Our users now have the front end of the application and formidable computing power to run it, right where all their regular applications run—on their computers, not on the other side of the Internet. The server, now directly accessible to the browser via Ajax, takes a more focused role as the real-time processor and supplier of the application's data.

This redistribution of responsibilities, with the work more equally and appropriately shared between client and server, gives you, the Web designer, a new, more powerful model for imagining and developing Web sites.

The brave new world of RIAs is driven by JavaScript. It's the language in which the client-side logic of today's Web applications is written; it controls the interface and directs the activities of the server. JavaScript, formally lurking in the wings as a poor cousin to HTML and CSS, and used mostly for browser-side data validation and simple animation effects, is now thrust center stage. So the key for you to open the creative and engineering doors to the potential of this new Web development model is to master JavaScript.

In the rest of this chapter, you will learn how to plan the coding of your pages so they can be readily enhanced with Ajax, and thereby transform your site into a more application-like experience.

Accessibility and Progressive Enhancement

Before I discuss JavaScript and Ajax, I'll talk about accessibility—in all its meanings. It is very easy when designing an RIA Web site to make it entirely dependent on JavaScript for its operation, but such a site can cause severe problems for many users. That super-cool, drag-and-drop feature is useless to someone who is physically disabled and can't use a mouse or who relies on an aural screen reader because of poor eyesight.

Also, some people use old browsers and low-powered computers that can't support the technical capabilities required to experience your RIA, or they simply have JavaScript turned off because of perceived security risks. This also is an issue of accessibility.

A common response to any suggestion that a Web site should be accessible is: "Oh, it doesn't matter for our site because it's only for (*pick one: in-house users, a small group of our customers, our preferred vendors, Superman and Batman*) who all use a (*enter some outrageously powerful computer here*) and none of them are (*enter some disability here*), and anyway my boss told me not to worry about it."

Rather than get into a heated debate, my position on accessibility is this: If you make the decision from the get-go, it is totally feasible to create a site that offers a rich user experience for fully capable users and browsers, and a more simple but completely useable experience for the less empowered.

In short, if the user doesn't have JavaScript turned on or the browser doesn't support the modern JavaScript that operates on the W3C (World Wide Web Consortium) version of the Document Object Model (DOM), the site can still function. And this is not some trivial number of users we are talking about here. Six percent of all users don't have JavaScript running in their browsers *(The Counter, Feb. 2009 Global Stats)* for security or other reasons, which is a significant percentage of users to exclude from your site.

The methodology that enables you to offer appropriate, but always functional, experiences for all users is called progressive enhancement. If compliance with Section 508 of the Americans with Disabilities Act, the desire to reach as many potential customers as possible, or simply your conscience demands it, you, too, can build a JavaScript-driven RIA that still provides its essential functionality without JavaScript.

However, it should be noted that despite the best intentions, some JavaScript-driven interface interactions (and drag-and-drop is a very good example) don't degrade nicely to regular HTML interface components when JavaScript is not present. If you want your site to be accessible, you may have to forgo such components for even your most empowered users, or provide an alternative non-JavaScript means of completing that task. In the latter case, JavaScript normally hides the alternate HTML component; if JavaScript is not present, the HTML component is displayed.

What I (and the accessibility community) am suggesting is that you plan your site so that it can work without JavaScript if JavaScript is not available. In this chapter, I'll show you a simple form implemented with HTML and PHP, and later enhance it with Ajax, so it works with and without JavaScript. You'll have to decide if this "maximum accessibility" approach is one you want to take—I hope it is.

A lot of advice is available on the Web about this subject, and you can find it by searching for Accessible Ajax or progressive enhancement. The W3C has an interesting initiative called ARIA (nice acronym) to address accessible RIAs through special markup and techniques, and Yahoo's YUI team, and the Dojo and jQuery framework developers are amongst those who are adopting its recommendations. In his succinct and excellent book, *Bulletproof Ajax* (New Riders, 2007), Jeremy Keith offers this advice to those who would make their sites as accessible as possible: "Plan for Ajax first, implement Ajax last." Sounds good, but how do we do that?

Three Steps to Progressive Enhancement

The steps to making an application that runs with or without JavaScript are based on layering enhancements onto the basic functionality of the site.

1. **Make it functional.** Get the site working with just an HTML front end and the server technology of your choice (PHP, .NET, Java, etc.).

2. **Make it look good.** Style the HTML with CSS in external style sheets (linked to the page with LINK elements).

3. **Enhance the experience.** Add interface behaviors that provide more intuitive responses and controls, and provide Ajax connectivity to enable "no-page-refresh" access to the server-side functionality.

If you think in this layered fashion, then should your awesome RIA suddenly find itself in a no-JavaScript environment, it will fall back to the old "round-trip" model of sending data to the server and waiting for a page to be served back in response. The user won't know the difference; the site will still be nicely styled, and it will still work. In an even more limited environment, where neither CSS nor JavaScript are supported, the site, looking rather less attractive perhaps, will still function. As long as users have the capability to support just HTML, they will be able to use your site.

The rest of this chapter illustrates with a simple example how to create a site that is based on the first two steps to progressive enhancement and is ready for JavaScript interface interactions and Ajax server communication to be added, or to use a commonly used and more accurate term, "layered on." I'll just discuss the third step in this chapter but actually demonstrate it in Chapter 5.

Let's start with step 1—Make it functional—to see what it takes to create a form that enables a user to sign up on your site.

1. Make It Functional

In this example I'll create a working form. To do this, I only need HTML markup to create the form and a server-side language (I'll use PHP) to validate and record the data on the server when the form data is submitted.

HTML—CREATING THE DOM

HTML is for structure. If you start by writing good HTML, you will have a great foundation on which to layer the CSS and JavaScript.

Here are some simple guidelines for writing your HTML.

First, use the right element for marking up each piece of your content. Study an HTML glossary and learn how each element should be used and the required and optional attributes that can be added to them. A common markup mistake is to omit the `label` element on a form's `input` element (text field). The `label` element should also have a `for` attribute with the same value as the `input`'s ID to semantically tie the element and the label together. In this way, if the site is being accessed with a screen reader, the label will be read aloud when the user moves the cursor into the field.

For an HTML quick reference listing, go to http://w3schools.com/tags/default.asp. For a more complete HTML tutorial, try http://dev.opera.com/articles/view/12-the-basics-of-html.

I can't emphasize enough how important it is to understand the various HTML elements and use them appropriately. If you are bolding the text in paragraph tags to create headings or do not understand the difference between block and inline HTML elements, you need to improve your knowledge of HTML so you are using its elements in semantically meaningful and technically valid ways.

Second, to this last point, validate your markup at validator.w3c.org or use the Web Developer toolbar so you can be sure that your markup is well-formed with all tags nested and closed correctly.

If you are wondering why I am obsessing over HTML markup in a JavaScript book, here's the reason. When you write HTML, you are actually creating the DOM, which is a hierarchical collection of nodes. There are three types of nodes: HTML elements, the elements' attributes, and the text inside of elements (white spaces in your code are also seen as nodes by modern browsers, and you will see how to take this into account in Chapter 2). Both CSS and JavaScript act upon these DOM nodes, but they can only do that if the document's structure is well-formed and if the appropriate ID and class are added onto elements where needed. Get the HTML markup right and JavaScript can then do its magic.

FORM MARKUP

Keeping in mind all that you have read so far, take a look at some simple markup for a form in which users can submit their email addresses to sign up for a newsletter. See **Figure 1.1**. This form will be brought to life using just HTML and PHP, and then styled with CSS. Later we will enhance it with Ajax to improve the user's experience, but it will be able to fall back to the non-Ajax interaction functionality if JavaScript is not available.

FIGURE 1.1 The red vertical lines overlaying this markup indicate the hierarchical relationship of the elements. Note that this code snip shows only the markup between the body tags.

CODE 1.1 simple_form_step1.php

```
Level 1
  Level 2
    Level 3
      Level 4
<body>
  <div id="sign_up">
    <h1>Sign up for our newsletter</h1>
    <form id="email_form" action="#" method="post">
      <label for="email">Email</label>
      <input id="email" name="email" type="text" size="20" />
      <input type="submit" value="Go!" />
    </form>
    <p class="msg"></p>
  </div>
</body>
```

Figure 1.2 shows how this HTML looks in the browser.

FIGURE 1.2 The unstyled form.

You may have noticed that there is no text in the last paragraph tag (the one with the ID msg) in the markup. This is because later I will use PHP to add a message into this tag that tells the user if the submitted address is invalid. Because it has no text in it yet, the empty element is not visible on screen.

INDENTING YOUR CODE

The first thing that you notice without reading any code is the indenting of the lines. You don't have to indent your code, but you definitely should, and here's both the why and how of code indenting.

A tab or a couple of spaces can be used to indent, and the general consensus according to Chris, my tech editor, is to use a couple of spaces.

The basic rule is simple: Indent nested tags.

An element should be indented if it's nested in (enclosed by) the previous tag. Put another way, you indent the current line if an element that opened earlier hasn't yet closed. For example, in the code in Figure 1.1, the div after the body tag doesn't close before the next (h1) element opens, so the h1 is indented. The label and input elements are indented further still because they are enclosed by the form element.

Correct indenting helps confirm that your markup is well-formed with all the tags correctly nested inside one another. Indenting naturally creates a code layout where the most deeply nested tags are farthest to the right, and if the markup is correctly formed, ends with the last line back at the left of the page. If you miss a closing tag somewhere, this won't happen. For example, note the closing div tag is exactly aligned with its opening tag higher up in the code. This will always be the case with any enclosing element if you have correctly nested all the tags within it. By following the indenting rule mentioned earlier, each child element is indented from its parent element. Sibling elements, such as `label` and `input` in the form, have the same indent.

So correctly indented code is not only easier to understand, but it also lets you see your DOM structure at a glance.

CHILD NODES

The next step in understanding the DOM is to know that the text within an element is a child of that element. For example, the text "Sign up for our newsletter" is a text node and a child of the p element in which it lives. An element's attributes are also child nodes of that element, so the `id="sign-up"` attribute on the `div` is a child node of the `div`. JavaScript can access and change element nodes *and* their child attribute nodes and text nodes; CSS, with the exception of the pseudo-classes `:before` and `:after` that can enable a rather limited means of adding content to the page, can only access the element and attribute nodes.

From the markup in Figure 1.1, I can draw a hierarchical tree version of the DOM of the code that looks like **Figure 1.3**.

FIGURE 1.3 The DOM hierarchy.

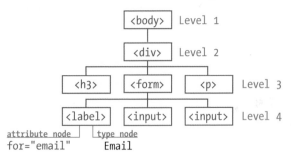

Compare this diagram with the markup. You want to be able to see this tree-like DOM view in your mind by looking at the markup. If you study the indenting and each element's text and attributes, it's not that hard to do. With this mental model, it's easy to look at any HTML markup and determine how to use CSS and JavaScript to access the nodes you want to modify.

PROCESSING THE DATA

As mentioned earlier, I'll use PHP to process the form. I could write an entire book about PHP (actually, I did), but here I will just cover a couple of key points, and then simply present the code along with a line-by-line explanation.

My book, Codin' for the Web *(New Riders, 2007), covers PHP and SQL.*

PHP is a server-side language for generating HTML pages. PHP is written in text files with the filename extension .php. Such a page is known as a PHP script. A PHP script is a mix of HTML and PHP that generates HTML. Whenever you request a PHP script URL, a new HTML page is served back to you. So a PHP script can be thought of as a template that generates an HTML page.

In the case of this form, each time the form data (the email address) is submitted to the PHP script, PHP serves up a slightly different version of the HTML page to the browser based on whether the email is valid or not. If the address is invalid, the PHP code will add a message to the page requesting that the user try again; if the email address is valid, PHP will record it into a text file and add thank-you text into the page instead.

Let's look at this process step by step. Writing a list of the tasks you want your code to perform is a worthwhile, time-saving step to take before you write the actual code. I'll often start my coding with a list of comments like this, and once I have them in the right order, add the actual code in between them.

1.   The PHP script is requested the first time, and the HTML in the script (the layout of the form) is served back to the browser.

2.   When the user submits the form, the form data is submitted back to the same script.

3.   PHP detects that the form data has been submitted.

4.   PHP tests the email address and determines if the email is correctly formatted.

5.   If the email address is valid, the email address is recorded in a text file on the server and the message text is set to the Success message.

6.   If the email address is invalid, the message text is set to the Invalid Email message.

7.   PHP writes the message into the HTML "message" element of the page and serves up the page to the user.

Note that PHP is never sent to the browser—only the HTML that PHP generates is sent. Clicking the "Go!" button passes the form data to the same PHP script each time the form is submitted, and PHP will serve up one of two slightly different versions of the HTML page in response.

PHP and HTML can be freely mixed on the page. You simply write `<?php` to indicate that you are switching from HTML to PHP and write `?>` to indicate you are switching back to HTML again. PHP only processes code inside the `<?` and `?>` tags, and writes everything else (the HTML) directly to the page it is generating.

Before I write the code to process the form, there are three bits of PHP I need to add to our markup.

1. Enable any error message generated by PHP to be added into that empty p element at the end of the markup.

    ```
    <p class="msg"><?php echo $msg; ?></p>
    ```

    Here I can create a PHP variable (temporary data store) called `$msg` that will hold the message that PHP selects after looking at the email address. PHP will then add that message into the HTML element with the ID "message" when it writes out the page.

    `echo` means "add to the page output" so the text in the `$msg` variable will get added here in place of `<?php echo $msg; ?>`. Remember, PHP is never added to the page.

2. Modify the form tag as follows to make the page submit to itself.

    ```
    <form id="tiny_form_vert" action="simple_form_step1.
    php" method="post">
    ```

    The highlighted text is the filename of the current page.

3. Echo the email address the user submitted into the form field, because then the user can modify it if necessary and not have to entirely retype it.

    ```
    <input id="email" name="email" type="text" size="20"
    value="<?php echo $email;?>" />
    ```

    The email address will replace the highlighted PHP.

    This is called making the field "sticky"—the info stays in the field between form submissions. Users will hate you, especially if the form has many fields, if you don't make form elements sticky; they really don't want to have to reenter all the data to correct an error.

Here's the entire PHP script with these three pieces of PHP highlighted.

this code runs only if the form was submitted—specifically, if there is anything from the form in the POST array	`<?php` `if ($_POST) {`
move the email address from the POST array to a variable	`    $email = $_POST['email'];`
$validis set if email is valid	`    $valid = verifyEmail($email);`
if the email passed validation	`    if ($valid) {`
pass email address to writeToFile function to record it in a text file	`        writeToFile($email);`
	`        $msg= 'Thanks for signing up! Please visit our <a` `            href="members.php4"> members only area.</a>';`
	`    } else {`
the $msg will get written into the markup as PHP generates the page	`        $msg = 'Please type a valid email address.';`

end if POST–
the two functions that follow are required by the above code
	`    }`
	
	`}`

checks for a well-formed email address–i.e., in format: someTextAndNumbers@ someTextAndNumbers.2-4 characters	`function verifyEmail ($testString) {`
returns 1 (TRUE) if email is well-formatted	`    return (eregi("^([[:alnum:]]|_|\.|-)+@` `        ([[:alnum:]]|\.|-)+(\.)([a-z]{2,4})$", $testString));`

gets the current date and time in March 14, 2009, 3:30 pm format–
see http://us2.php.net/date
for date format info
	`}`
	
	`    $dateNTime= date("F j Y H:i");`

assembles the email, a tab, the date and time, and a line break	`    $form_data = $email . "\t" . $dateNTime . "\n";`
open a file (creates one first if needed)	`    $myPointer = fopen("../../../form_data/data.txt", "r+");`
writes to the file	`    fputs ($myPointer, $form_data);`
closes the file	`    fclose($myPointer);`
	`}`
end of the PHP	`?>`

CODE 1.2 simple_form_step1.php

Although this page's code is all HTML and the previous page's code is all PHP, the code on both pages is part of the same file.

```
<!DOCTYPE html PUBLIC "-//W3C//DTD XHTML 1.0
    Transitional//EN" "http://www.w3.org/TR/xhtml1/DTD/xhtml1-
    transitional.dtd">

<html xmlns="http://www.w3.org/1999/xhtml">

<head>

    <title>Sign-up Form</title>

    <meta http-equiv="Content-Type" content="text/html;
        charset=iso-8859-1" />

</head>

<body>

    <div id="sign_up">

        <h1>Sign up for our newsletter</h1>

        <p>This info is only used to send you emails.</p>

        <p>We don't share your info with anyone.</p>

        <form id="tiny_form_vert" action="simple_form.php"
            method="post">

            <label for="email">Email</label>

            <input id="email" name="email" type="text" size="20"
                value="<?php echo $email;?>" />

            <input type="submit" value="Sign me up!" />

        </form>

        <p id="msg"><?php echo $msg; ?></p>

    </div>

</body>

</html>
```

If you don't know PHP, this can all look rather daunting. If this is the case, just focus on the results this code achieves—which is what really matters. There are two possible outcomes when the user submits the form. If the user supplies a badly formed email address or leaves the field empty, an error message is added to the page, as illustrated in **Figure 1.4**. If the email address is well-formed, the email and date are written to a file on the server and a link is displayed that provides access to the Member's page.

FIGURE 1.4 Unstyled form with incorrect field entry and user prompt.

If the email address is valid, the page looks like **Figure 1.5**.

FIGURE 1.5 Unstyled form with valid message.

Note that the first ten lines of the PHP code on page 14 are the main path of the code—the "procedural" steps taken to process the file. Two functions below these ten lines help in this work—one tests the email address and the other records the validated email address into a text file. These functions are called from the procedural code and return their results to it, but they are not in the main code flow.

Functions allow you to separate out pieces of code that are frequently needed by the "main flow" procedural code instead of repeatedly adding the same code into the main code flow. However, there is another important advantage to these "stand-alone" functions—you can call them directly from the browser using Ajax. In the case of my form, I will use Ajax to send the email address directly to the email validation function in this code to test the email address and have it return the result (1 or 0—valid or invalid) without running the rest of the code. In this way, I am planning for Ajax now, even though I will implement it last (Jeremy would be proud of us). You will see functions in detail when I cover the basics of JavaScript in Chapter 2.

The form is now functional using only HTML and PHP. Now let's see how the look can be improved with CSS.

A Note on Security

Accepting user input opens your site to the potential for code injection and XSS (cross-site scripting) attacks. The PHP code that starts on page 14 illustrates some steps you can take to protect yourself when receiving data and writing it into your file system. First, the input is validated. This not only mitigates the chances of the user typing in an incorrect email and then wondering why you didn't send him anything, but it makes it more difficult to pass malicious code to your server via the form. Second, the action of the form (the URL to which the form will be submitted) includes only the page name, not the entire URL into the page. In that way, you don't expose your folder structure in your code—information that could help a potential hacker. Third, when you write the file, you do not let PHP create a file if one is not there already—you create that file manually. Then, when you set the file mode to "r+", you allow read/write access for the file but no file creation. Because you now don't have to provide folder-level write access, which you would have to do if you allow PHP to create a file, you prevent anyone from writing a file to your file system. Fourth, the file to which you put this file is in a folder above the root folder of the Web site, making access to it much more difficult. These simple steps combine to make it much harder to break in through this form.

Security is a major issue with JavaScript because, unlike PHP, the code is running in the browser and is visible and modifiable by anyone. Learn more about JavaScript secutiry issues on the DevArticles Web site at www.devarticles.com/c/a/JavaScript/JavaScript-Security.

2. Make It Look Good

Every browser has a built-in style sheet that makes headlines larger than paragraph text, makes links blue, and controls the default presentation of HTML. By using a style sheet you can override any aspect of the default layout, which is predominantly full width elements one under the other running down the page. With CSS, you can lay out the HTML in columns if you wish, and style each element to your own liking.

My book, Stylin' with CSS *(New Riders, 2008), covers CSS and XHTML.*

CSS works by accessing the DOM. Again, I won't get into a full-on CSS lesson here (I already wrote that book, too) but instead will demonstrate how the DOM is accessed by CSS and how to use CSS in ways that support progressive enhancement.

A CSS rule has the format

`selector {property:value}` as in `p {color:red;}`, which colors all paragraph element text red. The property/value pair is collectively known as the declaration. This basic rule format can be extended with multiple selectors and rules

makes h1 and h2 headings blue and italicized

`h1, h2 {color:#069; font-style-:italic;}`

See **Table 1.1** for some selectors that target by context—using an ID, or a class, or by referencing an element's ancestor (parent and above)— elements in the DOM:

SELECTOR	DESCRIPTION
p	all paragraph selectors
#email { }	an element with the ID email (every ID on a page must have a unique name)
.warning { }	any elements with the class warning (the same class name can be used on multiple elements on the same page)
div#email { }	a div with the ID email
p.warning { }	a paragraph with the class warning
div p { }	a paragraph with a div ancestor
div#email form input { }	an input with a form ancestor that has a div ancestor with the ID email
a[title] { }	a link with a title attribute*
input[type="submit"] { }	an input that has a type attribute with the value submit*

TABLE 1.1 **CSS selectors.**   *doesn't work in IE6*

CSS rules should live in an external style sheet, which is simply a text document with the extension .css and is linked to the HTML by adding a link tag into the head of the HTML page like this:

```
<link type="text/css" rel="stylesheet" href="sign_up_form.
css">
```

You want to avoid using CSS to add presentational styles to your HTML as inline tags, like this:

```
<p style="color:red;">Warning: don't add inline CSS!</p>
```

or embedding CSS in the page in style tags, like this:

```
<style>
p.bignono {color:red;}
</style>
```

(and certainly don't use deprecated presentational HTML like FONT, COLOR, and ALIGN).

You permanently assign these styles to your markup when you add the styles to the tags, or to the page when you use embedded CSS. A linked style sheet gives you maximum flexibility. You can change either the markup or the CSS without affecting the other, and you can link that style sheet to as many pages as you wish to save repetitive CSS coding and provide consistent styling across all the pages of your site.

Many CSS properties are inherited—that is, passed down to their descendant elements. For example, if you set a font size on the body to 80%, all the font sizes in the document become 80% smaller because font size is inherited and body is the great granddaddy element of them all. Any inheritable properties set on an element affect all of its descendants too, unless that property is specifically restyled by a rule that targets an element farther down the DOM.

Armed with this *CliffsNotes* quality overview of CSS, here is some CSS that provides a more pleasing look for our form page.

```css
* {
    margin:0;
    padding:0;
}
body {
    font-family:verdana, arial, sans-serif;
    font-size:.8em;
}
div#sign_up {
    width:28em;
    color:#069;
    border-top:3px solid #069;
    border-bottom:2px solid #069;
    margin-top:2em;
    margin-left:auto;
    margin-right:auto;
    padding:0 1em;
}
div#sign_up h1 {
    margin-bottom:.2em;
}
div#sign_up p {
    margin-bottom:.4em;
```

sets all margins and padding to 0

makes the overall font size smaller

centers the div on the page (and everything in it)

CODE 1.3 simple_form_step2.php
with sign_up_form.css

```
}

div#sign_up label {

    font-weight:bold;

}

div#sign_up input[type='submit'] {

    color:#069;

    background-color:#EEF;

}

div#sign_up p.msg {

    margin-top:.3em;

    font-style:italic;

}

div#sign_up p.msg a {

    color:#963;

}
```

Figure 1.6 shows what this CSS does to the page.

FIGURE 1.6 Styled form.

Note the use of relative units—in this case ems. I could have also used percentages—not just for sizing text but for the width of the containing div. By specifying everything in ems, I make my page more accessible. If the user presses Ctrl-+ (PC) or Command-+ (Mac) to enlarge the onscreen text, the entire layout also resizes to accommodate the new text size.

I now have a functional and nicely styled page, but the HTML and CSS are completely separate. The page would still work without the CSS, and the CSS could easily be linked to other pages that could share its styles.

3. Enhance the Experience with JavaScript and Ajax

Now we come to JavaScript. I'll end this chapter with an overview of how JavaScript and Ajax are used to enhance the user experience. In Chapter 5, I will return to this email form example and use JavaScript to create an Ajax interaction with the server so I can validate the email address using the PHP code on the server before the user submits the form.

Let's start with three simple ideas: JavaScript is a powerful coding tool, is DOM scripting capable, and is Ajax capable.

A POWERFUL CODING TOOL

JavaScript is a full-featured scripting language that runs in the user's browser. It lets you manage data in variables, arrays, and objects, and write code logic that is common to almost every programming language, such as if-then-else, that allows you to infuse your code with decision-making capabilities. You can write code in either a procedural, step-by-step style—where each line of the code is executed sequentially—or in an object-oriented style—where objects composed of properties and methods (variables and functions) can communicate with one another to accomplish the work of the program. In reality, your script will probably be a mix of both. You will learn about these concepts in Chapter 2.

Java and JavaScript are not related in any way, except they are both used to program computers. Their relationship, or rather lack thereof, was summarized in a now infamous blog comment, which read: "Java is to JavaScript as car is to carpet."

Unlike well-known, industrial-strength programming languages such as C# (c-sharp) and Java, JavaScript does not need to be compiled (that is, processed into low-level computer machine code) before it can run. This makes it easier to test your code as you write it—you just open the page in a browser and it runs. Because it does not get complied, JavaScript is known as a scripting language, not a programming language. PHP is also known as a scripting language for the same reason. However, with today's more powerful computers, being compiled no longer gives a programming language such a big speed advantage over a scripting language.

Being a powerful and robust scripting language is only part of JavaScript's appeal. Where it shines is in the area of DOM scripting.

DOM SCRIPTING CAPABLE

As the name suggests, DOM scripting is JavaScript's capability to manipulate the DOM and thereby dynamically change the content and appearance of the page as the user interacts with it.

CSS only allows you to *set* the properties of DOM elements, and then only the style-related properties, such as color and position. JavaScript, on the other hand, lets you get *and* set all the properties of not only the DOM elements but also their attributes and text. This enables you to do things like add and remove content and navigation elements as needed. It also creates a very interesting relationship between CSS and JavaScript.

With JavaScript, you can override CSS styles dynamically or add classes and IDs to elements on the fly, and thereby have CSS rules for these classes and IDs suddenly come into effect on those elements. A simple example of this latter technique would be to set up a CSS background-color class called `tr.odd` that defines an alternate table row color. JavaScript can then zip through an HTML table and add the `odd` class name onto alternate rows, resulting in striped rows in the table to make it more readable (**Figure 1.7**).

FIGURE 1.7 A striped table.

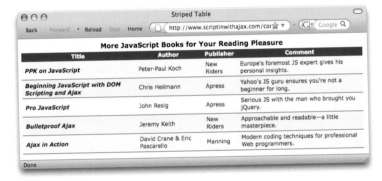

This is also a nice little example of JavaScript's power to get, process, and then set DOM properties. I'll show you how to code striped tables in Chapter 3.

PHP can only write out HTML elements that are included within the PHP page template, even though its code logic allows you to determine what gets written out and when. JavaScript, on the other hand, can be thought of as a programmable HTML writing machine; it has the capability to create HTML elements, add text and attributes to them, and then write them into the page.

AJAX CAPABLE

JavaScript can perform what are known as Ajax transactions and move data between the server and browser.

Ajax is actually a lot less than some people think. By that, I mean that Ajax is purely a technique that uses JavaScript's `XMLHttpRequest` object to request and receive data from the server without refreshing the page. It's not all the interactions of the cool, new interface components that are included with many Ajax frameworks (code tool kits), and with which the term Ajax has become associated. These interface components, such as sliding panels and auto-populating tree menus, might use Ajax to get their data, but the interactions are not Ajax. Ajax is about the movement of data and has nothing to do with the actual interface. This ultimately becomes something of a technical distinction, because although Ajax is just about moving data "behind the scenes," just about every aspect of the interface can be improved because of this capability.

In the old "round-trip" model, the user must receive a new, complete page from the server to update any part of the current page, as you saw when adding just a single line of text to the form example earlier in this chapter. Using Ajax and a little DOM scripting, it's easy for JavaScript to grab the email address as soon as the user finishes typing it, send it to the server, get back a simple yes or no, and add the appropriate text to the page. There is no page refresh, and in most cases, no discernible delay between action and response. After all, you are sending an email address of maybe 30 characters to the server and getting back not a page of HTML but a single character, 1 or 0, to tell you if the address is valid or not. That doesn't take long even over a slow connection—and it's certainly faster than serving back an entire page. I will add this Ajax capability to the form example as soon as I cover the basics of Ajax in Chapter 5.

Summary

I hope what you take away from this chapter is that JavaScript does not live in isolation on your page. Its comprehensive access to the DOM offers you the developer the means to write code that can change the structure, styling, and data in a Web page in response to user action or in response to the state of data on either the client or the server. This means that you must take extra care and planning to construct your HTML, CSS, and server-side code so that JavaScript can access them efficiently.

Now it's time to look at how to write JavaScript. In the next chapter, I will cover JavaScript from the ground up, using lots of simple hands-on examples that will help you understand and become familiar with writing the basic structures of JavaScript code.

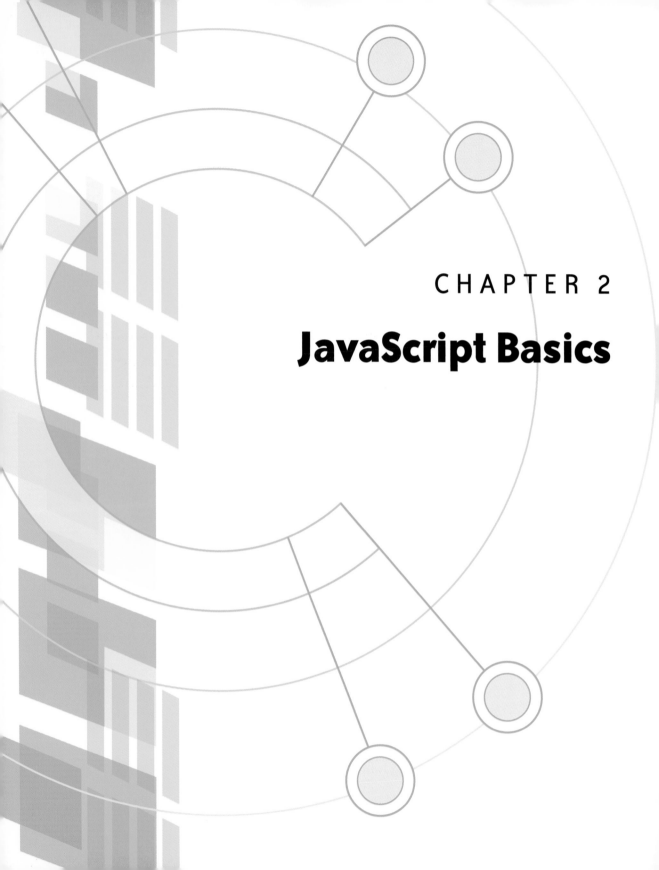

CHAPTER 2

JavaScript Basics

NOW IT'S TIME TO LEARN THE BASICS OF JAVASCRIPT. This chapter and the next two chapters on objects and events combine simple examples with general discussion about how the various aspects of JavaScript work. In later chapters, I will bring these ideas together in practical and useful ways.

When I am asked how programming works, my simple reply is: There is data, and there is code that acts on data. Most of this chapter is divided into two sections around this thought. First, you will see all the ways that data can be stored within JavaScript. Second, you will see all the code structures that allow you to run various kinds of tests and processes on that data. These code structures make up the basic building blocks of a fully functional application.

In preparation, let me briefly show you how to make the code examples run in your browser so you can follow along. I'll illustrate this with a very simple JavaScript example and an overview of how to format your code.

You can download and review the code examples for several of the examples in this chapter. The names of these files are listed next to the related code example.

Running the Code Examples

To run any code example in this chapter, place it within the following HTML markup in a text file, save the file with a name of your choice and the extension .html, and open it in your Web browser.

CODE 2.1 html_template.html

```
<!DOCTYPE HTML PUBLIC "-//W3C//DTD HTML 4.01 Transitional//
    EN">
<html>
 <head>
  <title>My JavaScript Test</title>>
 </head>
 <body>
  <script type="text/javascript">v
    // replace this line with the code example
    // remove the opening and closing script tags also if
       they are in the example
  </script>
 </body>
</html>
```

Because the browser needs to know when it is processing HTML and when it is processing JavaScript, I'll use the HTML `script` element with a `type` attribute of `"text/javascript"`, as highlighted in the preceding example, to indicate that I am switching from HTML to JavaScript. At the end of the JavaScript, I'll close the script element with `</script>` and the browser reverts to interpreting the code as HTML. The empty lines are only then there to make the code easier to read; the browser ignores white space that is longer than a single space in your code.

Hello, JavaScript

It seems like every good book about programming starts with a Hello World example where you learn how to display the message "Hello World!" In terms of data and code that acts on data, the text string "Hello World" is the data. To make the data display, in this case in an alert dialog, the code you use is the `alert` function. A function requires parentheses, which can contain any data it needs to act upon—in this example the text string:

CODE 2.2 hello_world.html

```
alert ("Hello World!");
```

So, grab the markup from the previous section (Code 2.1 example) and insert this function. As soon as the page loads into the browser, the JavaScript runs, and you see the dialog in **Figure 2.1**.

FIGURE 2.1 Alert dialog.

Inspired by the incredible simplicity of this display of JavaScript's capabilities, let's now learn the basics of writing JavaScript.

Scripts, Statements, and Comments

A script is a number of lines of JavaScript and is also used as a kind of general term for the JavaScript that you write—as in "I wrote a new script that does xyz." Within a script are statements and comments.

Scripts

A script can be placed between `script` tags within your HTML file or in a separate text file with the filename extension .js that is linked to your HTML page using a `script` tag. In the examples in this book, I added the JavaScript into the page so you can see it with its associated HTML markup. In a Web site of any size, you will want to link separate JavaScript files to your pages instead of adding the JavaScript directly into your document. The scripts are then downloaded only once and cached (stored) on the user's browser, and can be shared between all the pages of the site.

Statements

Each line of script is a statement. A statement is an instruction that JavaScript can evaluate (make sense of). Statements end with a semicolon, and it's standard practice to start each statement on a new line, although the code will still work if you don't.

ON FORMATTING JAVASCRIPT

As a formatting demonstration, here is a four-line script that adds two numbers together:

CODE 2.3 demo_2_plus_3.html

```
var x=2;

var y=3;

alert (x+y);

// displays 5
```

Each of the first three lines is a statement that JavaScript can evaluate, and each ends with a semicolon and a line break (press Return). You can separate statements by using line breaks only, but this is considered poor practice and makes the code confusing to read if statements wrap to more than one line. Always end a statement with a semicolon. The fourth line is a comment, which in this case states the anticipated outcome as shown in **Figure 2.2**.

FIGURE 2.2 An alert dialog displays the result of the calculation.

Comments

It's worth taking the time to put comments in your code so you know what that code is meant to do when you or someone else works on it in the future. Comments are entirely ignored by JavaScript and are simply meant to be read by anyone looking at the code.

A single-line comment starts with //

```
// this is a comment
```

Everything after the // is ignored by JavaScript until a new line starts, so you don't need to explicitly end a single-line comment—just start a new line. Often, you will add a single-line comment after a code statement on the same line:

```
var myFavAxe;   // my favorite guitar
```

You can also write a multiline comment, which starts with /* and ends with */.

A multiline comment might look something like this:

```
/*  This next piece of code handles any errors.

    Errors will be written into the error array.

    Errors are processed after all tests are completed. */
```

If you want to prevent the execution of a number of lines of code within a script temporarily, perhaps while you are troubleshooting a problem, you can simply enclose that code in a multiline comment.

Also, if you want to strip out comments to "minify" the scripts before you put them into production, use a minifying tool such as Douglas Crockford's JSMin (www.crockford.com/javascript/jsmin.html).

Now it's time to look at the ways in which JavaScript can store data.

Am I Writing HTML or JavaScript?

At first, it's easy to forget at any given moment if you are writing JavaScript or HTML, especially when adding comments. It's a common mistake to write JavaScript outside of the `script` tags where only HTML is valid or to write HTML inside a `script` and things then don't work right. You just have to learn to change gears mentally to the right language for the right part of the page.

Data and Ways to Store It

JavaScript classifies data into different types and offers different ways to store it. For your code to perform optimally, you need to understand and correctly use these options.

Variables

Variables, as you saw in the 2+3 example earlier, are the locations in which you can store various kinds of data so your JavaScript code can act on them. That data might come from sources such as a form the user filled out or be returned from an Ajax request to the server. A server could return data from its database, from a file on disc, or from an XML file far, far away across the Internet. Wherever your data comes from, you first put it in variables so your code can go to work on it.

NAMING VARIABLES

You can give a variable any name you want, but that name can't begin with a number and it can't contain spaces. It's a good idea to give a variable a name that makes sense when you and others read the code later; for example:

```
var userName;

var productId;

var totalWithTax;
```

These variables are written in a style called "camel case" where you join several words together to give a variable a meaningful name. Make the first word lowercase and capitalize subsequent words—without any spaces, of course. This will always give you a single `easyToReadOneWordVariableName`. This format is called camel case because of the visual humps created by the uppercase letters.

DECLARING A VARIABLE

When you first declare (create) a variable, you should put var in front of it, as shown in the three examples in the preceding section. In all future references, you can simply use the variable name. If you do not use var, you create a variable with global scope, which you usually do not want to do. I'll discuss scope in more detail when I introduce functions later in the chapter.

In the previous three variable examples, I didn't use the equals sign to set these variables to a value, so their current value would be "undefined"—meaning not set to any value. Undefined should not be confused with 0, which is the value zero. Sometimes you want to create an undefined variable so it is ready to receive a value that is generated later by your code.

However, you can declare (create) and set (put something into) a variable in a single step. The contents of a variable are known as its value, and when you reference a variable in your code, JavaScript effectively replaces that reference with the variable's value. Both these points are demonstrated by this next simple, two-line example:

| uses var when variable is first declared |

```
var myNickname = "Charlie";
```

| no need to use var in subsequent references to the variable |

```
alert (myNickname);

// displays Charlie
```

Now that you have a basic understanding of variables, let's look at the different data types variables can contain.

A variable can contain any of the following data types:

- a string
- a number
- a Boolean (true and false, or 1 or 0)
- an array (a group of related variables)
- a function
- an object

Let's take a look at each of these data types.

Strings

Strings are simply text characters. You can put any characters you want in a string. A string is always quoted—that is, enclosed in single or double quotes—your choice. When quoting strings, make sure your characters are "straight up-and-down" quotes and not "curly" quotes that may be automatically formatted by a text program. Here I put some strings into variables:

```
var joesGreeting = "Waaazup?";

var userPrompt2 = "Enter your name";

var carMake="Lotus", carType="Elan", carCategory="classic
sports car";
```

The preceding example shows that you can declare several variables on one line, separated by commas.

It's very important to realize that JavaScript does not attempt to evaluate strings (see the sidebar "Key Concept: Evaluation"), as the following example illustrates.

In this example:

> 2+3 is evaluated to 5

```
var answer = 2+3;

alert (answer);

displays: 5
```

whereas:

> the string is not evaluated

```
var answer = "2+3"

alert (answer);

displays: 2+3
```

"2+3" is a string, so JavaScript makes no effort to evaluate it and simply copies the string into the variable.

Conversely, JavaScript will attempt to evaluate anything that is *not* a string. So if you want to pop up a cheery greeting to your visitors and you write

> note the text is missing quotes

```
alert (Hello!);
```

The Error Console is a simple debugging tool that displays JavaScript error messages and their associated line numbers. It can be opened from the Firefox Tools menu, and it's very useful to have it open all the time as you test your work in the browser.

you will trigger an error because you forgot to put quotes around the string. In this case, JavaScript would assume that you are referring to a variable named Hello!, and if there was no variable called Hello! (probably not), would display the error message *Hello! is not defined* in your error console.

Forgetting to quote a string like this is an easy mistake to make, as you may soon discover when you start writing your own code.

With this in mind, note the problem with this string:

```
"She said "Go away!" and went back to her book."
```

The string closes (ends) right before the G of Go because that's where the second double quote is located—the rest of the text is considered outside the string, so JavaScript will then try to evaluate Go away" and went back to her book". You may not be surprised to learn that this phrase is not part of the JavaScript language, so an error occurs. There are two ways to get around this issue of quotes within a string: One way is to "escape" the problem characters with a backslash:

```
"She said \"Go away\" and went back to her book."
```

Escaping a character causes it to be treated as a string character and not be evaluated as code, so now the string does not end until the closing quote at the end of the line.

The other way is to use single quotes around the string and double quotes within it (or vice versa):

```
'She said "Go away!" and went back to her book.'
```

Key Concept: Evaluation

In JavaScript, and most programming languages, the common statement structure

```
someVariable = someExpression;
```

sets the value of the variable on the left to the *evaluated* result of the expression on the right. In this context, "evaluated" means "processed by JavaScript". For example, if you use a variable name on the right side of the statement, JavaScript will evaluate that variable name to its value and set the variable on the left to that same value. Every expression you write must be able to be evaluated by JavaScript or an error will result.

JavaScript can automatically add escape characters to strings to prevent these problems, as you will see later.

Numbers

Numbers can be positive or negative and can be

- **Integers.** Whole numbers such as 1, 45, -34, 2354564

- **Floating-point numbers.** With numbers to the right of the decimal point, such as 3.142, -.000001, and so on

- **Exponentials.** In JavaScript you can use e to mean "to the power of," so you can represent the number 10^9 as 10e9

You can also represent numbers in octal (base 8) and hexadecimal (base 16) formats. Hexadecimal is useful when working with colors because they can be expressed in three groups of two-digit hexadecimal values, such as #FF0000, which is red.

Booleans

Boolean values are special values known as constants. They can only be true and false, and can also be represented as 1 and 0, respectively. Note that although they are words, they are not strings and should not be quoted. Booleans are used to represent entities that can only have one of two states, such as on or off, yes or no, equal or not equal. You will learn more about Boolean values when we look at if statements later in this chapter.

Arrays

Arrays can be thought of as a variable that can hold more that one value. Often you want to keep a set of related values together, and arrays are the way to do this. Arrays are powerful structures: Every array you create is a child of the global Array object, so your arrays have access to a complete set of methods that enable you to easily create, access, add, remove, and perform operations on an array's values. You can find a listing of the Array methods in Appendix B.

An array is capable of holding any list of items, such as this list of animals:

dog, cat, pig, horse, sheep

Let's see how to create and manage an array with these items in it.

Keep Track of Your Data Types

In strongly typed languages, such as C++ and Java, you must declare what type of variable you are creating—string, number, Boolean, array, and so on—when you create it: You can only use it to hold that kind of data. In JavaScript, which is weakly typed, you can simply declare a variable and put any type of data in it. This makes JavaScript more flexible because you can change your mind about what type of data you want in a particular variable at will. However, if you don't keep track of the type of data in your variables, you can write code that produces unexpected and unwanted results. You can always use the typeOf operator to test what type of data you are dealing with before you use it.

CREATE AN ARRAY

Here's how to create an array:

| left and right square brackets |

```
var animalArray = [];
```

CODE 2.4 array_demo.html

You now have a new empty array called animalArray that you can start to populate as your code runs.

INDEXED ARRAYS

Indexed arrays are a list of items whereby each item is referenced by its index—its numerical position in the array.

Let's begin by creating and populating the array in a single step, separating the items with commas:

```
var animalArray = ["dog", "cat", "pig", "horse", "sheep"];
```

Note that the names are strings. If you didn't quote them, when your code later accessed the array, JavaScript would look for variables elsewhere in the code with these names.

Each part of an array is known as an element; the array now has five elements.

READING AN ELEMENT FROM AN ARRAY

To read from an array, use the format

```
arrayName[arrayIndex];
```

For example:

```
alert ( animalArray[2] );

// displays pig
```

The [2] reads the element in the third position, not the second, because the array indexing starts from 0, not 1. This concept of counting from index 0 is common in programming languages.

This system of indexing from 0 instead of 1 may seem strange at first, but once you start extracting elements in a programmatic way using loops, it will make more sense.

ADDING AN ELEMENT TO AN ARRAY

You can add elements into an array at any time. Let's add goat to our array, like this:

```
animalArray.push('goat');
```

array now contains:

```
var animalArray = ["dog", "cat", "pig", "horse", "sheep",
"goat"];
```

The Array method push (more on methods later) adds the stated element to end the end of the array, so "goat" is now added as a new element in the last position in the array.

SORTING AN ARRAY

You can sort the array alphabetically, using the sort method:

```
sort(animalArray);
```

Then the array sequence changes to:

```
var animalArray = ["cat", "dog", "goat", "horse", "pig",
"sheep"];
```

If you display the element where "goat" was located in the previous example

```
alert (animalArray[3]);
```

you now get "horse" because it is at index 3 in this alphabetized array.

ASSOCIATIVE ARRAYS

So far you've seen an *indexed* array where you can reference the elements by their index (numerical position). But there is a second kind of an array known as an *associative* array that has elements that are each made of two parts: a key and a value. The key is a text string that allows you to associate each value with an actual name.

The format to populate an associative array is

```
arrayName[key] = value
```

In the next example, a country name is the key and the name of the country's capital city is the value.

Here's how to build an associative array of countries and their capitals

creates the array

CODE 2.5 array_game_capital_cities.html

```
var capitalCitiesArray[];

capitalCitiesArray["USA"] = "Washington DC";

capitalCitiesArray["England"] = "London";

capitalCitiesArray["France"] = "Paris";

capitalCitiesArray["Italy"] = "Rome";
```

The power of an associative array is that you can easily find a value, regardless of its position in the array, by referencing its key.

The format is the same as that for an indexed array except instead of using the index number you use the key name. The key here is a string, so you have to remember to put it in quotes:

sets thisCapital to Paris

```
var thisCapital = capitalCitiesArray["France"];
```

To reinforce what you saw earlier, note that the variable on the left, `thisCapital`, is set to the *evaluated result* of the expression `capitalCitiesArray["France"]`, which is Paris.

Even if you sort this associative array, this line of code will still find the correct capital because you locate the value by its key, not the indexed position.

You can also use an object literal in place of an associative array, as you will see in the next chapter on objects. An object literal is a simple structure in which to store properties and other values. Generally, it's best to use an object literal because the syntax is simpler.

Code that Acts on Data

Now you have seen the different data types and ways you can store them. Let's look at code structures you can use to work on that data.

Operators

Operators go between data elements to indicate how JavaScript should evaluate them. In most cases, an operator indicates the process that the right side should perform on the left side. There are several types of operators.

MATH

We're all familiar with the basic math operators:

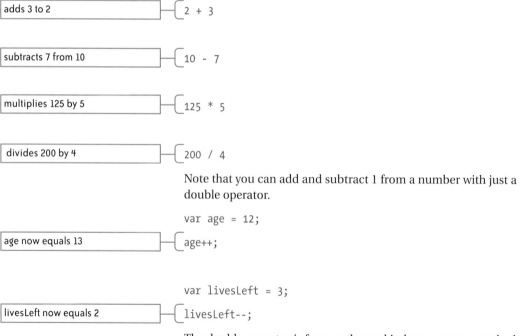

adds 3 to 2 — `2 + 3`

subtracts 7 from 10 — `10 - 7`

multiplies 125 by 5 — `125 * 5`

divides 200 by 4 — `200 / 4`

Note that you can add and subtract 1 from a number with just a double operator.

```
var age = 12;
```
age now equals 13 — `age++;`

```
var livesLeft = 3;
```
livesLeft now equals 2 — `livesLeft--;`

The double operator is frequently used in loops, so you can look at each element in a set of data sequentially—see "Loops and Iterating over Data" later in this chapter.

COMPARISON OPERATORS

Often you will want to use a comparison operator to see if two values are the same or to see if one is greater or less than the other. I introduced Booleans earlier—now you can see them in action. A comparison always evaluates to one of the two Boolean values: `true` or `false`. You can make comparisons with an `if-then-else` control structure, which is formatted like this:

```
if (this comparison evaluates to true) {

    // then do these things

} else { // the else part is optional

    // do these other things

}
```

For example:

| "less than" comparison |
```
if (yourHeight < minHeight) {

alert "You are too short to ride!";
```

| no else statement in this example |
```
}
```

| "greater than" comparison |
```
if (livesLeft > 0) {

    alert "Play again!";

} else {

    alert "You die!";

}
```

| equality comparison (are both same value and type?) |
```
if (a === b) {

    alert "Identical!";

} else {

    alert "Not the same!";

}
```

If the comparison evaluates to `true`, then the statements inside the first set of braces execute; if the statement evaluates to `false`, the optional `else` part of the statement inside the second set of braces executes.

THE =, ==, AND === OPERATORS

You may have noticed the triple equals sign (===) operator in the preceding example, so this is a good moment to clarify the possible meanings of the equals sign.

A single equals sign does *not* mean equal to; it means "set," as in

The space on either side of the equals signs is optional. I add the spaces to improve clarity such as between long variable names. In short math formulas, I forgo the spaces. It's a matter of personal style.

```
var a=15+10;
```

The element on the left, a, is set to the result of the evaluated expression on the right, which is 25.

== is an equality operator and means equal to.

By contrast, == "loosely" compares two values to see if they are the same, but they don't have to be of the same type. Because the == operator equates values of differing types, the following comparisons all evaluate to true:

a string and a number	`1=="1"`
a Boolean and a string	`false=="false"`
two different falsey values	`undefined==null`

=== means exactly equal to. This is a more stringent comparison than == because both values must be the same *and* of the same data type:

sets x to an integer	`x=4`
sets y to a string	`y='4'`
true	`(x==y)`
false—not both same type	`(x===y)`

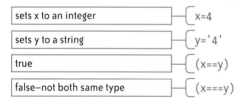

You almost always want to use the === operator and avoid the == operator. Be sure that you want the looser == comparison if you use it. It is important to keep track of what type of data your variables hold, and if in doubt, check a variable's data type with the typeOf() operator before using it, like this:

```
if (typeOf myVar==='number') { /* do something with a
number here */ }
```

When you are sure of the data type, you can confidently use === . If you use ==, your code can return incorrect and a hard-to-debug comparison results. You will see more of the == and === operators as you go forward. For now, just know that they are both used in comparisons, and that === is the one you want to use except in specific cases where a looser comparison is required.

THE ! (NOT) OPERATOR

To see if two values are *not* the same, you can use the ! (NOT) operator. Now you are effectively testing for false instead of true.

inequality comparison (are not same value)

```
if (a !== b) {

    alert "Not the same value!";

} else {

    alert "Identical!";

}
```

Note that the !== operator is stringent in its comparisons and behaves like the negative version of ===.

THE AND AND OR OPERATORS

You can make comparisons with more than one operator as you saw with the equality and NOT operators in the NOT operator example.

Other comparison operators you might want to add to your comparisons are && (which means AND) and || (the double pipe symbol, which means OR and is written by pressing Shift-\ [at least it is on U.S. and U.K. keyboards]). These operators allow you to do more complex comparisons.

```
if (a && b < c) {

    // do this if both a and b are less than c

}


if (a || b < c) {

    // do this if either a or b are less than c

}


if (a < b && b < c) {

    // do this if a is less than b and b is less than c

}
```

USING THE OR OPERATOR TO SUPPLY DEFAULT VALUES

Then there is the very interesting and handy use of the OR operator to supply a default value, as shown here:

```
var userName = logInName || 'Visitor'
```

Here, I want to set the userName variable to the name the user supplied when that user logged in. However, if logInName is undefined (the variable was never set because this person hasn't logged in), the user name will be set to "Visitor". When the OR operator is used in this format, the value to its right is a fallback value in case the one to the left is not set. This is very handy for setting a variable to a default value when the primary value is not provided, as demonstrated in this example.

THE + OPERATOR—ADDITION AND CONCATENATION

The + (plus symbol) operator actually has two uses. The first, as you have seen, is its familiar role of adding numbers together.

```
alert (123+456)   //displays 579

alert 100++      //displays 101
```

However, the + operator will also concatenate (join together) two expressions, such as strings—a common task you will often perform.

```
alert ("lap" + "top")   //displays laptop
```

Be aware that the + operator will only add two values together if they are both numbers; otherwise, it will concatenate them.

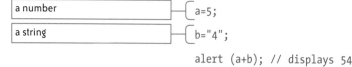

```
a number          a=5;
a string          b="4";

alert (a+b); // displays 54
```

This displays 54, because you are adding a string to a number, so JavaScript treats both values as strings and concatenates the two values.

If you want to use a number that is stored as a string, you can use the string methods parseInt() and parseFloat() to convert it to an integer or a floating-point number, respectively. Just put the number, or the variable that contains it, in the parentheses, like this:

```
parseInt(b);
```

Now you can add the integer to the string in the previous example if you rewrite the code like this:

evaluates to 9

```
a+parseInt(b);
```

You will want to use `parseInt()` when a data source serves up a string like this

```
"25 pounds weight"
```

and you need to use the value 25 in a calculation.

The `parseInt()` method only sees the numbers at the start of a string and ignores the rest, so

```
var perPound= 5;
```

```
var totalWeight="25 pounds weight";
```

* means multiply

```
alert (perPound * parseInt(totalWeight)); // displays 125
```

Because JavaScript is weakly typed, you need to keep in mind the types of data that are stored in your variables. As illustrated earlier in the chapter, use the `typeOf` operator to determine what type of data your code is dealing with, and if necessary, convert it to an appropriate format before using it.

Here is a real-world example of concatenation. I want to display the user's first and last name, but they are stored in two separate variables. I can concatenate them with the + operator.

When I do this, I also want a space between the first and last names, so I also include a string with a just a space in it:

```
firstName="Austin";
```

```
lastName="Markus";
```

```
alert (firstName+" "+lastName)   // displays Austin Markus
```

Note that the string is located between the two + signs (highlighted). It has a single space in it. By concatenating this between the first and last name variables as an additional expression, the displayed first and last names are separated by a space.

THE "SETNESS" TEST

Very frequently, before you access a variable, function, array, or object, you want to check if it has data in it or if it simply exists at all. This is particularly true if the process you want to run will cause an error or even cause the application to fail entirely if the required data is not present. So, a very common true/false test is to check if a variable is set or not. This can be done in a simple, shorthand way—you don't even need a comparison operator.

Let's imagine you want to check if a visitor to your site is logged in (has provided a user name and password) before you allow the visitor to access the site's "Members Only" area. You might create a userLoggedIn variable for this purpose:

```
var userLoggedIn;
```

Here you have declared a variable but have not assigned a value to it. When the user successfully logs in, it is set to true. Then at any time you can check if the user is logged in or not, like this:

```
if (userLoggedIn) {
    // code here takes user to member content
    // code only runs if userLoggedIn evaluates to true
}
```

In this case, the expression

```
if (userLoggedIn)
```

is the shorthand equivalent of

```
if (userLoggedIn===true)
```

If the variable is set to anything except a falsey value, the test will evaluate to true.

JavaScript's falsey values are

0	(Number)
NaN	(Not a number)
false	(Boolean)
""	(Empty string)
null	(Object)
undefined	(Undefined)

It doesn't matter which of these falsey values are returned—any of them cause the expression to evaluate to false. You initialized the userloggedIn variable when the user arrived at the site, but you didn't define a value for it. So currently, because undefined is a falsey value, the user will not get to see your Members Only content. However, if the variable didn't even exist, the test would also return undefined, and the test would still evaluate to `false`.

This neat little structure appears somewhere in just about every script, and you can use it to check if a field has text in it, to test if an element with a particular ID exists in the markup before you attempt to modify it, or to determine if you received a `false` result back from a function.

Its big benefit is that you don't have to know or explicitly state in your test what the variable should be set to. You might choose to put the user's session ID or first name in this variable when you change it from 0—it doesn't matter.

All that matters is that the variable is set to something other than the falsey values listed earlier. This structure could be thought of as a test for setness, and yes, I made up that word.

THE SWITCH STATEMENT

The final comparison structure I'll show here is switch.

```
switch (value to test) {
   case 1:
      // case 1 code here
      break;
   case 2:
      // case 2 code here
      break;
   case 3:
      // case 3 code here
      break;
   default:
      // default code runs if no case matches
}
```

It's similar to the `if` statement and should be used when you want to test if a variable is one of several possible values.

```
switch (upgradeOptions) {

  case "silver":

    additionalCost=100

    break;

  case "gold":

    additionalCost=500

    break;

  case "platinum":

    additionalCost=1000

    break;

  default:

    additionalCost=0;

}
```

The variable we want to test here is `upgradeOptions`—the argument for the `switch` statement. It is compared with the value for each case. You can have as many case tests as you want. If there is a match, the code for that case runs. Note that the last line of each case is `break`, which terminates the end statement. You will rarely find a situation where you want more than one case to match, so remember to add `break` to each `case` statement. If none of the cases match the switch argument, the optional default `case` runs, if present. When you find yourself testing the same variable for several possible values by writing a laundry list of `if` statements, it's probably time to refactor your code as a `switch` statement.

Loops and Iterating Over Data

Sometimes you'll want to examine a set of data, typically held in an array, and test each item in that set for some particular characteristic—values greater than 10, as a random example. Examining each item of a data set is a process known as iteration, and it's a common programming task.

To help you in this work are code structures called loops. A loop is a code structure that runs the same piece of processing code repeatedly on a data set and uses a counter to keep track of which item of data it should process next until some exit condition is met, and then it stops. Let's look at these ideas in more detail.

COUNTERS AND EXIT CONDITIONS

Loops use a variable that acts as the counter. The counter usually starts at 0 and increments (goes up by one) each time the loop runs. It is used, for example, as the index reference when processing the elements of an indexed array. Each time the loop runs, the next element in the array is processed by the code within the loop.

When programming a loop, you must ensure that some event occurs that triggers an exit condition or the loop will not stop and your code will eventually error out, or lock up and crash the browser. So, each time a loop runs, the exit condition is checked; if the exit condition evaluates to false, the loop stops. Let's see these ideas in action.

THE WHILE LOOP

The structure of the while loop looks like this:

```
while (some condition is true) {

    // repeatedly do these things

}
```

I use the document.write() *method to display the output on the page here because it is simple to understand and use at this early stage in the book. It is pretty much obsolete now that I can reliably use DOM scripting (see Chapter 3) to add data into HTML elements. Generally,* document.write() *should be avoided.*

Let's use a while loop to simply write out the numbers 1 to 10 in the browser window.

```
var x = 1;

while (x < 11) {

    document.write (x + "<br />");

    x++;

}

// lists the numbers 1 thru 10
```

In this example, the loop keeps running as long as x is less than 11. Without the line x++ (which increments x each time the loop runs), x would always equal 1, the exit condition (x becoming equal to or greater than 11) would never be met, and you would have the infamous infinite loop condition.

THE DO WHILE LOOP

A variation on the while loop is the do…while loop. It looks like this:

```
do {

    // these things

    }

    while (some condition is true);
```

Unlike the while loop, the do…while loop runs at least once, even if the test evaluates to false. This is because, as you can see from its format, the test is at the end of the loop, not the start. Look at this do…while variation on the while loop example:

```
var x = 1;

do {

    document.write (x + "<br />");

    x++;

    }

    while (x > 11);

// displays: 1
```

In this example, I changed the test around so the loop runs while x is *greater* than 11. Because the initial value of x is 1, the test resolves to false; however, the loop runs once before stopping.

THE FOR LOOP

A more complex but more useful loop is the for loop, which requires three values in order to work.

```
for (counterInitialValue;  exitCondition;  counterIncrement)
{

    // do this repeatedly

}
```

A common use of this loop is to iterate over (examine each element of) an array. I first set up an array that holds the names of my five favorite Web languages (yes, I know, some of them technically aren't languages!). The loop will extract each element's value in turn.

```
var languages=["HTML", "CSS", "JavaScript", "PHP", "SQL"];

for (var arrayPos=0; arrayPos<languages.length; arrayPos++) {

   alert(languages[arrayPos]);

}
```

A sequence of alert dialogs displays each item.

The meanings of the three (highlighted) elements of this for loop are

1. Set a variable called arrayPos to 0. This variable is the counter that will keep track of the position in the array as I check each element and will automatically increment, moving to the next element each time the loop runs.

2. Each time the loop runs, check if the counter is less than the number of items in the array (note that languages.length evaluates to 5, the length of the array as an integer), and if so, the loop runs again.

3. Each time the loop runs, increment the counter, in this case by one.

Now let's look at the code within the loop:

```
alert(languages[arrayPos]);
```

This code will extract the element whose index is equal to the value of the counter arrayPos and display it in a dialog. So the first time the loop runs, I retrieve the element at index 0 because the counter's initial value is 0. The counter increments before the loop runs again and, because the counter (now 1) is still less than the number of items in the array (5), the loop runs again and I get the element at index 1. Eventually, when the loop runs for the fifth time, I extract the item at index 4 (the fifth and final item) and I increment the counter to 5. Now the test of the counter being less than the number of items in the array evaluates to false (they are now equal), and the loop stops.

The workings of the for loop can be a little hard to grasp, but it's worth getting your head around this structure, because you will use it frequently when examining the data within arrays and objects.

Functions

Functions are the building blocks of your page's functionality, as their name suggests. Each function performs a task, such as validating an email address, adding numbers together, or moving an element onscreen. What makes functions so useful is that they can be written to accept items of data, called arguments, which they use in their work.

Imagine you owned a very smart robot that could do your bidding. It has a very useful shopping function that enables the robot to look up store locations, find its way to the store, track down items, pay for them, and get home with the goods. All you have to do is call the shopping function on your robot, remembering to include the required store and item arguments

```
goShopping("Borders", "Codin' for the Web");
```

and soon after, it returns with a nice book with a blue cover. The enormous quantity of code to get your robot to do this is hidden away in a function that you don't have to worry about. You just call the function with the required arguments and everything else is already taken care of.

Functions also keep things nice and tidy. The main flow of your code doesn't contain all those miles of instructions telling the robot how to walk or pick up things. All these individual, and often complex, tasks are abstracted (out of sight but useable) into functions that can be called with a single instruction from anywhere in your code.

In short, you call a function, passing it any arguments (data) it needs to do its job, and then it returns the result to you. That function can have a million lines of code in it, but you can call it and obtain the returned result with a single line.

The basic format of a function is

```
function functionName(parameter1, parameter2,…parameterN) {

    // code that executes when function is called

}
```

This structure is know as a function literal, and it comprises the reserved word `function` (you can't use it for any other purpose in your code), the optional function name, any parameters you choose to add within the required `()` operator, and the statements within the curly braces that execute when the function is called.

When JavaScript first loads in the browser, code within functions is not executed. Code within functions is only executed when the function is called, using a function call. The basic format of a function call is

CODE 2.6 simple-addition_
function.html

```
function functionName(arg1, arg2,…argN)
```

For example, here's a function that adds two numbers together:

the function

```
function addThese(firstNum, secondNum) {

    return firstNum + secondNum;

}
```

When you call the function with this code

the function call

```
var theAnswer = addThese(5478, 430672);
```

the variable `theAnswer` is set to 436,150.

Variables Declared Within a Function Are Local Variables

Variables declared within functions are local variables, which means they are only useable by the code within the function and last only as long as the function in which they are declared is running. Once the function ends, those variables are disposed of. Next time the function runs, they are created again.

This is a good thing. A local variable's scope is limited to the function, so it cannot conflict with a variable with the same name in another function. The only other kind of variable scope in JavaScript is global where the variable can be accessed from any function. It is rare that you'll need a global variable, and it's a recipe for bugs if you create one inadvertently. If you need to create a variable that sticks around, create it as the property of an object. You will learn how to do this in the next chapter.

Another advantage of using local variables is that the memory they use can be retrieved after the function completes and the variables are no longer needed. JavaScript performs a regular process called garbage collection that frees up unused memory. This is another reason to put `var` in front of variables when you declare them. If you don't use `var` when you create variables, they become global variables, and unless you then explicitly dispose of them, the memory they use is not garbage collected. Depending on how your application is coded, you can accumulate large numbers of global variables by constantly (and usually inadvertently) creating new ones, and your application can eventually grind to a standstill as JavaScript tries to juggle an ever-diminishing amount of memory. Using local variables, unless global variables are absolutely necessary, is very important in an Ajax-driven world where a user can be in your application for hours; those little "memory leaks" can really add up with prolonged use of your application.

How Functions Work

1. A function is a block of code that is called (triggered) by a function call.

```
                          var a = 250;
                          var b = 170;
                            variable name  function name  arguments
                          var theAnswer = addThese(a,b);
                          alert (theAnswer);
                                   function name        parameters
                          function addThese(firstNum, secondNum) {
                              return firstNum + secondNum;
                          }
```

function call

function

2. The function call can pass data arguments (data items) into the corresponding parameters of the function.

```
                          var theAnswer = addThese(a,b);
                          alert (theAnswer);

                          function addThese(firstNum250, second170Num) {
                              return firstNum + secondNum;
                          }
```

3. The function uses the parameter values in its code.

```
                          var theAnswer = addThese(a,b);
                          alert (theAnswer);

                          function addThese(firstNum, secondNum) {
                              return firstNum250 + second170Num;
                          }
```

4. The result of the function's work is returned to the calling code, which evaluates to that value.

```
                          var theAnswer = addThese420(a,b);
                          alert (theAnswer);

                          function addThese(firstNum, secondNum) {
                              return firstNum + secondNum;
                          }
```

5. Here the variable that was set to the evaluated value of the function call is displayed.

The page at http://www.scriptinwithajax.com says:

420

OK

If you're confused about the difference between arguments and parameters, remember this: The arguments of the function call set the parameters of the function.

Here's how this works. The function has two parameters, firstNum and secondNum, which are special kinds of variables that are set to the values of the arguments passed to the function by the function call. In this example, the parameters' values are added and the result is returned to the code that made the function call. In functions, the right side of the line of code that calls the function evaluates to the returned result, so the left side, in this case theAnswer, is set to that value. Now you can use the variable theAnswer later in your code, and it will evaluate to the number 436,150.

The return keyword is not required, but its purpose is to pass back the result of the function's work to the code that called it. Sometimes you don't need to return anything from a function, so you can omit return (in which case it will return undefined). However, note that once the function encounters return, it stops running and the calling script regains control.

Once you have written a function like this, you can use it over and over in your code by simply calling the function with the two numbers you want to add.

Any time you find yourself writing the same piece of code or something very much like it a second time, it makes sense to break it out into a function. You can then write and maintain it in one place, and use it whenever the code logic requires it.

FUNCTIONS DON'T REQUIRE ARGUMENTS

Sometimes you won't want to pass any arguments with a function. Perhaps your function just returns the current time, for example, and doesn't need any additional information to do that.

corresponding function not illustrated

```
var rightNow = currentTime();
```

Even if you don't pass arguments, you still need to include the parentheses or the function will not be called.

PASSING ANONYMOUS FUNCTIONS AS VARIABLES

An interesting aspect of JavaScript functions is that they can be passed around in your code like variables.

If you want to stop a function from running during testing, adding return; *as the first line of the function's code is an alternative to commenting out the function. Just don't forget to take it out when you are done.*

It's common in programming languages to set the value of a variable to the value of another variable, like this:

CODE 2.7 big_woof.html

```
var thisVar = 20;

var thatVar = thisVar;

alert (thatVar); // displays 20
```

What's remarkable about JavaScript is that you can do the same kind of thing with functions. Here, I set a variable to a function:

```
var bigWoof = function() {

    return ("WOOF!");

}
```

I can then call the function using the name of the variable in which it is stored, like this:

note the parenthesis because I am calling the function

```
var bark = bigWoof();
```

Now the variable bark is set to "WOOF!", as seen in the display in **Figure 2.3**.

```
alert (bark);
```

FIGURE 2.3 The dialog displays the result of the passed function.

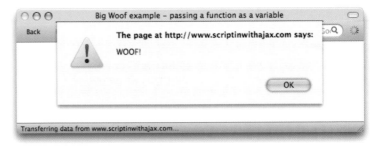

The function doesn't have a name after the word function as you saw in earlier function examples; it's what is called an anonymous function. It doesn't need a name because you reference it with the name of the variable in which it is stored. It's very handy to be able to pass an anonymous function to other parts of your code like this, giving it whatever appropriate variable name you want as you do so. You will see anonymous functions used in many later examples.

A common use is to pass a function to an Ajax call as the callback, which is the code that runs when the requested data comes back from the server. Normally, you just pass the name of the function to run, but you can give it the entire function instead and let the Ajax request response run it for you as illustrated on pages 187-188.

CALLING A FUNCTION FROM A LINK

User actions are the trigger for many of the functions you will write. User actions actually trigger *events*, which are messages that are fired off by the browser when the user does any of a number of actions, such as clicking the mouse, moving on or off an element, or pressing a key on the keyboard. Events are a large and important topic that will be the subject of Chapter 4. However, in the interest of being able to follow Chapter 3, "Objects," just understand for now that you can easily detect a click event and use it to trigger a JavaScript function. Here's an example of how that works:

```
<a href="dogs.html" onclick="bigWoof();">Bark and Go!</a>
```

Adding an onclick *handler directly to a link like this is no longer considered a good way to associate an event with a link because it mixes the JavaScript with the HTML. However, it's simple and easily understood, so I will use this technique until I cover events in depth in Chapter 4.*

The (highlighted) onclick event handler is triggered when the click happens and in this case, the bigWoof function is then called. The event handler (onclick) receives the click message before the href. So in this case, you would first get the WOOF! and then the dogs. html page specified in the href would load. Often, you don't want the href to work if the JavaScript function is called (for example, if you are using Ajax to get the data and only want the regular page to reload as a backup if the JavaScript isn't present). To prevent the href from receiving the event after the JavaScript event handler, you do this:

```
<a href="dogs.html" onclick="bigWoof(); return false;">Bark
and Stay!</a>
```

Now the click event triggers the function, but it is not passed on to the href of the element and you remain on the current page.

Summary

In this chapter, you've seen the basic concepts of how JavaScript works. You've seen how data is stored and the ways you can perform processes, such as conditional tests and iterative looping, on that data. You've also seen how functions are the basic building blocks of your application's capabilities.

Next, I'll show you objects. Because JavaScript is so heavily based on objects and the Document Object Model (DOM) is an object, let's start a new chapter and take a close look at objects and the DOM.

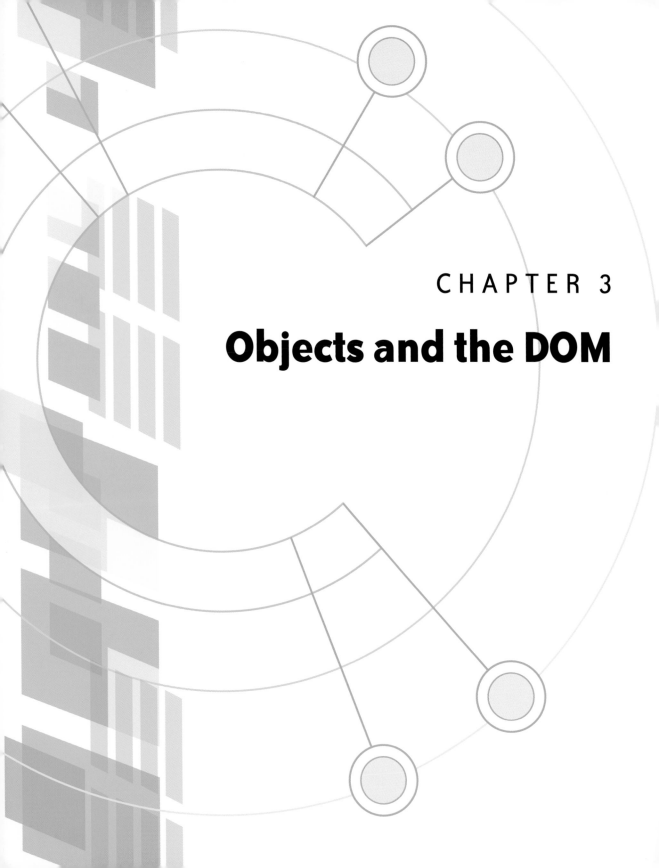

CHAPTER 3

Objects and the DOM

OBJECTS ARE THE FOUNDATION of object-oriented programming (OOP), which is the way the logic of most modern applications and Web sites is written. As you will start to discover, everything in JavaScript is an object. For example, when you create a function or an array, you are actually creating a specialized kind of object. As its name implies, the Document Object Model (DOM) is simply, from JavaScript's view, a large data object. When you use JavaScript to add HTML elements to your markup, you are extending this object with new properties.

If you have worked with JavaScript a little and have added some simple functionality to a page, you may find that this chapter takes your understanding to a new level. If you are new to JavaScript, get ready to see JavaScript's power to create interactive interfaces.

Objects

There are numerous advantages to using objects in your coding work. The primary advantage is that they provide a high level of organization to your code. If you try to write anything but the most basic functionality without using objects, you'll soon find that you have numerous functions that call one another and you'll find yourself playing "pass the parcel" with the arguments as you move data from function to function. The code gets hard to read, because it becomes difficult to see which functions relate to which task. It's much easier to take the variables and functions that relate to a particular task and package them into an object.

An object is a named collection of variables and functions. To indicate that they are part of an object, a variable inside an object is known as a property, and a function inside an object is known as a method.

You access an object's properties and methods with "dot syntax," which separates elements with dots (periods) and looks like this:

```
objectName.aPropertyOfTheObject;
```

```
objectName.aMethodOfTheObject();
```

You will see dot syntax a great deal in this book. As mentioned earlier, *everything* in JavaScript is an object, or at least can be treated as an object, and accessed with dot syntax.

However, you can also use the array syntax to access an object. You would do this when you need to select the property to read based on some condition in your code and don't want to hard-code the property name in your script. In that case, you can use a variable as the property name, in this format:

```
var theProperty = changeableValue
```

```
objectName[theProperty]
```

There are two types of objects: predefined objects that already exist as part of the JavaScript language ready for you to use, and user-defined objects that you write yourself for some purpose specific to your application.

Predefined JavaScript Objects

JavaScript has a hierarchy of predefined objects, each with built-in methods and properties ready for use. At the top of this hierarchy is the Window Object, and its immediate descendant is the Document Object, which contains the DOM of your document. There are a number of other predefined objects that help with particular types of tasks, such as the Number, Math, and Date Objects. Listings of these predefined objects and their methods are in Appendixes A, B, and C, and you will see many examples of each as we go forward. However, the Window and Document Objects warrant further discussion here.

THE WINDOW OBJECT

The Window Object gives you access to a hierarchical representation of the browser-related properties and methods that can be accessed and sometimes set via the Window Object. For example, the Window Object stores the history of pages visited and can be used to move to pages previously visited—it's like operating the Back button right from the code.

To move the user to the previous page visited, write

```
window.back();
```

This calls the back method of the Window Object, and the browser goes back one page.

The Window Object has methods that can open, load content into, and close additional windows. Other Window Object methods display some basic dialogs (alert, prompts, and confirm), set and remove the focus on elements, and set up time delays to control time-based events such as animation.

THE DOCUMENT OBJECT

As its name suggests, the Document Object gives you access to the DOM. The DOM is a hierarchical representation of an HTML document. JavaScript enables you to manipulate the DOM in sophisticated ways, including adding, changing, and removing HTML elements from the document as the code runs—a capability that is integral to the use of Ajax in your work.

The Document Object's predefined getElementById method is one of the ways you can "get" an HTML element as an object so that you can use dot syntax to extract a property from it. For example, you can extract the text from within this h1 element:

```
<h1 id="headline">Big news!</h1>
```

like this

```
var theElement=document.getElementById("headline");

alert(theElement.innerHTML);

// displays Big news!
```

In the first line, I put the h1 element into a variable. In the second line, I get the text of the h1 element and display it. To do this, I use the innerHTML property, which references whatever is in between that element's opening and closing tags. I'll show you how to access the DOM in detail later in this chapter, but for now, note that you use dot syntax to access the DOM because it is an object.

You may already know that CSS also uses the DOM as the basis for its operation on the document, and the selector of a CSS rule (the part before the curly braces) defines which elements of the DOM the CSS rule affects.

selects all list items in element with ID "nav"

```
#nav li {code goes here}
```

CSS is capable of setting the style-related properties of an element—its text color or its position onscreen, for example.

JavaScript takes this DOM relationship much further and allows you to not only set style properties, but also to get and set all the values of the properties and attributes of the DOM. This means that with JavaScript you have programmatic control of the entire DOM and can manipulate the document structure in response to user actions. I'll get right to the specifics of how to do this after we look at user-created objects.

User-created Objects

While JavaScript has many predefined objects, you can also create your own objects to manage large tasks and data sets within your application. Within an object, you define its properties and the methods that can act on those properties.

OBJECT LITERALS

The simplest way to create an object is to use a format called an object literal. The format of an object literal is

```
objectName={

   propertyName1:value,

   propertyName2:value,

   functionName1: function() {

      // code for function

   },

   functionName2: function() {

      // code for function

   }

}
```

Here is a simple example of an object created using the object literal format. This object does math using the constant π (pi)—the ratio of the radius of a circle to its circumference, as we all remember from high school.

```
circleMath={

   pi:Math.PI,

   calcCircumf:function(rad) {

      var circum = rad * circleMath.pi;

      alert (circum + " inches");

   },

   calcArea:function(rad) {

      var area = (rad * circleMath.pi) * rad;

      alert (area + " square inches");

   },

   calcVolume:function(rad) {

      var volume = (4/3) * circleMath.pi * (rad * rad * rad)

      alert (volume + " cubic inches");

   }

}
```

CODE 3.1 circle_math_obj.html

The object is called `circleMath`, and it contains one property—the value of π, which is obtained from the built-in Math object—and three methods that calculate the circumference, area, and volume of a circular object. (For simplicity here, I've assumed the units to be inches.)

By writing

```
circleMath={

    // all the properties and methods of the object

}
```

I set `circleMath` variable to the value of the object itself, so we use dot syntax to access the properties and methods within. Here, in each case, I pass 10 as the radius of the circle:

```
circleMath.calcCircumf(10) // displays 31.416 inches
```

```
circleMath.calcArea(10) // displays 314.1592653589793 square
    inches
```

```
circleMath.calcVolume(10) // displays 4188.790204786391 cubic
    inches
```

Object literals are very unforgiving of formatting errors, so have the Firefox Error Console open while you test your object literals, and any errors will be identified. Some common formatting errors can be avoided if you remember the following points about object literals:

- Property names and values are separated by a colon; don't use the equals sign to set them, as you would with variables.

- Every time you refer to a property or method in your code, even within the object itself, you must precede its name with `objectName.`—as in `circleMath.calcCircumf(10)` when calling the `calcCircumf()` method—or you will get a "not defined" error.

- The first line of each function is formatted differently from the functions you have seen so far. With an object literal the format is function name, colon, the keyword `function`, and then the ( ) parentheses. This is then followed by the curly braces, that contain the function's code, like this

  ```
  functionName:function() {

      // function's code

  }
  ```

As you can see, JavaScript can return some very long floating-point numbers. To keep the code as simple as possible, I left them that way, but I could shorten the circum value to three decimal places using the `toFixed(x)` *Number object method, where* x *is the required number of decimal places, like this:*
`var circum=circum.`
`toFixed(3);`

Technically, an object literal is just a list of properties, and the value of a property can be a function. However, I find it easier and more consistent simply to refer to the properties that contain functions as methods.

- An object literal is simply a comma-separated list of properties and methods, so don't forget those commas. Take a close look at the placement of the commas in the circleMath example on page 61. Note that no comma is used after the last item's }, right before the object's closing }.

The key takeaway here is that object literals are a powerful organizational structure for your code. Use meaningful names for the objects you create because they are effectively the name of the object's collection of properties and methods.

The benefit that this extra level of organization that object literals (and objects in general) brings to your code cannot be overstated. I am constantly improving my code by identifying functions that are "loose" in my scripts and moving them into object literals along with other related functions and variables.

In short, with good use of objects, you organize your code into the tasks that your application performs. It's so much easier to understand what is happening if you do this. In contrast, if you have to work on a large script that's just made up of dozens of functions, you have to work out how they all relate to one other by reading every one of them line by line.

Object literals are a great organizational tool, but the power of objects is revealed when you understand how to create instances of the objects you create.

Objects and Instances

Often, you will use an object to manage a set of data where each entity in the data set has the same types of properties (a set of products may each have a brand name, a model number, and a price, for example). You can then create an instance of the object for each product—each instance with its own set of property values for the object's properties—and then use the object's methods to perform all kinds of operations on the instances.

To help you understand this concept, in this example, I'll create an object to hold information about my guitars.

I'll first write an object, again using an object literal format, called Guitar that can help me do this. It's standard practice to start an object name with a capital letter if instances can be created from it.

CODE 3.2 guitar_object.html

the object's method

the object's properties

end object

```
var Guitar = function (theName, theBrand, theModel) {

    this.guitarName=theName;

    this.guitarBrand=theBrand;

    this.guitarModel=theModel;


    this.describeGuitar= function() {

    var description = this.guitarName+" - "+this.guitarModel+
    " by "+this.guitarBrand;

    return (description);

    }

}
```

This is what is called a constructor function; instances can be "constructed" from it. Because I use the `this` keyword as a prefix to each property name, instances can be created where the values of these properties are different for every instance.

In technical terms, the keyword `this` is bound to the instances of the object, but the easy way to think about `this` is that it means "this instance of the object." The value of a property that is preceded with `this` can be different for each instance. For example, the word `this` that you see here

```
this.guitarName = theName
```

means "this instance's value for the property `guitarName`". So the entire line above means, "set this instance's value of the property `guitarName` to the passed-in value of the parameter `theName`."

Note also that the object has one method, `describeGuitar`. A method is simply a function inside an object, but methods are different from functions in a very important way.

When you call a function, you pass the data the function needs to do its work as arguments at the time you call the function.

When you create a new instance of an object, you set its properties at that time. When you later call the methods of an object, it simply needs to know which instance of the data you want it to use, and it can get the data for itself. Method calls don't need no stinkin' arguments! That is, unless you need to change any property values later as your code runs. Most of the time, all you need to pass is

Here, I just create two instances, but if you are working with a large data set, creating numerous instances of an object can use large amounts of memory. To prevent such memory use, the Prototype Property allows you to store the methods of the objects you create in a way that they can be shared by the instances instead of being duplicated in every instance as I have done here. You can learn more about the Prototype Property at www.packtpub.com/ article/using-prototype-property-in-javascript.

CODE 3.3 guitar_object.html

My eight-year-old daughter has named each of my guitars and now everyone refers to them by these names like they are pets or something.

the instance name to which the values of its properties are already associated. This is what makes objects so very efficient as a means of working on large data sets—you don't need to pass all this data around anymore. All the object's methods work on the predefined properties of whichever instance is passed to them.

Methods use the `this.methodName()` name syntax for their data, and they, like properties, effectively replace `this` with whichever instance's variable name precedes the method call. The code effectively acts as if it were written like this:

```
instanceVariableName.thisMethod();
```

I'll now instantiate (create) an instance of the `Guitar` object with the appropriate arguments for one of the guitars. By passing this data into the object at the time of creation of the instance, I will not need to pass it again when I later call the object's methods on the instance.

```
var instrument1 = new Guitar("Tiger", "Paul Reed Smith", "Hollowbody II");
```

Note the use of the word `new` in front of the object name—this is what causes the new instance to be created.

I'll now instantiate a second instance:

```
var instrument2 = new Guitar("Sunny", "Ibanez", "Roland G3 Synth Controller");
```

Now, at any time, I can call the object's methods for each instance, and the methods will act on that instance's data.

```
instrument1.describeGuitar();
```
```
displays: Tiger - Hollowbody II by Paul Reed Smith
```
```
instrument2.describeGuitar();
```
```
displays: Sunny - Roland G3 Synth Controller by Ibanez
```

Let's look at how this works, starting with the line that creates the `instrument1` instance.

```
var instrument1 = new Guitar("Tiger", "Paul Reed Smith", "Hollowbody II");
```

I pass three arguments to the `Guitar` object when I instantiate it, which are the data that relate to this specific instance of the object— the nickname of the guitar, its model, and its brand.

How Objects Work

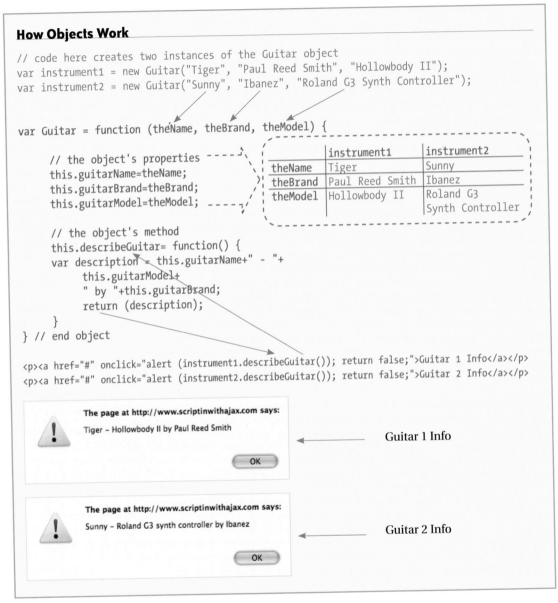

```javascript
// code here creates two instances of the Guitar object
var instrument1 = new Guitar("Tiger", "Paul Reed Smith", "Hollowbody II");
var instrument2 = new Guitar("Sunny", "Ibanez", "Roland G3 Synth Controller");


var Guitar = function (theName, theBrand, theModel) {

    // the object's properties
    this.guitarName=theName;
    this.guitarBrand=theBrand;
    this.guitarModel=theModel;

    // the object's method
    this.describeGuitar= function() {
    var description = this.guitarName+" - "+
        this.guitarModel+
        " by "+this.guitarBrand;
        return (description);
    }
} // end object

<p><a href="#" onclick="alert (instrument1.describeGuitar()); return false;">Guitar 1 Info</a></p>
<p><a href="#" onclick="alert (instrument2.describeGuitar()); return false;">Guitar 2 Info</a></p>
```

	instrument1	instrument2
theName	Tiger	Sunny
theBrand	Paul Reed Smith	Ibanez
theModel	Hollowbody II	Roland G3 Synth Controller

The page at http://www.scriptinwithajax.com says:

Tiger – Hollowbody II by Paul Reed Smith

OK

Guitar 1 Info

The page at http://www.scriptinwithajax.com says:

Sunny – Roland G3 synth controller by Ibanez

OK

Guitar 2 Info

These arguments set the values of the object's three parameters, theName, theBrand, and theModel. These values are then used to set the properties of this instance of the object.

Once the instance has been created, a copy of the object along with its new property values is stored in the variable instrument1. If you try to display the value of the instrument1 variable in an alert dialog, you will just see the words `object Object`. All that matters is that the variable `instrument1` now contains the `instrument1` instance's data.

```
instrument1.describeGuitar(); // calls the describeGuitar
method using the instrument1 instance data
```

When you call the object's method on this instance, the methods will be using the `project1` instance's property values and you get

Tiger - Hollowbody II by Paul Reed Smith

The important takeaway here is that each instance's unique data set can be run against a set of methods defined in the object. I'll extend the code I've used here into a more complete, real-world example in a later chapter. But before moving on, let's talk about object scope.

OBJECTS AND SCOPE

A big advantage of an object is the limited scope of its properties and methods—they are accessible only by explicitly referencing the instance of the object, as in

```
instrument1.describeGuitar();
```

This makes each object a self-contained entity and, if the names used for the object's methods and properties were to be used elsewhere in the code, there would not be a conflict. This concept is known as encapsulation, and it is very helpful when large teams are working on a project. As long as an object behaves in a predictable manner, accepts specific data, and returns predictable responses, only the team members working on that object need concern themselves about its internal implementation, which is immaterial to the rest of the code.

My brilliant wife, who is the Development Editor on this book, wrote a large "HUH?" next to this Objects section when she first read a printout. If she didn't get it…well, let's just say that I have reworked this section a few times to make it clearer. The fact is, objects is a concept that isn't easy to grasp and certainly can't be fully explained in a few pages like this. However, once you start to really understand objects and OOP, your coding abilities will reach a new level. So, if you are also saying "Huh?" right about now, come back to this section after you have seen some real-world examples later in this book, and I think it will all make more sense.

A concept called closure can be used to further protect an object's data from access by other code. Closures are not a simple subject, but here's the most basic tutorial I could find http://javascriptkit.com/javatutors/ closures.shtml.

DOMinating the Document

Other tag-based document types, such as XML, also define a DOM and can be manipulated by JavaScript in the same manner as I demonstrate in this section using an HTML document. There will be examples of XML in Chapter 5, "Ajax."

A must-bookmark reference on the various browsers' JavaScript capabilities is the Compatibility Tables at QuirksMode.org (www.quirksmode.org/compatibility.html).

Now let's look at an object you will work with extensively—the DOM—and see how it can be manipulated with a JavaScript technique called DOM scripting.

Much of the logic of your DOM-related code will go something like this: "Find the HTML element with the attribute 'x' and add a paragraph after it with the text 'blah, blah…'." Your ability to access an easy-to-get element such as one with an ID, move up or down the DOM from that element to the one you actually want, and then modify that element in some way is key to achieving DOM mastery.

The DOM is a family tree-like hierarchical representation of the elements, attributes, and text of an HTML document, known collectively as the document's *nodes*. When you use DOM scripting to modify a visible part of a document, such as the text of a paragraph, that change is immediately visible onscreen. Using the techniques you'll learn in this section, you can rewrite any part of the document's HTML and thereby change the appearance of the document as the user works.

Before I show you some DOM scripting examples, I'll mention that the way in which browsers provide access to a document's elements has changed over time, as those of you who worked years ago with Netscape's now-obsolete concept of layers will know. Today, the W3C's DOM model has become the de facto standard way of accessing the DOM. All modern browsers use it, and I will focus on it here. That said, Internet Explorer (6, 7, and 8) still has many incompatibilities, and I will discuss a number of these and show you how to work around them.

Getting Around the DOM

The DOM is a tree of linked nodes. There are three types of nodes: HTML elements, element attributes, and text within elements, which rather confusingly includes the white space between the HTML elements created by the formatting of your code.

If you add white space between two li's (list items), say by pressing Return and then indenting the next line a few spaces, that white space is contained within the parent ul and is a child node of that

Internet Explorer, unlike most other browsers, does not treat white space in the document as document nodes.

parent element. For this reason, you must be sure you are accessing the element you expect and not white space. It is quite simple to check, as

```
if (nodeType===3) { /* move to another node */ }
```

returns true if the node is white space. Later you'll see how you can move to an adjacent DOM element if this is the case.

A set of DOM-related methods—known colloquially as *getters* and *setters*—allow you to access the nodes.

You can access an element node with a getter, and then you can access the properties of it and its child elements, including the attribute and text nodes. You can also traverse (move around) the DOM to get nodes relative to the one you currently have. Once you have "got" the node you want, you can then modify that node or add a new one in a location relative to it using the DOM methods known as setters.

To get a node and put it into a variable, you need some kind of definitive reference to find it. This reference is often an ID attribute. As those of you who have read my book *Stylin' with CSS* (New Riders, 2008) will know, I strongly advocate dividing a page's markup into sections using div (division) elements and giving each div an ID. Because you are only allowed to use an ID name once on a page, IDs provide CSS with a unique reference, or hook, to the div and its child elements. Using this reference, CSS can be targeted accurately at the desired elements. IDs serve exactly the same purpose for JavaScript. The difference is that when using JavaScript, IDs enable you to get an element along with its child elements and store it in a variable so you can manipulate it. Let's see these ideas in action.

CODE 3.4 dom_exercises.html

Get, Set…DOM!

Here's some markup I'll work with in this section. The highlighted code contains the DOM elements I will get and set. The code that follows is simply links that trigger the demo functions.

```
// only document body shown to save space

<body>

<h1>Simple DOM exercises</h1>

<p>View Source to see the code</p>

<hr />

<div id="content" title="This is the div's title text!">

  <h2>Manipulating the DOM</h2>

    <p id="dom_description">The DOM is a representation of a
       Web page as a family tree-like structure of nodes.</p>


    <div id="demo_links">

    <p><a href="#" onclick="alertElementText()">Show text of
       the paragraph (by ID)</a></p>

    <p><a href="#" onclick="alertDivAttribute()">Show content
       div's title attribute (by ID)</a></p>

    <p><a href="#" onclick="alertHeadlineText()">Show headline
       text (by ID of parent)</a></p>

    <p><a href="#" onclick="displayHeadlineText()">Display
       headline text (add it into an existing element)</a></p>

    <p id="display">The displayed headline will appear here.
       </p>

    <p><a href="#" onclick="newElementForHeadlineText()">
       Display headline text (in a new element)</a></p>

    <p><a href="#" onclick="addStyle()">Add style</a></p>

    <p><a href="#" onclick="addClass()">Add class</a></p>

    </div>

  </div>

</body>
```

markup to be manipulated

each link element has an onClick event attached to it that triggers a JavaScript function when the link is clicked

I admit I am abusing links here by using them to trigger JavaScript while the hrefs of the links point to nowhere—not something I would do in production code. However, I did this here so I can demo styling these links with JavaScript later in this example. If not for this, I would have more correctly used buttons to trigger these examples.

Figure 3.1 shows how the preceding markup displays in the browser.

FIGURE 3.1 The DOM exercises code displayed in the browser.

I'll first show you the getters, the JavaScript methods that provide access to the nodes of the DOM. As with just about everything in JavaScript, what you actually get using these techniques is an object that contains all the properties of the element, including all its child elements and their properties. Because the "got" element is an object, you can read out its properties using dot syntax.

Frameworks such as jQuery greatly simplify getting and setting nodes by using a kind of shorthand. I'll discuss the pros and cons of frameworks in Chapter 6, "Frameworks."

GETTING THE TEXT FROM WITHIN AN ELEMENT

The text of an element node is a separate child node,

```
<p>This text is the child node of its paragraph element</p>
```

so to get the text of the paragraph in the markup that starts "The DOM is a representation…" and has the ID dom_description, I need to first get the element using its ID, and then get the element's first (and only) child node. Finally, I can get the child node's nodeValue—the text string. I'll do this in three steps, each time putting an element into a variable, and then extracting a "sub-element" from it using the variable name.

```
function alertElementText() {

    var myElement=document.getElementById("dom_description");

    var myNode= myElement.firstChild;

    myText=myNode.nodeValue;

    alert(myText);

}
```

put the div with ID "dom_description" into the variable "myElement"

put the firstChild node of "myElement" into "myNode"

put the value (the text) of the element's child node into the variable "myText"

show the "myText" variable in an alert dialog

CODE 3.5 dom_exercises.html

```
// displays The DOM is a representation of a Web page as a
family-tree-like structure of nodes.
```

I could also write these three lines as a single more complex line like this:

```
alert (document.getElementById("dom_description").firstChild.
nodeValue);
```

For beginners, going step by step, as in the preceding multiline code example is probably best, so that you can test for the correct value at each step. If you are a more experienced programmer who is confident of the syntax, writing out all the elements on one line separated by dots can makes your code clearer and more concise. I'll show you a step-by-step and a concise version of these examples as I go along.

Next, let's get the text of an element's attribute. It's easy if that element happens to have an ID, as in this example. Again, I'll first go step by step.

Checking for the Existence of an Element

As I illustrate in the downloadable file for this example, it's good practice to use an `if` statement to check that a child node actually exists before you try to get it, like this:

```
if (theTags[0].firstChild) { // is child node present?

    alert(theTags[0].firstChild.nodeValue);

    }

}
```

Checking for the existence of data before attempting to use it can bulletproof your code in situations where nodes may or may not be populated or exist at all.

GETTING AN ELEMENT'S ATTRIBUTE

It can be very useful to access an element's attributes, such as its class or title. In this example, I'll get the title attribute of the div with the ID content and display that attribute's text.

```
function alertDivAttribute() {

    var theContent=document.getElementById("content");

    var thisText=content.getAttribute("title");

    alert (thisText); // displays This is the div's title
        text!

}
```

put the div with ID "content" into the variable "content"
put the attribute value into var thisText
CODE 3.6 dom_exercises.html

The more concise form looks like this:

```
alert (document.getElementById("content").
getAttribute("title"));
```

GETTING THE TEXT OF A CHILD ELEMENT

Often the element you want is within a containing div that has an ID, so you would first get the div and then "drill down" to the element you want. In this example, the element I want—the text node of the h2 element—is the first child of the h2 element.

```
function alertHeadlineText() {

    var content=document.getElementById("content");

    var theTags=content.getElementsByTagName("h2");

    alert (theTags[0].firstChild.nodeValue);

    // displays Manipulating the DOM

}
```

put the div with ID "content" into the variable "content"
put all h2 elements within the div into variable "theTags" (in this case, there is only one h2)
get the text from the text node of the first (and in this case, only) element
CODE 3.7 dom_exercises.html

Here's the same thing in one line. As shown, you would normally put the result into a variable and only use an alert for testing.

```
var theText=document.getElementById("content").
getElementsByTagName("h2")[0].firstChild.nodeValue;
```

You can see how these single-line versions can become long and complex. Using a couple of extra lines and going step by step can make the code easier to read.

Now let's take a look at the setters, which as their name suggests, set the properties of an element and can even add a completely new element into the markup.

SETTING THE TEXT OF AN ELEMENT

Here I will use the text I got from the h2 element in the previous example and insert it into a different element. The only difference is the highlighted line.

```
function displayHeadlineText() {

    var content=document.getElementById("content");

    var theTags=content.getElementsByTagName("h2");

    var theText=(theTags[0].firstChild.nodeValue);

    document.getElementById("display").firstChild.
        nodeValue=theText;

}
```

Code 3.8 dom_exercises.html

get the text from the h2 element

add the text into the element with the ID "display", replacing its previous text

With a single line (highlighted) I put the text into the text node of the paragraph element with the ID display, replacing the text that was there.

CREATING A NEW ELEMENT AND ADDING TEXT AND AN ATTRIBUTE TO IT

In the final example that uses this markup, I'll grab the h2 text in the same way as the previous two examples. This time, however, I'll create a completely new element, add the text into that element, and then add the new element into the page.

```
// modifies the previous example, creating a completely new
    element for the text

function newElementForHeadlineText() {

var content=document.getElementById("content");

var theTags=content.getElementsByTagName("h2");

var theText=(theTags[0].firstChild.nodeValue);

var myPara=document.createElement("p");

var myTextNode=document.createTextNode(theText);

myPara.appendChild(myTextNode);

myPara.setAttribute("title","I created this paragraph using
    DOM scripting!");

content.appendChild(myPara);

}
```

Code 3.9 dom_exercises.html

create a new paragraph element

create a new text node

insert the text node into the new paragraph element

add an attribute to the paragraph

insert the paragraph as a child of the "content" div (automatically added as last element of the parent)

The comments in the preceding code example pretty much explain what is going on, but I'll also make two remarks here. First, when you create an element like this, it's just hanging around unseen in JavaScript "hyperspace" until you append it to the page.

Second, `appendChild` always adds the element right before the closing tag of the parent element; in this case, the `content` div. It would make more sense aesthetically to add the new text right after the link that we clicked to generate it, but JavaScript does not have an `insertAfter(someElement)` method. However, you can do this with the `insertAfter` helper function that you can find in the `scriptin_helper.js` file.

Modifying Element Styles

This final DOM scripting example will, I hope, give you a lot of inspiring ideas by showing you how JavaScript and CSS can work together. In short, because JavaScript enables you to change the attributes of an element, you have two interesting possibilities for applying CSS with JavaScript:

- **Style attribute.** As you probably know, you can use CSS to add a style attribute to an element to, say, bold its text or even change its visibility or position.

  ```
  <p style="font-weight:bold">As bold as you please!</p>
  ```

  You can do the same thing with JavaScript and ideally, you would use the `setAttribute` method like this

  ```
  myElementObject.setAttribute("style","font-weight:bold;")
  ```

  and indeed you could. However, IE6 doesn't use `setAttribute` predictably, so it's more reliable to treat the element as the object it is and use dot syntax like this:

  ```
  myElementObject.style.fontWeight="bold";
  ```

  All browsers including IE6 understand this syntax. See the sidebar, "Applying Styles with JavaScript," to learn more about applying styles in this way.

- **DOM scripting.** A second and very powerful technique for modifying the styling of an element is to use DOM scripting to add a `class` attribute. This can cause a number of CSS rules that have that class as a contextual selector to come into effect instantly on referenced elements. For example, any styles within these paragraph and link rules

```
.myClass p { /* CSS styles */ }

.myClass a:hover { /* CSS styles */ }
```

would be applied when the class of myClass is added by JavaScript to one of the paragraph's or link's ancestor elements (assuming that no more-specific styles override them).

So let's use the first of these two techniques by adding styles to bold each of the links.

ADDING A STYLE TO AN ELEMENT

Now I'll show you how you can add a style to an element. I'll get all the links that are used to trigger the demo examples and set the font of each one to bold.

CODE 3.10 dom_exercises.html

```
function addStyle() {

    var linkDiv= document.getElementById("demo_links");

    var theLinks= linkDiv.getElementsByTagName("a");

    for (var aLink=0; aLink < theLinks.length; aLink++) {

        // theLinks[aLink].setAttribute("style","font-
           weight:bold;");

        theLinks[aLink].style.fontWeight="bold";

    }

}
```

commented out

There is nothing here that you haven't seen in earlier exercises. I first get the div that contains the links, get all the links within it, and finally loop through all the links, setting each one's style attribute.

As I'll show you on page 109, instead of writing aLink < theLinks. length *in the* for *statement, it's actually best to set a variable for the array length so JavaScript doesn't have to count the elements every time the loop runs, but it's easier to understand written this way.*

The line of code that uses setAttribute and is commented out (highlighted) works perfectly in all W3C DOM-compliant browsers, but doesn't work reliably in IE6. On the line that follows, you can see the alternate, dot-syntax version that works in all browsers.

ADDING A CLASS TO AN ELEMENT

Changing a class on a containing element can have a much more far-reaching effect on the document than simply adding a style, because this can cause many CSS styles to be invoked on many elements from the style sheet at once.

I'll illustrate this by writing a couple of CSS styles (you can see them within a style tag in the head of the document in the downloadable

Applying Styles with JavaScript

Here's a little more detail on adding a style attribute to an element. If you were to manually add a style to the element in the HTML, you could write

```
<p id="myPara" style="font-weight:bold;">Here is some bolded text</>
```

Alternatively, the highlighted code can be added using JavaScript like this:

```
document.getElementById("myPara").setAttribute("style","font-weight:bold;")
```

Here, I format the style's declaration (its property/value pair—highlighted) just as I would write it if adding the style manually. However, because setAttribute is not reliable in IE6, I use use the dot syntax style to add the style in a way that is understood by both W3C DOM-compliant and IE6 browsers.

```
myElementObject.style.fontWeight="bold";
```

Now, instead of using JavaScript to simply write some CSS into the markup, I am setting the property via JavaScript. When I use JavaScript in this way, I change the format of the property name (highlighted), converting the hyphenated CSS format font-weight to its JavaScript camel case equivalent fontWeight. When using dot syntax to set styles, I can, in almost every case, simply change the hyphenated CSS version to the camel case version and get the right format for the property name. The exception is float which becomes cssFloat.

From a performance perspective, this approach also helps avoid looping through a large list of links, table rows, or whatever you are working on, and adding classes to each one, which can be very slow.

CODE 3.11 dom_exercises.html

example). These are styles for links (the a tags) and have the contextual class of important_links.

```
.important_links a {

    font-weight:bold;

}

.important_links a:hover {

    color:#666;

}
```

When I add the important_links class to the containing div, all links within it will immediately be affected by this CSS. Because the containing div has a nice hook—its ID—we can get and set this element with a single line of code.

```
function addClass() {

    document.getElementById("demo_links").className="important_
links";

}
```

Not only are all the links now bolded, but they also turn gray when the cursor moves over them.

Using this technique, you can have all kinds of extra styles in your style sheet ready to be invoked with the addition of a class to an element when the right moment arrives—as you will see in the following example.

Zebra Tables

Here I'll use DOM scripting to add a class to alternate rows of a table to create a striping effect. This effect helps guide the user's eye across the rows and is especially useful if the table is wide. You saw this table in Chapter 1—now I'll write the JavaScript to make it work.

Achieving this stripe effect requires some of the DOM scripting techniques you just saw. I'll also use the `onload` event handler to trigger the function that adds the stripes right after the page loads. Also, after you learn about event handling techniques in the next chapter, I'll come back to this table and make the table rows highlight as the user moves the cursor over them.

In this example, I'll add the class of `stripe_table` on the `table` element, as shown in this markup.

```
<table class="stripe_table" border="1">

    <caption>More JavaScript books for your reading pleasure
        </caption>

<thead>

    <tr>

        <th scope="col">Title</th>

        <th scope="col">Author</th>

        <th scope="col">Publisher</th>
```

Adding and Removing Classes

You can have multiple class names separated by spaces in a class attribute, like the three classes illustrated here:

```
<div class="nav links members"><!-- --></div>
```

In this situation, you can run into problems if you simply set a class, as I do in the "Adding a class to an element" example, on an element that already has other classes. Those existing classes will be replaced by the one you are adding. To avoid overwriting existing classes when you add new ones, you have to first get the classes that are currently there, store them in an array, add your new class, and then write the whole thing back, not forgetting the space that goes between each class name. There is a nifty helper function that will correctly add and remove classes in the scriptin_helper.js file in the downloads, and I will use it in later examples.

CODE 3.12 table_stripe_step0.html

```
      <th scope="col">Comment</th>
    </tr>
</thead>
<tbody>
    <tr>
      <td>PPK on JavaScript</td>
      <td>Peter-Paul Koch</td>
      <td>New Riders</td>
      <td>Europe's foremost JS expert gives his personal
        insights.</td>
    </tr>
    // etc...additional rows removed here to save trees
</tbody>
</table>
```

This markup uses `thead` and `tbody` tags to separate the header row from the table's data rows. Not only is this good semantic markup (that is, it meaningfully structures the content), but as you'll see, it also provides a targeting context for the rows I want to stripe. Those rows are all contained within the `tbody` tag, and by targeting only the rows within it, my code won't affect the header row, which I want to leave untouched. **Figure 3.2** shows how this unstyled markup looks in the browser.

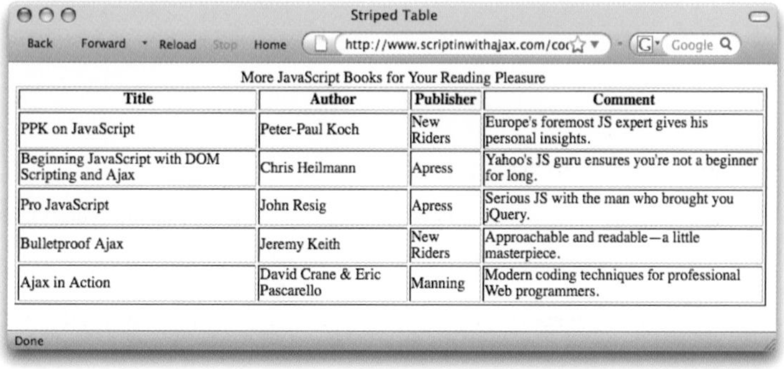

More JavaScript Books for Your Reading Pleasure

Title	Author	Publisher	Comment
PPK on JavaScript	Peter-Paul Koch	New Riders	Europe's foremost JS expert gives his personal insights.
Beginning JavaScript with DOM Scripting and Ajax	Chris Heilmann	Apress	Yahoo's JS guru ensures you're not a beginner for long.
Pro JavaScript	John Resig	Apress	Serious JS with the man who brought you jQuery.
Bulletproof Ajax	Jeremy Keith	New Riders	Approachable and readable—a little masterpiece.
Ajax in Action	David Crane & Eric Pascarello	Manning	Modern coding techniques for professional Web programmers.

FIGURE 3.2 A table with the default browser styling.

The browser's default styling of tables, with a border around the table and a border around every cell within, is unattractive, does not help show how the data elements are related, and distracts your attention from the data.

CODE 3.13 table_stripe_step1.
html

Fortunately, the look of a table can be improved easily with a little CSS (and the deletion of the `border` attribute from the HTML `table` element) as shown in **Figure 3.3**.

```
body {font-family:verdana, sans-serif; font-size:.8em;}

table.stripe_table {border-collapse:collapse;}

table.stripe_table {border:0;}

.stripe_table caption {margin-bottom:.3em; font-weight:bold;
    font-size:1.2em;}

.stripe_table th {color:white; background-color:#036;}

.stripe_table tr {background: #EEF; border-bottom:1px solid
    #036;}

.stripe_table tr:last-child {border-bottom:2px solid #036;}

.stripe_table td {padding:.3em;}

.stripe_table td:first-child {font-weight:bold;}

.stripe_table tr.odd {background: #DEE;}
```

"odd" class to be added to markup by JS

FIGURE 3.3 Removing the table borders and adding a little color and some thin horizontal lines improves the aesthetic, and brings out the relationships in the data.

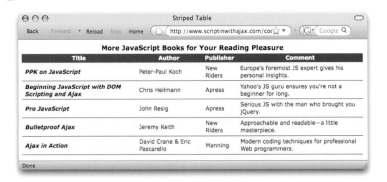

To set up the stripe effect, I write a CSS style like this (highlighted in the preceding code):

```
stripe_table tr.odd {background: #DEE;}
```

I could then manually add the `.odd` class to every other `tr` element of the table. However, in an application where the table is generated dynamically, I have JavaScript do this for me.

Let's start with a list of the steps that add the stripes to the table.

1. Set up an `onLoad` event handler that triggers the `getTheTables-ToStripe` function as soon as the page loads.

I'll use this example to show you how to develop your code step by step, adding a few lines at a time and then checking that you are getting the anticipated result. By doing this, you can be confident that your code works as expected when you complete it.

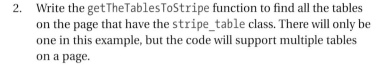

2. Write the `getTheTablesToStripe` function to find all the tables on the page that have the `stripe_table` class. There will only be one in this example, but the code will support multiple tables on a page.

3. Pass the name of any tables with the `stripe_table` class to a second function that adds the `.odd` class (highlighted in the preceding CSS) to every other row of the table.

Here's step 1—setting up the load event:

```
window.onload=getTheTables;
```

Because this line of code is not contained within a function, it will run as soon as it loads into the browser. The `getTheTables` function will then be called as soon as the rest of the page's content has loaded and the `load` event fires. You will learn about the `onload` event handler in more detail in the next chapter. For now, just accept that you can't add stripes to a table that hasn't loaded in the browser. Using the previous line of code ensures the `getTheTables` function doesn't get called until the page has loaded.

As its name suggests, the `getTheTables` function will go out and get all the tables on the page and identify any that need the stripe effect; that is, those that have the `stripe_table` class.

Before I add the code to do that, I'll simply check that the function is being called by the `onload` event.

```
window.onload=getTheTables

function getTheTables() {

    alert ("getTheTables function called");

}
```

When the page loads, the alert dialog appears, as shown in **Figure 3.4**.

Of course, I only show one table on the page in this example, but this code allows me to determine which of several tables on a page will have the stripe effect.

Note that I delete each line of code with an alert *before moving on to the next step.*

CODE 3.14 table_stripe_step2.html

FIGURE 3.4 The `onload` event handler successfully calls the function when the page finishes loading.

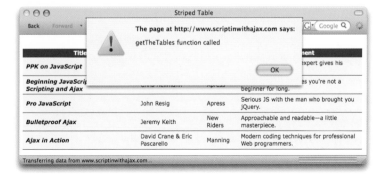

With the function being called successfully from the onload event, it's time to add the real code into it. I'll first check if the browser offers support for the DOM scripting method I want to use, and exit the function if it doesn't. Note that this is the "setness" test from Chapter 2.

```
if (!document.getElementsByTagName) {return false;}
```

In browsers that pass this test, and these days most browsers including IE6 will, I can now use the getElementsByTagName method to find all the page's tables and store them in a variable that I've called theTables. I'll ensure this step is working by checking how many tables were returned; in this case, there should be one, of course. The getElementsByTagName method returns an array-like node list. I can use the length method to determine the number of elements in it, but note that other array methods, like sort, push, and pop, won't work on a node list.

CODE 3.15 table_stripe_step3.html

get all the tables

```
function getTheTables() {

if (!document.getElementsByTagName) return false;

    var theTables = document.getElementsByTagName("table");

    alert (theTables.length+" table(s) found");

}
```

When we run this code, the alert dialog shows that one table was found (**Figure 3.5**).

FIGURE 3.5 The table array holds the anticipated single element.

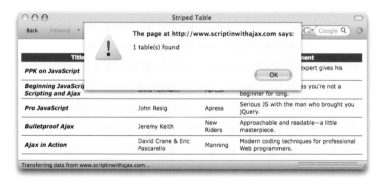

CODE 3.16 table_stripe_step4.html

Next, I'll loop through the elements in the node list to check if any of them have the class stripe_table.

```
function getTheTables() {

if (!document.getElementsByTagName) {return false;}
```

then this is not a W3C DOM-capable browser–bye-bye!

| get all the tables as objects |
| loop through them |
| if a table has the required class |
| pass it to the function that adds the stripes |
| end of if |
| end of for loop |

```javascript
var theTables = document.getElementsByTagName("table");

for (var i=0; i < theTables.length; i++) {

    if (theTables[i].className == "stripe_table") {

        addStripes(theTables[i]);

    }

}
```

Here I use a `for` loop to iterate over the tables I found in the earlier step. In this case, there is only one table, but for the code to be considered robust, it must be able to cope with however many tables might appear on the page.

Within the loop, I test each table to see if it has the `stripe_table` class. If it does, I pass it to the `addStripes` function to add the `.odd` class to every alternate row.

I'll start by writing the structure of the `addStripes` function and check that it's being called from the `getTheTables` function.

```javascript
function addStripes(theTable) {

    alert("addStripes function called");

}
```

As ilustrated in **Figure 3.6**, I then get confirmation that the function was successfully called.

FIGURE 3.6 The `getTheTables` function is now calling the `addStripes` function.

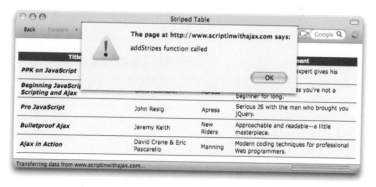

I'll use the `getElementsByTagName` method again—first to get the `tbody` element and a second time to get the rows within it. As a sanity check, I'll display the length of the node list.

adds stripes (the "odd" class) to any table passed to it

get the table body

get the table body's rows

set rowCount to the number of rows

CODE 3.17 table_stripe_step5.html

```
function addStripes(theTable) {

    var theTableBody = theTable.getElementsByTagName("tbody");

    var theTableRows = theTableBody[0]
    getElementsByTagName("tr");

    var rowCount=theTableRows.length //

    alert (rowCount+ " rows in this table");

}
```

When you run the code, you see the result shown in **Figure 3.7**

FIGURE 3.7 There are five rows in this table including the header.

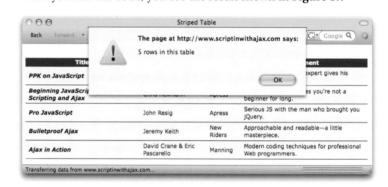

Now I know I am successfully getting the five rows of this table that are within the tbody tag.

All that's left is to write a loop that adds the .odd class to every alternate row.

CODE 3.18 table_stripe_step6.html

```
function addStripes(theTable) {

    var theTableBody = theTable.getElementsByTagName("tbody");

    var theTableRows = theTableBody[0].
    getElementsByTagName("tr");

    var rowCount=theTableRows.length
```

run the loop on each row

add the "odd" class to every other row

give the counter a second increment here so you skip every other row

```
    for (var i=1; i < rowCount; i++) {

        theTableRows[i].className = "odd";

        i++;

    }

}
```

As **Figure 3.8** shows, the table is now nicely striped

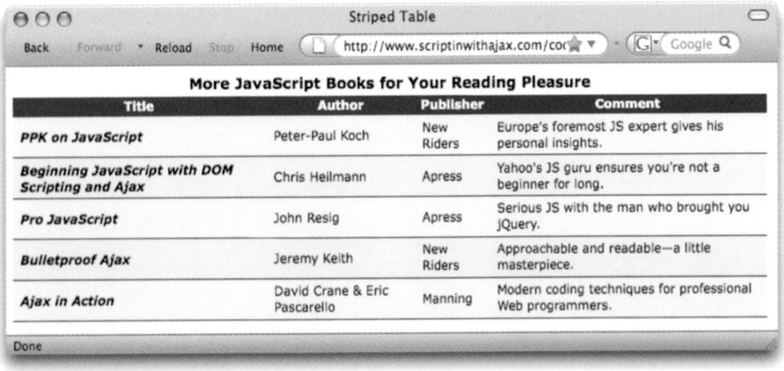

FIGURE 3.8 The stripes are now added to the alternate rows.

There are three interesting points I want to explain about this code.

First, this example is a good illustration of JavaScript's object-oriented nature. When I get the table elements, they are stored in an array-like node list object. This node list can be queried for its length, and each element of the node list can then be queried for its properties using a loop.

Second, note also how `theTables[i]` (where `i` is the loop's current counter value) can simply be passed to another function. It's the reference to the object that contains that table, so the receiving function can immediately work on that table. Once you understand that you are passing around references to objects and can at any time access that object's properties using `objectName.propertyName` dot syntax, reading and working with JavaScript gets much easier.

Third, let's examine the counter in the loop. When adding the class to the alternate rows, the loop uses `i++` in the `for` statement to increment its counter by one in the standard manner. However, in this case, because I only want to apply the class to every *other* row, I give the counter a second increment within the code. This causes the counter to be incremented by two each time the loop runs, and the class is thereby added to every other row, not every row.

Refactoring the Code

In the next chapter I'll add more functions to this code. In preparation, I'll refactor the two functions into the methods of an object literal that I will call `stripeTable`.

Refactoring is the process of improving your code without altering its functionality. You might do this to make it run faster, to make it more secure, or in this case, to simply make it more organized, readable, and easier to extend. I'll start by creating the basic structure of the object.

```
var stripeTable={

}
```

Now, I drop the functions inside this object, indent them within the object, and rework each one's first line. I also add the object name in front of the call to the addStripes method.

```
var stripeTable={

  getTheTables:function() {

   if (!document.getElementsByTagName) return false;

     var theTables = document.getElementsByTagName("table");

      for (var i=0; i < theTables.length; i++) {

        if (theTables[i].className == "stripe_table") {

          stripeTable.addStripes(theTables[i]);

        }

      }

  },

  addStripes:function(theTable) {

     var theTableRows = theTable.getElementsByTagName("tr");

     var rowCount=theTableRows.length;

     for (var i=1; i < rowCount; i++) {

        theTableRows[i].className = "odd";

        i++;

      }

    }

  }
```

CODE 3.19 table_stripe_objlit_
step7.html

I also need to modify the onload event to call the getTheTables function. You would think that this simple modification

doesn't work!!!! ──┤ `window.onload=stripeTable.getTheTables` would do the job, but the dot syntax doesn't work in this context. So, I'll add a simple function called `init` (initialize) that I'll call from the event and add the call to the object there.

```
window.onload=init;

function init() {

    stripedTables.getTheTables();

}
```

Now it works. Also, if I wanted to call other functions when the page loads, I could now add them to this initialization function.

I now have a nicely organized object called `stripeTable`, which I will extend with additional functionality in the next chapter.

Summary

Objects are the fundamental nature of everything in JavaScript. The examples in this chapter will start you down the road to deeply understanding how JavaScript works and how to write code that takes full advantages of its capabilities. By using objects to contain related code elements, you take control of your code as it grows and prevent scoping conflicts. By creating objects from which you can create instances, you have a powerful mechanism for managing large data sets.

DOM scripting enables you to manipulate the user interface and takes your Web page from a fixed layout to a fluid canvas that you can modify at will.

Now it's time to look at events and discover how to detect and provide appropriate responses to the user's interaction with your application.

CHAPTER 4

Events

IN A MODERN WEB SITE or browser-based application, JavaScript's primary purpose is to provide responses to the user interactions with the interface, or to be more technically precise, to handle events that are triggered by user actions.

Events are messages that the browser fires off in a constant stream as the user works; for example, every time the user moves the pointer over an HTML element, clicks the mouse, or moves the cursor into a field of a form, a corresponding event message is fired. JavaScript receives these messages, but does nothing unless you provide an event handler that provides a response to them.

Your ability to write code that can monitor and respond to the events that matter to your application is key to creating interactive interfaces.

To make your application respond to user action, you need to:

1. Decide which events should be monitored

2. Set up event handlers that trigger functions when events occur

3. Write the functions that provide the appropriate responses to the events

You'll see the details of this process throughout this chapter. For now, just get the idea that an event, such as `click`, is issued as the result of some specific activity—usually user activity, but sometimes browser activity such as a page load—and that you can handle that event with an event handler. The event handler is always the name of the event preceded by "on"; for example, the event `click` is handled by the `onclick` event handler. The event handler causes a function to run, and the function provides the response to the event. **Table 4.1** lists the most commonly used event handlers.

Techniques to Handle Events

In this section, I'll show you four techniques that you can use to trigger JavaScript functions in response to events. The first two require adding JavaScript into the markup, so I try to avoid them, preferring techniques where event handlers are programmatically added to and removed from elements as needed. In small projects, such as simple Web sites, the first two techniques work just fine, but with important caveats that I will discuss for each one.

JavaScript Pseudo Protocol

If you worked with JavaScript in years past, you may have used the the JavaScript pseudo protocol to trigger a function from a link:

```
<a href="javascript:someFunctionName();">Link Name</a>
```

When the user clicks the link, the function `someFunctionName` is called. No `onclick` is stated; this technique simply replaces the `href` value. The problem with this approach is that it completely replaces the URL that normally would be the `href` value. If the user doesn't have JavaScript running or the associated JavaScript function fails to load for some reason, the link is completely broken. This approach also adds JavaScript into the markup, an issue I'll discuss after I show you the second method. In short, avoid triggering events with the pseudo protocol.

EVENT CATEGORY	EVENT TRIGGERED WHEN...	EVENT HANDLER
Browser events	Page completes loading	onload
	Page is removed from browser window	onunload
	JavaScript throws an error	onerror
Mouse events	User clicks over an element	onclick
	User double-clicks over an element	ondblclick
	The mouse button is pressed down over an element	onmousedown
	The mouse button is released over an element	onmouseup
	The mouse pointer moves onto an element	onmouseover
	The mouse pointer leaves an element	onmouseout
Keyboard events	A key is pressed	onkeydown
	A key is released	onkeyup
	A key is pressed and released	onkeypress
Form events	The element receives focus from pointer or by tabbing navigation	onfocus
	The element loses focus	onblur
	User selects type in text or text area field	onselect
	User submits a form	onsubmit
	User resets a form	onreset
	Field loses focus and content has changed since receiving focus	onchange

TABLE 4.1 This table contains a list of the most commonly used event handlers.

Inline Event Handler

An inline event handler, as you saw briefly in Chapter 2, attaches an event handler directly to an element.

```
<input type="text" onblur="doValidate()" />
```

Here, a form text field has the JavaScript function doValidate associated with its blur event—the function will be called when the user moves the cursor out of the field by pressing Tab or clicks elsewhere. The function could then check if the user actually typed something in the field or not.

Focus and Blur

When the user clicks into a text field, the `focus` event message is fired because the focus of the keyboard is now on that field, and anything the user types then appears in that field. If the user then presses Tab or clicks elsewhere to move the cursor out of that field, the field loses focus and the `blur` message is fired.

Inline event handlers have been the standard way of triggering events for years, so if you have to work on a Web site that has been around for a while, you will no doubt see inline handlers all over the markup. A benefit of inline handlers is that the `this` keyword is bound to the function that is called from an inline handler. To illustrate this point, here's a link that calls a function named `addClass`

```
<a href="somePage.html onClick="addClass()">
```

so in the function you can simply write

```
this.className="hilite";
```

without having to first "get" the element.

Additionally, you don't have to worry about users triggering JavaScript events that act on the DOM before the DOM has loaded into the browser, because the event handler is attached to the markup. We'll examine this DOM ready issue in "The First Event: load" section of this chapter.

However, both benefits can be realized using the two other ways of associating events with elements. Before I describe them, keep in mind that neither of the first two techniques is ideal in that they mix JavaScript with the HTML. In the previous example, the `addClass` function is permanently associated with this HTML element. If you change the function's name or remove it from your code, you'll also have to find and remove every occurrence of the handler in the markup. Also, if for some reason the `addClass` script doesn't load, JavaScript will throw an error when the link is clicked. In a modern Web application—in the interests of accessibility, maintainability, and reliability—you want to keep JavaScript and CSS out of your HTML markup.

Because inline handlers are still widely used, it would be remiss of me not to show you how they work in some detail, because they will be around for years to come. In later chapters, I'll show you examples of inline handlers and how to use them. That said, I hope they will be fading into obscurity as programmers become more aware of Web standards and the advantages of using JavaScript to register events with their associated elements. With all this in mind, let me now show you the ways you can create responses to events without adding JavaScript into the HTML markup.

Handler as Object Property

```
var clickableImage=document.getElementById("dog_pic");
```

```
clickableImage.onclick=showLargeImage;
```

This example shows a two-step process. First, I assign an object—an HTML element with the ID dog_pic—to a variable. In line 1 of the example, the object representing the HTML element is stored in the clickableImage variable. Second, I assign the event handler onclick as a property of the object, using a function name as the onclick property's value. The function showLargeImage will now run when the user clicks on the element with the ID dog_pic.

While this technique has the desirable quality of keeping the JavaScript out of the markup, it has a couple of serious drawbacks.

First, only one event at a time can be assigned using this technique, because only one value can exist for a property at any given time. I can't assign another event to the onclick property without over-writing this one, and for the same reason, another event that was previously assigned is overridden by this one.

Second, when the user clicks on this element and the function is called, that function has to be hard-coded with the name of the object so that it knows which element to work on.

```
function showLargeImage() {

   thePic=document.getElementById("dog_pic");

   // do something with the pic

   }
```

If you change the object that is the source of the event, you will also have to modify the function.

For this reason, the "handler as object property" technique is suitable only when you just want to assign one event to one object, such as running an initial onload function once the page is first loaded (see "The First Event: load" section later in this chapter). However, for the reasons noted, it really doesn't provide a robust solution for use throughout an RIA, where events commonly get assigned and removed from objects as the application runs. In almost every case, the best way to manage events is to use event listeners.

Event Listeners

Introduced with the W3C DOM model, event listeners provide comprehensive event registration.

An event listener does what its name suggests: After being attached to an object, it then listens patiently for its event to occur. When it "hears" its event, it then calls its associated function in the same way as the "handlers as object properties" method but with two important distinctions.

First, *an event listener passes an event object containing information about its triggering event to the function it calls.* (I emphasize this point because it is so important.) Within the function, you can read this object's properties to determine the target element, the type of event that occurred—such as `click`, `focus`, `mousedown`—and other useful details about the event.

This capability can reduce coding considerably, because you can write very flexible functions for key tasks, such as handling clicks, that provide variations in their response depending on the calling object and triggering event. Otherwise, you would have to write a separate, and probably very similar, function for every type of event you have to handle. You will learn how to write functions with this kind of flexibility later in the chapter.

Second, you can attach multiple event listeners to an object. As a result, you don't have to worry when adding one listener that you are overwriting another that was added earlier, as you do when simply assigning an event as an object property.

While both the W3C and Microsoft browsers enable event handlers, they differ in the way those handlers are attached to elements and in the way they provide access to the event object. I'll start with the W3C approach, which will be the de facto standard in the future, and then discuss how event listeners work in Microsoft browsers.

W3C EVENT MODEL

Here's the W3C technique for adding listeners to elements. I'll add two listeners to a form's text field that will cause functions to run when the user clicks (or tabs) into or out of the field:

get the object	`emailField=document.getElementById("email");`
add a focus listener	`emailField.addEventListener('focus',doHighlight,false);`
add a blur listener	`emailField.addEventListener('blur',doValidate,false);`

Now the function `doHighlight` will be called when the cursor moves into the field, and the function `doValidate` will be called when the cursor moves out of the field. (The third argument, `false`, relates to *event bubbling,* a concept that can wait until later in this chapter.) I can attach as many event listeners as I want to the object in this manner.

I can remove the events from the element in a similar way using the `removeEventListener` method.

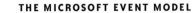

get the object

```
emailField=document.getElementById("email");

emailField.removeEventListener('focus',doHighlight,false);

emailField.removeEventListener('blur',doValidate,false);
```

THE MICROSOFT EVENT MODEL

You only need to explicity remove event handlers if your application requires that an element no longer respond to an assigned event. In most cases, you only add event listeners and don't explicity remove them. They only persist for as long as the page is loaded in the browser.

Microsoft's event registration model is slightly different. The equivalent of this W3C style

```
emailField.addEventListener('focus',doHighlight,false);
```

in the Microsoft model is

```
emailField.attachEvent('onfocus',doHighlight);
```

and the equivalent of this W3C style

```
emailField.removeEventListener('focus',doHighlight,false);
```

in the Microsoft model is

```
emailField.detachEvent('onfocus',doHighlight);
```

Note the use of `on`, as in `onfocus`, in the name of the event for the Microsoft version. Clearly, there are some syntax variations here, so let's look at how to write code that works on both browsers.

AN ADDEVENT HELPER FUNCTION

To add event listeners to elements correctly, regardless of the user's browser type, I'll use an existing helper function written by John Resig that can determine the correct event models to use. This function accepts the following arguments:

- The element to which the listener should be attached

- The type of event to listen for

- The name of the function to call when the event occurs

It will then use these arguments to construct a correctly formatted event listener registration for the user's browser.

The function first tests if the browser supports Microsoft's `attachEvent` method (highlighted) and then branches the code accordingly.

```
function addEvent( obj, type, fn ) {
```

it's a Microsoft browser

```
    if ( obj.attachEvent ) {

        obj['e'+type+fn] = fn;

        obj[type+fn] = function(){obj['e'+type+fn]
            ( window.event );}

        obj.attachEvent( 'on'+type, obj[type+fn] );
```

it's a W3C browser

```
    } else {

        obj.addEventListener(type, fn, false);

    }

}
```

Removing events can be achieved with a second, similar helper function.

```
function removeEvent( obj, type, fn ) {

    if ( obj.detachEvent ) {
```

W3C

```
        obj.detachEvent( 'on'+type, obj[type+fn] );

        obj[type+fn] = null;

    } else {
```

Microsoft

```
        obj.removeEventListener( type, fn, false );

    }

}
```

These functions, as you can see, are somewhat complex, but fortunately you don't have to understand them; you just have to be able to use them. If you wanted to add an event listener to the email field from the preceding example, all you would have to do is call the `addEvent` helper function like this:

```
addEvent(emailField, 'focus', doHighlight);
```

The three arguments are the element, the event, and the function to call when that element receives that event. The function then

---

Software Design Patterns

If you are a designer, you may be aware of the classification of common user interface interactions into design patterns—such as Wizard, multiple undo, and drag-and-drop to name just a few—that define each interaction's appropriate use and implementation. Design patterns document successful user interactions, give designers a common vocabulary, and most of all, provide users with familiar interactions across the sites they visit. Jenifer Tidwell's *Designing Interfaces* (O'Reilly, 2005) is the seminal work on this subject and essential reading for all interface designers.

A similar set of design patterns exists in software also and provides a standardized way to solve and discuss common programming problems. The first major classification of software design patterns was published in *Design Patterns: Elements of Reusable Object-Oriented Software* (Addison-Wesley, 1994) by Erich Gamma, Richard Helm, Ralph Johnson, and John Vlissides (known as "The Gang of Four").

Most of the helper functions used in *Scriptin' with JavaScript* are simple implementations of the Façade pattern, where "a common interface is provided to two or more interfaces in a subsystem." The code addresses a single interface—in the case of adding event listeners, the addEvent function—and the interface takes care of addressing, in a syntactically correct manner, one of two objects—addEventListener or attachEvent—depending on the user's browser. By using these Façade pattern helpers, you abstract away cross-browser issues and simply pass your requests to these intermediate objects that resolve them for you.

As your skills grow, studying design patterns can help you write better code, because you're then using best coding practices and can avoid struggling to discover solutions to coding problems that were discovered and proven long ago.

Event listener registration is yet another example of the cross-browser issues you face with JavaScript. However, once you have a nice little collection of helpers or a framework such as jQuery, you don't have to worry about them as much.

---

takes care of formatting the event registration appropriately for the browser on which it is running.

A common time at which to add listeners to elements is when the page first loads, or to be more specific, upon an event that virtually every JavaScript application must detect and handle—the load event that is triggered when the page is fully loaded and rendered in the browser.

The First Event: load

Typically, the first thing you want JavaScript to do is set up the initial state of the page so it's ready for use. A very common part of this initialization process is to attach event listeners to the elements in the DOM that will respond to user actions, and you can't do that until the DOM has loaded into the browser.

For example, you might want to attach blur events to the text fields of a form so you can detect when the user clicks or tabs away from them. You can then immediately validate the text the user entered.

To help you ensure that you are working with a DOM that actually exists, a load event is issued when the page is entirely loaded into the browser window. You can use the onload handler to detect this event and trigger the JavaScript functions that will set up the initial page state for the user. Then you know that the DOM is ready.

Here's a simple example of how to do this:

note the use of the "event as object property" style of event assignment here

```
window.onload=init;

function init() {

    alert ("The page is fully loaded!");

    // normally, code to set up initial page state (such as
        adding event listeners) would be here

}
```

In the highlighted line that calls the init function, you can see that there are no parentheses after the init function name. You would normally add parentheses after a function name because you would want the function to run immediately at that point in the code. However, because you are setting up an event that will call the function at a later time, you don't do that here. If you wrote

```
window.onload=init();
```

How onLoad Can Work Against You

There are two ways that you can run into problems with the onLoad event:

- **Delay in assigning listeners.** Be aware that linked content, such as images, loads after the DOM (the HTML markup), and that the load event does not fire until after all linked content is loaded. So if your page contains many large images, there can be a substantial delay between the DOM loading and the onLoad event. In this interval, the user may try to type into a search field or click a link—after all, the DOM is loaded and those elements are visible. If you then wait until after a number of large images are loaded before you get the load event that registers the event listeners, the user may be clicking on links that as yet do nothing.

    As a workaround for this problem, there are now some helper functions that can cause a "DOM is ready" type of event to be called as soon as the DOM is ready. For example, the jQuery framework has a .ready method that is called after the DOM and CSS (but before images and other linked content) are loaded to avoid this delay in assigning listeners.

- **Competing for the onLoad event.** Because of the importance of waiting for the DOM to be ready, third-party scripts that you use might also want to set the window.onLoad property, and this can override your setting or you can override theirs, depending on who loads last. Thanks to a contest organized by Peter-Paul Koch, there is now a robust helper function called addLoadEvent that allows multiple events to be assigned to the window.onload property. I will use this function in later examples and it is included in the Scriptin' helper file. I recommend you use this function to assign your initialization functions.

the function would run immediately (setting the `onload` property to the result of the function!) and not wait for a page load event to be sent.

Also note that you write `window.onload=init` because `onload` is a method of the window object, so you must always precede it with `window.` for it to work.

By omitting the parentheses when you assign the `init` function to the `onLoad` property, the function does not run immediately; instead, it runs when the `load` event occurs after the page is fully loaded.

The `onload` handler is very important in every JavaScript application because it is used to initialize the page state; that is, to set up all the event responses that the interface will provide to the user. If you are looking at an existing piece of JavaScript and trying to determine what it does, the best place to start is with the function that is called by the `load` event—everything flows out from there.

Also note that any JavaScript statement not enclosed in a function and just "loose" on the page runs as soon as it loads. For this reason, it's very unusual to place any JavaScript except the `onload` event assignment outside of a function.

Adding Event Listeners on Page Load

After all this discussion, I'll now show you a simple example of event listeners that are added to an element when the page loads. In this case, when the `onload` event handler calls the `init` function, it will add event listeners to a text field.

As a result of the functions called by these event listeners, the text field will highlight (its `background` property will be set to `green`) when the field receives focus; it will unhighlight (the default white background will be restored) when the focus is removed. I'll do this using the `addEvent` helper function I showed earlier, so that it works on both W3C and Microsoft browsers.

Here's the form field input.

```
<input id="email" name="email" type="text" size="24" />
```

It's the only HTML element that is relevant to this demo, so I'll leave the rest of the markup to your imagination—you can see it in the download file.

Step one is to ensure the `load` event is triggering the function that will set up the event listeners.

CODE 4.1 hilite_field_basic1.html

```
window.onload=setUpFieldEvents;


function setUpFieldEvents() {

    alert ("called");

    }
```

Figure 4.1 shows that when the page loads, the function is called.

FIGURE 4.1 The function is successfully called from the onload event handler.

Next, I'll add the code that actually adds the event listeners to the field. To do this, I'll use the addEvent helper function.

```
// add event helper function

function addEvent( obj, type, fn ) {

    if ( obj.attachEvent ) {

        obj['e'+type+fn] = fn;

        obj[type+fn] = function(){obj['e'+type+fn]
            ( window.event );}

        obj.attachEvent( 'on'+type, obj[type+fn] );

    } else

        obj.addEventListener(type, fn, false);

}
```

CODE 4.2 hilite_field_basic2.html

```
window.onload=setUpFieldEvents;


function setUpFieldEvents() {
```

get the field
```
    var emailField=document.getElementById("email");
```

add focus event
```
    addEvent(emailField, 'focus', addHighlight);
```

add blur event
```
    addEvent(emailField, 'blur', removeHighlight);

    }
```

CODE 4.3 hilite_field_basic2.html (cont.)

Because it's not contained in a function, the highlighted `onload` event is set up when that line of code loads in the browser, and then the `setUpFieldEvents` function is called when the page has completely loaded. This causes the two event listeners to be added to the field via the `addEvent` helper function. Now, when the field gets focus, the `addHighlight` function will be called; when the field loses focus (blurs), the `removeHighlight` function will be called.

To ensure this step is working, you can simply add the functions, with temporary alerts, for the two events.

```
function addHighlight() {
    alert("addHighlight called");
}
function removeHighlight() {
    alert("removeHighlight called");
}
```

Then click in the field, and you will see the alert dialog shown in **Figure 4.2**.

FIGURE 4.2 When the field receives focus, the `addHighlight` function is called.

OK the alert and then click away from the field. You will see the alert dialog shown in **Figure 4.3**.

FIGURE 4.3 When the field loses focus, the `removeHighlight` function is called.

Once the functions are successfully triggered by the events, all you need to do is replace the alerts with the code to highlight and unhighlight the field.

CODE 4.4 hilite_field_basic3.html

```
function addHighlight() {

    var emailField=document.getElementById("email");

    emailField.style.backgroundColor ="#6F3";

}

function removeHighlight() {

    var emailField=document.getElementById("email");

    emailField.style.backgroundColor ="";

}
```

restore field's default settings

Now the field's background becomes green when it receives focus as shown in **Figure 4.4**. The normal white background color is restored when the field loses focus as shown in **Figure 4.5**.

FIGURE 4.4 The background of the field now changes color when it receives focus.

FIGURE 4.5 The background of the field is restored to its default color when it loses focus.

While this example serves to show a simple implementation of event listeners, it does not take full advantage of the power that event listeners offer. In the preceding example, the functions that were called by the event listeners then use getElementById to get the field before changing its background style. Hard coding the event's element into the function in this way limits its flexibility: This function can only provide a response to events on this one field.

It is, in fact, unnecessary to get the element at this point because, as mentioned in the introduction of the chapter, event handlers provide the functions they call with access to the name of the object to which they are attached and their triggering event. Once you understand how to take advantage of this feature, you will be able to write event handling code that is both versatile and compact.

The Event Object

When a W3C event listener's event occurs and it calls its associated function, it also passes a single argument to the function—a reference to the event object. The event object contains a number of properties that describe the event that occurred.

Table 4.2 lists the names of the most commonly used properties of the event object, which of course usually differ between the W3C and Microsoft models.

W3C NAME	MICROSOFT NAME	DESCRIPTION
e	window.event	The object containing the event properties
type	type	The event that occurred (click, focus, blur, etc.)
target	srcElement	The element to which the event occurred
keyCode	keyCode	The numerical ASCII value of the pressed key
shiftKey altKey cntlKey		Returns 1 if pressed, 0 if not
currentTarget	fromElement	The element the mouse came from on mouseover
relatedTarget	toElement	The element the mouse went to on mouseout

TABLE 4.2 This table contains a list of the most commonly used event object properties.

Several other less commonly used event object properties are not listed in Table 4.2, including mouse coordinates. Peter-Paul Koch provides an in-depth discussion and demos of the event object properties at www.quirksmode.org/js/ events_advanced.html.

By convention, the parameter name e is used in event-triggered functions to receive the event object argument. If I wanted to determine the type of event that occurred, such as a click, I would write:

```
function myEvent(e) {

    var evtType = e.type

    alert(evtType)

    // displays click, or whatever the event type was

}
```

This code would not work on a Microsoft browser, because the Microsoft model does not pass an event object reference like the

W3C model; instead, it uses a central global object that contains the properties of the most recent event. I'll start with the W3C approach and then show you how to work with the Microsoft event object.

To demonstrate the W3C model, I'll use two event object properties as I modify the two functions in the preceding example so that those functions no longer have to get the target element before modifying it.

This takes two simple steps: I'll add the parameter to accept the event object, and then replace the "get" of the field element with the target property of the event:

CODE 4.5 hilite_field_basic4.html

```
function addHighlight(e) {

    var emailField=document.getElementById("email");

    var emailField=e.target;

    emailField.style.border="3px solid #6F3";

    }

function removeHighlight(e) {

    var emailField=document.getElementById("email");

    var emailField=e.target;

    emailField.style.border="";

    }
```

There is no visual change—see Figures 4.4 and 4.5.

You could now assign this same event listener to multiple input fields, and those fields would all display the highlight behavior. Instead of stating "highlight this field," the code now states "highlight the field to which the event occurred."

The Event Object's Type Property

With access to the event object, I can now also determine the type of the event that occurred (focus, blur, click, etc.), so I can use a single function to detect both the focus and blur events.

To do this, I'll change the event listeners to call the same function, checkHighlight. This name makes more sense for the new function, which will add *and* remove the highlighting.

add focus event

```
addEvent(emailField, 'focus', checkHighlight);
```

add blur event

```
addEvent(emailField, 'blur', checkHighlight);
```

I'll then change the name of the addHighlight function to checkHighlight, delete the removeHighlight function entirely, and modify the checkHighlight function to look like this:

```
function checkHighlight(e) {

    switch (e.type) {

        case "focus":

            e.target.style.backgroundColor="#6F3";

            break;

        case "blur":

            e.target.style.backgroundColor="";

            break;

    }

}
```

There is no visual change—see Figures 4.4. and 4.5.

This function is pretty self-explanatory. The switch statement checks if the event type (highlighted) is focus or blur and branches the code accordingly.

The Event Object in Microsoft Browsers

So far you've learned that when an event listener triggers a function in W3C-compliant browsers, a reference to an object containing properties that describe the triggering event is passed to the function; this event object can be accessed through the e parameter.

In Microsoft browsers, the model is slightly different. There is one global object, window.event, that holds the last event that occurred. Because it's global, it doesn't have to be passed to the function like the W3C event object; it's always available to your code. For comparison, these two lines are equivalent in their respective browsers:

W3C—e must be stated as function parameter ──{ `e.type`

Microsoft—direct access of global event object ──{ `window.event.type`

The simplest way to write cross-browser event object code is like this:

```
function eventType(e)
```

then it's a W3C browser ──{ `if (e) {`

CODE 4.6 hilite_field_basic5.html

If you are wondering why I used a switch *instead of an* if *statement, here's the reason: An* if *statement only checks one case for truthiness and does the* false *part if there is no match, regardless of what that "false" condition might be. By using* switch, *I am absolutely explicit; if any other case than* focus *or* blur *is passed to this function, it will be ignored. Also, I can easily add* click *or other events to this function if I want to extend it later.*

```
                            alert (e.type)
```

it's a Microsoft browser

```
                        } else {
                            alert (window.event.type)
                        }
                        // displays the triggering event (click, focus, etc)
```

While this works fine, branching your code for every event object property you want to use gets old fast. A better solution is to get the object, whichever kind it is, and give it a new name. Peter-Paul Koch uses the OR operator very neatly to achieve this.

```
var evt = e || window.event;
```

If e evaluates to true (a W3C event object exists), the evt variable is set to e—the W3C event object with all its properties. If not, evt is set to the Microsoft object instead. So now this works in both browsers:

```
var evt = e || window.event;

alert (evt.type)
```

The preceding example works because, unlike many event object properties, the property name for the type of event that occurred is the same—type—in both kinds of browsers. If you want to get the event target, which is target for W3C and eventSrc for Microsoft, you can build on the previous step and again use an OR statement to create a common cross-browser name (highlighted) for the event target, too:

```
var evt = e || window.event;

var evtTarget = evt.target || evt.srcElement;

alert(evtTarget);
```

Once you start working with the event object, you can manage collections of events within a single function. I'll now add this idea into the code.

```
function checkHighlight(e) {
```

sets evt variable to either W3C or Microsoft event obj

```
    var evt = e || window.event;
```

gets the target of the event

```
    var evtTarget = evt.target || evt.srcElement;
```

type is the same name in both objs

```
    switch (evt.type) {
```

CODE 4.7 hilite_field_basic6.html

```
        case "focus":

            evtTarget.style.backgroundColor="#6F3";

            break;

        case "blur":

            evtTarget.style.backgroundColor="";

            break;

    }

}
```

Again, there is no visual change, just much better code. See Figures 4.4 and 4.5.

Now you have a working cross-platform version of a single form field. The next step is to make the event handlers attach themselves to as many text inputs as the form might contain. Let's add a couple more form fields to the markup so users can also enter their first and last names.

CODE 4.8 hilite_field_basic7.html

```html
<div id="sign_up">

    <h3>Sign up for our newsletter</h3>

    <form id="email_form" action="#" method="post">

      <label for="first_name">First Name</label>

      <input id="first_name" name="first_name" type="text"
        size="18" />

      <label for="last_name">Last Name</label>

      <input id="last_name" name="last_name" type="text"
        size="18" />

      <label for="email">Email</label>

      <input id="email" name="email" type="text" size="18"
        />
      <input id="submit" type="submit" value="Go!" />

    </form>

</div>
```

Figure 4.6 shows this revised markup.

FIGURE 4.6 The new markup has three form fields.

Because I am now working with several form elements, my hook into the DOM will be higher up at the form element's ID, email_form. Once I have this parent element I can get at all the form's child elements within. I'll start by modifying the setUpFieldEvents function to tell me how many input tags are within the form.

```
function setUpFieldEvents() {
```

get the form

CODE 4.9 hilite_field_basic7.html (cont.)

```
    var emailForm=document.getElementById("email_form");

    var theInputs=emailForm.getElementsByTagName("input");

    var inputCount=theInputs.length;

    alert(inputCount);
```

temporarily commented out

temporarily commented out

```
    // addEvent(theInputs[i], 'focus', checkHighlight);

    // addEvent(theInputs[i], 'blur', checkHighlight);
}
```

The number of fields is shown in an alert dialog (**Figure 4.7**).

FIGURE 4.7 The new code indicates the form has four inputs.

I first get the form element and then all the elements inside it with the tag name input. My alert test shows me I have four inputs, not three as you might expect. The reason there are four is that the button, to which I don't want to add the event listeners, is also an input tag: The only thing that makes it appear as a button is that it has a different type attribute—submit. Without step-by-step testing like this, I might have missed that and would have baked in a weird bug that changes the background color of the button every time it's clicked.

I'll worry about filtering out the button in a moment. I'll first just loop through all the input fields and apply the event listeners to each of them, so that I can see that I'm able to highlight all the fields.

```
function setUpFieldEvents() {

    var emailForm=document.getElementById("email_form");

    var theInputs=emailForm.getElementsByTagName("input");

    var inputCount=theInputs.length;

    for (i=0; i < inputCount; i++) {

        addEvent(theInputs[i], 'focus', checkHighlight);

        addEvent(theInputs[i], 'blur', checkHighlight);

    }

}
```

get the field

add focus event

add blur event

CODE 4.10 hilite_field_basic8.html

The first highlighted line counts the number of inputs and then puts that number in a variable; doing this allows me to write a more efficient loop. I could have skipped that line and simply written the loop like this:

```
for (i=0; i < theInputs.length; i++) { // etc.
```

The problem with this version is that JavaScript then has to determine the length of the `theInputs` node list (highlighted) every time the loop runs; counting items in arrays and node lists is a relatively slow process in JavaScript. It isn't such a big deal with a few items like this, but if you are looping over a big data set or hundreds of table rows, the wasted time can add up. It's always good practice to get the number of items once and store that in a variable that you then use as the loop count, as I have done here.

Now, when I click in each of the fields, they highlight and then return to their initial appearance when I click away. The event listeners are now successfully attached to each one, as illustrated in **Figure 4.8**.

FIGURE 4.8 Each field now highlights when it receives focus.

The problem, as I knew would happen when the earlier test returned four inputs, is that the button, which is also an input, now also gets the background color when I click it. **Figure 4.9** shows that this looks very strange.

FIGURE 4.9 Applying highlight events to all the form's inputs has the undesired effect of highlighting the button as well.

What makes the button different from the text inputs is that its type attribute is submit not text, so I can create a simple if statement filter based on this difference to identify and exclude it from having event listeners added.

I'll first simply check that I can access the type attribute of each input by adding this line of code into the for loop.

CODE 4.11 hilite_field_basic9.html

```
alert (theInputs[i].getAttribute("type"));
```

This pops up a sequence of four dialogs, which read text, text, text, and submit.

Now that I know I can differentiate the submit input, I'll work up this bit of code into an if statement inside the for loop.

CODE 4.12 hilite_field_basic10.html

```
function setUpFieldEvents() {

    var emailForm=document.getElementById("email_form");

    var theInputs=emailForm.getElementsByTagName("input");

    var inputCount=theInputs.length;

    for (i=0; i < inputCount; i++) {

        var theInputType=theInputs[i].getAttribute("type");
```

only true if input's type attribute is "text"

```
        if (theInputType==="text") {
```

```
add focus event                          addEvent(theInputs[i], 'focus', checkHighlight);

add blur event                           addEvent(theInputs[i], 'blur', checkHighlight);

                                    }

                                }

                            }
```

Now, the `text` input form fields are still highlighting correctly, but the button no longer has event handlers added to it.

That completes this example. The code that you saw developed here will work reliably across today's Web browsers and even back to IE5.5. It has dynamic capabilities to add the field highlighting effect to as many inputs as are present in the form. The actual end result of highlighting the field is rather simplistic and not what is important. What you should take away from this example are the key concepts illustrated here: cross-browser event listeners, event object handling, and the selective addition of event listeners to a number of like elements while filtering out unwanted elements. These are common tasks you will perform many times while making your applications respond to events.

I'll now return to the stripe table example that I showed you in Chapter 3 and use events to make each table row highlight as the cursor moves over it. Along the way, I'll illustrate the concepts of event bubbling and event delegation.

The Secret Life of Events

You saw that an event message (e.g., `click`) can trigger an event handler (`onclick`) that is attached to a DOM object. However, an event message isn't just received by that one DOM element: Events travel up and down the DOM and are received by any elements they pass through along the way. This feature, known as *event propagation,* gives you some interesting options in how and where events get handled, and which elements the event affects.

In this next example, I want to highlight a table row when the cursor moves over it, and remove the highlight when the cursor moves off it. The problem, as you will see, is that although I want to highlight the table row, the mouse events that tell whether the cursor is moving in or out of a given row are in fact triggered by the table cell within the table row, or by the link within the table cell within the table row, if a link is present.

In other words, unlike the examples I've shown you so far, the event's target is not the element I want to change when the event occurs. To understand how to find and modify elements that are not the target of the event, let's first discuss the concepts of *event capturing, event bubbling,* and *event delegation.*

Capturing and Bubbling

When an event message is fired (and let's say it's a `click` event for the sake of this discussion), that `click` message does not go directly to the target of the event. It is first sent to the object at the top of the DOM hierarchy, `body`, and then moves down through the document tree to the target—the object that actually received the `click`. The message's downward journey to the target element is known as the *capturing phase.*

Once the message reaches the target object, it then travels back up the DOM to the `body` tag: The upward journey is called the *bubbling phase.* After the message makes it all the way back up to the `body` tag, like a salmon swimming upstream to its spawning grounds, its life ends.

You can add an event handler to any element that receives the `click` message as it makes this "down-and-then-up-again" journey. This can bring great efficiencies to your code, because you can now apply a technique called *event delegation.*

Event Delegation

Event delegation is the technique by which you place an event handler on an element that is not the target element of the event. The most advantageous use of event delegation is when you attach the event handler to the parent of a large number of child elements that must all provide a response to a particular event.

Significant coding economies can be realized by taking advantage of event delegation. Instead of attaching individual event handlers to every child, the message of interest is allowed to bubble up from whichever child triggered it and is handled by a single handler that is attached to the parent element. I'll show this process in the next example. If needed, the event object can supply the name of the target element: Then just that one "downstream" element—out of the many that might have triggered the parent's event handler—can be modified.

The W3C model supports both the capturing and bubbling phase. The third argument of a W3C event registration (highlighted)

```
someElement.addEventListener('focus', doHighlight, false)
```

is set to `true` if the event is to be handled in the capturing phase and `false` if it is to be handled in the bubbling phase.

However, the capturing phase is not supported in IE, and event delegation really only makes sense as the message travels up the DOM from children to parents. For these reasons, you will almost always use the bubbling phase to delegate events. In the W3C model, that third argument will, almost without exception, be `false`.

All these concepts will be illustrated as I add the rollover effect to the striped table.

Striped Table with Rollovers

In Chapter 3, I showed you how to add stripes to the rows of a table. You can see the complete JavaScript code on page 86. Now I'll modify this code so that each table row highlights as the cursor moves over it.

I'll start by modifying the HTML markup in two places. I'll first add a link into one cell of the table.

```
<td><a href=http://ajaxinaction.com>Ajax in Action</a></td>
```

It's very common to have links and other elements in a table cell, and the code needs to be robust enough to cope with such circumstances. This one link will represent an additional level of content hierarchy within the `tds` while I test.

Using an Element as a Debugging Tool

Next, I'll manually add a `p` tag with the attribute `id="display"` right after the table.

```
</table>

<p id="display">Display Area</p>

</body>
```

This element will display the kinds of test values that I have displayed with alert dialogs in earlier examples. When I start testing these rollovers, events will be generated so rapidly that I would soon tire of clicking the OKs in all those alert dialogs. Instead, I'll write my test results into the text of this element, which currently reads "Display Area", and see the results right in the page—no alerts needed. Now, any time I want to check a value, I can use this line of code

```
document.getElementById("display").innerHTML = valueToDisplay
```

and the words "Display Area" will be replaced by the value of *valueToDisplay*. Just remember, whenever you see

```
document.getElementById("display").innerHTML = someValue
```

in subsequent code, you'll know I am just displaying a test value.

The final preparatory step is to add a CSS style that will be the highlight background color for the rows—in this case, white.

the rollover color ──{ `.stripe_table tr.row_hilite {background:#FFF;}`

The sole purpose of the code I'll write is to add and remove the `stripe_table` class name from the table rows as the cursor passes over them.

Mouse Events

JavaScript is very chatty when it comes to mouse events. Every time the mouse moves on or off an element, or even moves the smallest amount, events are fired off describing these activities.

To detect if the cursor is over a table row, I'll use the mouse events `mouseover` and `mouseout`, which occur when the mouse enters and leaves an element, respectively.

Event Delegation

Because events bubble up, I'll add the two event listeners for these events at the `tbody` level. I want only table rows within the body of the table to highlight, so `tbody` is the highest level at which I can detect them without also receiving events from the table rows that are in the header, which I don't want to stripe.

I am already getting the `tbody` element in the existing striping code, so it's easy to add event handlers in the line right after that one.

get the table body	`var theTableBody = theTable.getElementsByTagName("tbody");`

```
                        // add event listeners to the tbody tag

                        addEvent(theTableBody[0],'mouseover', stripeTable.
                            checkEventSource);
```

note: don't use mouseleave– it doesn't work	`addEvent(theTableBody[0],'mouseout', stripeTable.` `    checkEventSource);`

```
                        // stripe the table rows
```

get the table body's rows	`var theTableRows = theTableBody[0].` `    getElementsByTagName("tr");`
set rowCount to the number of rows	`var rowCount=theTableRows.length`
add rollover event handlers and "odd" class for stripes	`for (var i=0; i < rowCount; i++) {`
add the "odd" class to every other row	`    theTableRows[i].className = "odd";`
increment counter a second time	`    i++;`

```
                        }
                    },
```

called when the user mouses over the table rows	`checkEventSource:function() {`

```
                        document.getElementById("display").innerHTML = "row
                            event triggered"; // temporary display

                    },
```

CODE 4.13 table_stripe_roll1.html	`etc`

In the first piece of highlighted code, I again use the addEvent
helper function to add the event listeners, specifying that the
mouseover and mouseout events will be attached to the tbody element. Both of these events will call the same function, checkEvent-
Source.

As its name suggests, the checkEventSource function will check
which element was the source of the event when the mouse moves
over the table rows and then add the hilite class to the related
table row. That functionality will come later. For now, as you can see
in the second piece of highlighted code, I've added the checkEvent-
Source function and within it simply used the "Display Area" element to display a bit of text confirming that the function was called.

When I first load the page, I see the "Display Area" default text in the
lower-left corner, as shown in **Figure 4.10**.

FIGURE 4.10 The page with the default Display Area text.

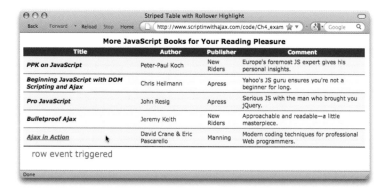

When I move the cursor over the bottom row of the table, as shown in **Figure 4.11**, the checkEventSource function is called and the "Display Area" message is updated.

FIGURE 4.11 The Display Area text is replaced with the text from the function.

This confirms that at least one of the two event handlers, mouseover, is attached successfully. I can be fairly confident that mouseout was too—I'll soon find out.

From the perspective of this code, I know that the mouseover event is bubbling up to the event listener on the tbody, but I don't know the triggering element, so I don't yet know which row I need to stripe.

Determining the Target Element

The next step is to determine the target element—the element that is actually triggering the event. To do this, I need to get the target element's nodeName, which in the case of an element gives the name of the tag—a, td, or tr, for example.

```
checkEventSource:function(e) {
```

CODE 4.14 table_stripe_roll2.html

```
    var evt = e || window.event;

    var evtTarget = evt.target || evt.srcElement;

    document.getElementById("display").innerHTML =
        evtTarget.nodeName;

    }
```

You've seen the first two lines of code within this function before—they get the event target. The highlighted code in the third line simply gets the node name of that target element; you can see the node names displayed in the lower-left corners of **Figures 4.12** and **4.13**.

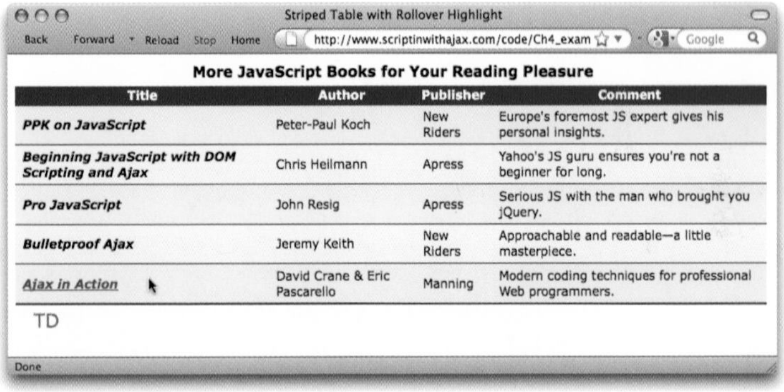

FIGURE 4.12 When the cursor is over a table row, the event target is a table cell.

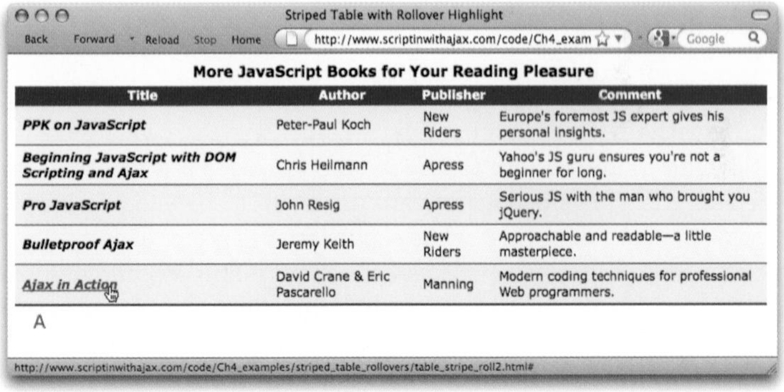

FIGURE 4.13 When the cursor is over a link within a table row, the event target is the link.

This test shows that the table row elements don't trigger events when the mouse goes over them, because they are entirely filled with their child tds. There simply is nowhere you can place the cursor to get the tr to trigger a mouse event. The target element—the element directly under the mouse—will always be the td unless you explicitly add padding or margins to create space between it and the tr. The td, because it's a child of the tr, will always be on top of the tr in the element stacking order and will therefore always be the target of any mouse event. You can also see in **Figure 4.14** that if the mouse moves over a link within a td, as you might expect, that link will be the target.

```
<body>
 └<table class="stripe_table">
    <caption>More JavaScript Books for Your Reading Pleasure</caption>
    <thead>
      <tr>
        <th scope="col">Title</th>
        <th scope="col">Author</th>
        <th scope="col">Publisher</th>
        <th scope="col">Comment</th>
      </tr>
    </thead>
  └<tbody> Event listener on tbody has mouseover handler that triggers checkEventSource function

      <!-- 4 table rows removed here -->            ┌──┴──┐
    └<tr>                                          mouseover
      └<td>                                         message
        └<a href="#">Ajax in Action</a>           bubbles up
      </td>                                      User rolls over link
      <td>David Crane &amp; Eric Pascarello</td>
      <td>Manning</td>
      <td>Modern coding techniques for professional Web programmers.</td>
    </tr>
  </tbody>
 </table>
</body>
```

FIGURE 4.14 The event bubbles up to the event listener on tbody.

The most important thing that this test shows is that the target of the event, be it the td, a link, or some other element that might appear within a table cell, is a child of the row that you want to highlight.

Traversing the DOM

To find the event target's ancestor table row so I can apply the row_hilite CSS class to it, all I need to do is start moving up the DOM from the target element until I find an element with the node name tr and apply the highlight class to that element. This process of moving up, down, or across the DOM to an adjacent element is known as *traversing*.

```
checkEventSource:function(e) {
    var evt = e || window.event;
    var evtTarget = evt.target || evt.srcElement;
    while (evtTarget.nodeName.toLowerCase() !== "tr") {
        evtTarget=evtTarget.parentNode;
    }
    document.getElementById("display").innerHTML =
        evtTarget.nodeName;
}
```

set up cross-browser event obj names

if the event didn't happen to the tr

move up from any child element to the tr

temporary—for testing

CODE 4.15 table_stripe_roll3.html

You can see the way I do this in the preceding highlighted code. I simply change the event target property from the target element to the parent of that element. This effectively moves me up the DOM—if the target was a, a link, I am now at the level of its parent table cell. I keep moving up like this until my test returns tr. (Note that I use the String method toLowerCase to convert the node name to lowercase for cross-browser compatibility. Some browsers, such as Firefox, return the node name in uppercase, as you can see in the lower-left corners of Figures 4.14 and 4.15.)

By the time I get a tr and the loop stops, my event target is already set to tr because each time the loop runs, I set the target to the parent element of the current target element before the loop determines if it should run again. The event target is now set to the element I want to modify and is no longer set to the original target of the event. In short, now when the mouse rolls over the table, the target element, whether a link or a table cell (or anything else), is instantly changed to the tr ancestor of that target element, as illustrated in **Figure 4.15**.

FIGURE 4.15 Even though the cursor is over a link, the reported event target is now the table row.

Adding the Highlight

Now that I have the row I want to highlight as the reported target for the mouseover and mouseout events, a few lines of code within a switch statement are all that's needed to add and remove the hilite class.

```
checkEventSource:function(e) {

    var evt = e || window.event;

    var evtTarget = evt.target || evt.srcElement;

    while (evtTarget.nodeName.toLowerCase() !== "tr") {

        evtTarget=evtTarget.parentNode;

    }

    switch (evt.type) {

        case 'mouseover':

            stripeTable.oldClass = evtTarget.className;

            evtTarget.className="row_hilite";

            break;

        case 'mouseout':

            evtTarget.className=stripeTable.oldClass;

            break;

    }

}
```

set up cross-browser event obj names

if the event didn't happen to the tr

move up from any child element to the tr

then respond to the event type case "mouseover" or "mouseout"

store the current class—either "odd" or undefined

change it to the hilite class—table row hilites

restore the orginal class—table row returns to original appearance

CODE 4.16 table_stripe_roll4.html

Figure 4.16 shows that the row that has the cursor over it now highlights, and the rollover effect code is complete.

FIGURE 4.16 Each row now highlights when the cursor is over it.

This is an good example of event delegation, because three separate elements are involved. The event happens to the link, the event handler attached to the table head responds to the event, and the link's table row is modified. This relationship is illustrated in **Figure 4.17**.

checkEventSource function asks…

► …is target now tr?
Yes, so highlight class is applied to tr.

► …is target now tr?
No, target is td.
Target is set to target's parent–tr.

► …is target now tr?
No, target is a.
Target is set to target's parent–td.

```
<body>
    <table class="stripe_table">
        <caption>More JavaScript Books for Your…</caption>
        <thead>
            <tr>
                <th scope="col">Title</th>
                <th scope="col">Author</th>
                <th scope="col">Publisher</th>
                <th scope="col">Comment</th>
            </tr>
        </thead>
        <tbody>                                    Event listener


            <!-- 4 table rows removed here -->

            <tr>                                   Modified element
                <td>
                    <a href="#">Ajax in Action</a>  Event target
                </td>
                <td>David Crane &amp; Eric Pascarello</td>
                <td>Manning</td>
                <td>Modern coding techniques for…</td>
            </tr>
        </tbody>
    </table>
</body>
```

FIGURE 4.17 The checkEventSource function determines the parent table row of the event target.

You can see in the code that before I set the row_hilite class on the tr, I store any class that is currently on that element. This is because there is a 50 percent chance that the row already has the odd class that does the striping. So, if the event handler is mouseover, which means I need to add the row_hilite class, I put any existing class name in a variable called oldClass and then change the class on the element to row_hilite. When the user moves off the row and the mouseout handler fires, I set that row back to the class name in the oldClass variable.

Mouse Coordinates

When an event is triggered by mouse activity, the event object holds several sets of x and y coordinates for the mouse, which give the mouse position with respect to the event target, the browser window, and the screen. These coordinate sets are unevenly supported by the various browsers and will not be covered here. Also, you will find you rarely actually need the mouse coordinates; knowing which element is under the cursor is usually sufficient information when working with mouse events. However, if you want some cross-browser code to help reliably obtain the mouse coordinates, check out the research of Peter-Paul Koch at www.quirksmode.org/js/events_properties.html#position. His book, *ppk on JavaScript* (New Riders, 2007), also has an in-depth discussion on working with mouse coordinates.

As illustrated in the previous diagram, what is really interesting about this example is that the element with the event listener is tbody, the element that triggers the event is td or a, and the element that is modified as a result of the event is tr. By combining event listeners, event delegation, event bubbling, and DOM traversing, you can have a single event handler manage events from dozens, hundreds, or thousands of child elements and then have the event affect any element that you choose.

Now that you've seen some ways to work with mouse events, let's take a look at the other way the user interacts with your application—the keyboard.

The Up and Down Life of Keys

It's easy to have a simplistic view of the keyboard: The user just presses a key and a character appears, right? The reality—JavaScript's reality, at least—is rather more complex. A keystroke is several discrete events, each with its own event message. When a key is pressed, the sequence of events is as follows:

1. keydown is sent when the key makes contact and is immediately followed by keypressed.

2. keypressed is a general event that summarizes a complete key press/release cycle.

   Then the character actually appears at the location of the keyboard's focus.

3. keyup occurs when the key breaks contact.

   If you hold the key down until it starts to repeat the character, keydown and keypressed repeat as well. (I think it's wrong for keypressed to repeat here, but it does.)

Generally, I work with keyup or keydown. Which one I use depends on the circumstance. Usually, I'll use keyup but sometimes keydown when I want to test the character before it appears onscreen. For example, if you have a numbers-only text field, you might use keydown so you can test the character, and reject it without letting it appear in the field if it is not a number.

Text Fields with Character Limits

Those of you who have tried to pack the excitement of what you are doing *right now* into a 140-character Twitter tweet have encountered a text field with a character limit. As soon as you type that hundred-and-forty-first character, the Update button dims and you can't send your tweet. Ahhhh, now the world will never know all the tasty details of that bologna sandwich!

Limiting text input can help ensure you are getting correctly sized data (U.S. zip codes and phone numbers for example) and compel those who would rant via your site to at least organize their thoughts.

I'll demonstrate how to set character limits on fields with a textarea (multiline) text field, as shown in **Figure 4.18**.

FIGURE 4.18 This is the finished example. A display below the text area shows how many more characters the field will accept.

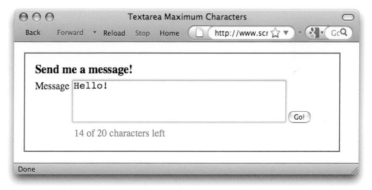

For this example, I've limited the field to 20 characters, but this can easily be changed.

The strategy for designing such a control is simple.

1. Each time the user types a character in the field, count the total number of characters in the field.

2. Update an onscreen display so users can see how many characters they still have left to type.

3. If the limit is reached, highlight the onscreen display to warn the user and delete any characters over the limit.

4. If the user deletes characters to reduce the text to below the maximum, remove the warning highlight.

This layout requires some simple HTML and CSS, which you can see in the download file. The only HTML that interacts with the JavaScript code is the text area and the display text.

```
<textarea id="msg_field" cols="35" rows="3"></textarea>

<p id="display"></p>
```

The p tag is currently empty, but I will add text into it as I go along. The initial code file, text_field_max_chars1.html, is displayed in the browser in **Figure 4.19**.

FIGURE 4.19 The initial markup for the text field displayed in the browser.

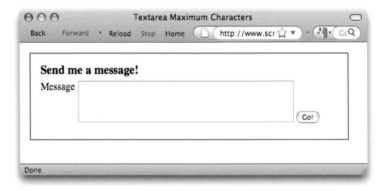

Setting Up the Message Display

Here's a start to the code.

```
window.onload=init;

function init() {

    limitChars.setUp();

}

limit_chars={

    theMaxChars: 20,

    setUp:function() {

        limitChars.theDisplay=document.
            getElementById("display");
```

the element to receive user feedback text

```
    limitChars.displayMsg("Message limit: " + limitChars.
        theMaxChars + " characters.")

},

displayMsg:function(toShow) {

    limitChars.theDisplay.innerHTML=toShow;

    }

}
```

In this first step I set up theMaxChars property to specify the character count limit (highlighted) and define the setup method, which is called when the page loads. For now, this method simply passes a text string stating the character limit to the displayMsg helper function (also highlighted), which then updates the display with the text string, as shown in **Figure 4.20**.

FIGURE 4.20 The display now indicates the 20-character limit defined by theMaxChars property.

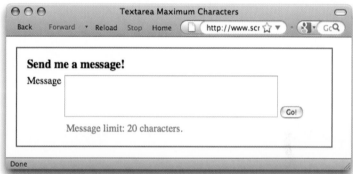

The next step gets the text the user types in the field so I can determine how many characters have been typed. To do this, I'll set an event listener on the field that calls its function on keyup events; in other words, the function will be called every time the user types a character into the field.

```
limitChars={

    theMaxChars: 20,

    setUp:function() {

        limitChars.theField=document.getElementById("msg_field");
```

```
        addEvent(limitChars.theField,"keyup", limitChars.
            checkField);
```

```
        limitChars.theDisplay=document.
            getElementById("display");

        limitChars.displayMsg("Message limit: " + limitChars.
            theMaxChars + " characters.")
    },
    checkField:function() {

        var theText=limitChars.theField.value

        limitChars.displayMsg(theText);

    },
    displayMsg:function(toShow)  {

        limitChars.theDisplay.innerHTML=toShow;

    }
}
```

get the current text

display the typed text

CODE 4.18 table_stripe__roll3.html

There is nothing here you haven't seen in earlier examples in this chapter. In the first block of the preceding highlighted code, I get the message field and then add an event listener to it that calls the `checkField` function whenever the `keyup` event occurs. To test that this arrangement is working, I'll have the `checkField` function display the user text in the display area (second highlighted code block). You can see this happening in **Figure 4.21**.

FIGURE 4.21 The `keyup` event successfully triggers a function that, for now, simply shows the text in the display area below.

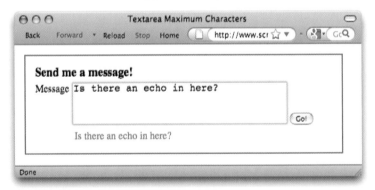

Every time the user types a character, the text in the text field immediately appears in the display area below. Capturing the text every time a character is added is crucial to the functionality I am creating here.

Monitoring the Character Count

Now it's time to do something more useful with this capability than to simply display the text—let's add some real functionality to the checkField method.

```
setUp:function() {

    limitChars.theField=document.getElementById("msg_
        field");

    addEvent(limitChars.theField,"keyup", limitChars.
        checkField);

    limitChars.theDisplay=document
        getElementById("display");

    limitChars.displayMsg("Message limit: " + limitChars.
        theMaxChars + " characters.");

},

checkField:function() {

    var theText=limitChars.theField.value

    limitChars.theField.value = theText.substring(0,
        limitChars.theMaxChars);

}
```

| called every time a key is pressed |
| get the current text |
| trim off excess chars |

CODE 4.19 text_field_max_chars4.html

I've removed the test display code and replaced it with a piece of code that deletes any characters in the field that exceed the number defined by theMaxChars property—20.

To do this, I use a String object method substring, which returns part of a string—known as the substring. The substring method accepts two parameters: the index of the first character to be returned and the length of the substring.

The highlighted line states "return a 20-character substring of the text in theText object starting from index 0 (the first character), and then set the contents of theField to that text."

This code is a sort of circular reference: The text is being read from the field in which the user is typing, trimmed to the first 20 characters, and put back into the same field. When there are less than 20 characters in the field, this has no visible effect. Once the user exceeds 20 characters, however, the effect is that the twenty-first and subsequent characters are deleted as fast as the user types them.

It's impossible to show this effect in a static screenshot, but if you open text_field_max_chars4.html in your browser and start typing, you're 20 characters away from seeing it for yourself.

While this achieves the objective of limiting the amount of text that can be typed in the field, it's not a very nice user experience to simply delete the user's text without giving some kind of warning. To help the user understand the rules of the field, let's first create a countdown in the display that states how many characters can still be typed.

```
checkField:function() {

    var theText=limitChars.theField.value

    if (theText.length > limitChars.theMaxChars) {

        limitChars.theField.value = theText.substring(0,
            limitChars.theMaxChars);

    } else {

        limitChars.charsLeft = limitChars.theMaxChars -
            theText.length;

        theText=(limitChars.charsLeft +  " of " + limitChars.
            theMaxChars + " characters left");

        limitChars.displayMsg(theText);

    }
}
```

get the current text

maximum chars reached

trim off excess chars

max chars not yet reached

= max chars – current length

assemble string stating number of characters remaining

display string

CODE 4.20 text_field_max_chars5.html

There is actually no point in updating the text in the field until the user exceeds the character limit, so I've added an if statement to control when the field is updated. Once the limit is exceeded, I'll trim the text. As long as the character count is below the maximum allowed, I'll update the message below the field to read "x of y characters left." **Figure 4.22** shows that the user is still below the 20-character limit.

FIGURE 4.22 Now there is a countdown display that shows how many more characters can be typed.

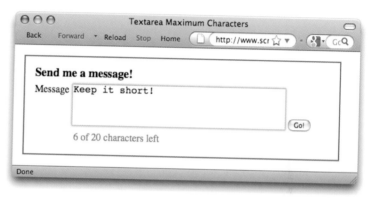

As a finishing touch, when the limit is exceeded, I'll make the display text bold and bright red. I'll add this one line to the CSS.

CODE 4.21 text_field_max_chars6.html

```
div#sign_up #display.hilite {color:red; font-weight:bold;}
```

Then I'll add the `hilite` class onto the display element when the limit is reached, as shown in **Figure 4.23**, and remove it if the user deletes enough text to get back below the limit again.

FIGURE 4.23 The display text now highlights when the character limit is exceeded.

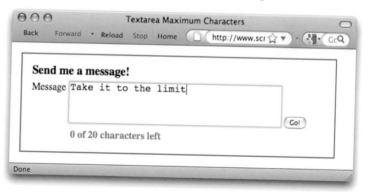

The Finished Code

Here's the complete code for this example with the two additional lines of JavaScript.

```javascript
// Note: addEvent helper function must be linked to page

window.onload=init;

function init() {

    limitChars.setUp();

}

limitChars={

    theMaxChars: 20,

    setUp:function() {

        limitChars.theField=document.getElementById("msg_field");

        addEvent(limitChars.theField,"keyup", limitChars.
            checkField);

        limitChars.theDisplay=document.
            getElementById("display");

        limitChars.displayMsg("Message limit: " + limitChars.
            theMaxChars + " characters.")

    },

    checkField:function() {

        var theText=limitChars.theField.value

        if (theText.length > limitChars.theMaxChars) {

            limitChars.theField.value = theText.substring(0,
                limitChars.theMaxChars);
```

checkfield() is called on every keyup

the element to receive user feedback text

get the current text

maximum chars reached

trim off excess chars

Which Key Was Pressed?

If you want to know which key the user pressed, perhaps to create keyboard navigation for a game, get the Event Object's keyCode property. This gives you the numeric ASCII code (see the ASCII code table in Appendix D for details) that you can convert to an actual character such as "A" by running it through the `String.fromCharCode(keyCode)` String method.

hilites info text if too many chars typed	`limitChars.theDisplay.className="hilite";`
	`} else {`
max chars not yet reached	
= max chars−current length	`limitChars.charsLeft = limitChars.theMaxChars -`
	`theText.length;`
	`theText=(limitChars.charsLeft +   " of " + limitChars.`
	`theMaxChars + " characters left");`
	`limitChars.displayMsg(theText);`
removes hilite if present by resetting default styles	`limitChars.theDisplay.className="";`
	`}`
end checkField	`},`
	`displayMsg:function(toShow)  {`
	`limitChars.theDisplay.innerHTML=toShow;`
	`}`
	`}`

That completes this example and this chapter.

Summary

In this chapter you have learned how to monitor and respond to events. The keyboard and mouse are the only ways the user can interact with your application (although touch, voice, and motion are beginning to offer alternatives), and providing meaningful responses to these inputs is what makes an interactive application interactive. The techniques you have learned are a basic toolkit for building responsive RIAs.

In the next chapter, I'll show you Ajax techniques that enable your application to respond even faster and smoother to those user inputs, by fetching data from the server and updating the page's content without making the user wait for a new page.

CHAPTER 5

Ajax

NOW IT'S TIME TO LOOK AT AJAX. In this chapter, you will not only learn how Ajax works, but also how it changes the way you think about and develop online applications. You will also see the different formats of data that Ajax allows you to access and how to process each format in the browser, ready for display on the page.

Ajax is an acronym for Asynchronous JavaScript and XML, even though it appears in this book as a regular noncapitalized word.

Ajax is a term coined by Jesse James Garrett of Adaptive Path in his now legendary posting, which you can read at www.adaptivepath.com/ ideas/essays/archives/000385.php.

Ajax is simply a catchy name given to a JavaScript programming technique that enables data to be moved between the browser and the server without the usual "round-trip to the server and a page refresh"—the only model by which the Web previously worked. In that model, even updating one word in the page required the server to send an entirely new page to the browser. A new page was the only context in which new data could arrive in the browser.

Ajax offers a new model. Using Ajax you can request data from the server and then use the DOM scripting techniques discussed in Chapter 3 to add that data into the page. This occurs without the user having to wait for an entire new page to load—in fact, without reloading the page at all.

This capability lets you deliver a more application-like experience. If the user has a reasonably fast Internet connection, there is often little or no perceivable delay between clicking a link and seeing new data appear in the page. Suddenly, the response of your site is less of the old click-and-wait experience and much more like a regular "sovereign" application running on the user's local computer. Things happen as soon as you click or select from a menu without the rest of the screen changing.

A more subtle but powerful change that Ajax brings is a sense of place; instead of perceiving the site as a series of discrete pages, the experience is now a workspace that changes and updates as the user works.

Understanding Ajax

Ajax is quite simple to understand and not too difficult to implement. Let's start at the beginning and look at why this programming technique was called Ajax in the first place.

Ajax by the Letters

The first A of Ajax stands for *Asynchronous*. The Merriam-Webster dictionary defines asynchronous as "digital communication (as between computers) in which there is no timing requirement for transmission." In other words, the Ajax request that is made by the browser does not affect the browser's other activities.

In the regular round-trip model, the user can do nothing after, say, submitting a form except wait until a new page is served back to

To Ajax or Not to Ajax?

The technical and user experience changes that Ajax brings also create new design challenges. For example: If a small amount of the page content changes, will the user notice? How can I direct the user's attention to these changes? What if the request to the server has no response and the required data is not delivered? How will my page respond under this circumstance, and how can the user be made aware of any problems this causes?

It's also important to understand that Ajax is not appropriate for every browser/server transaction. If you simply want to add a line of text—perhaps a validation message on a form—it makes perfect sense to get that little piece of data from the server as an Ajax request and add it into the page with DOM scripting. If the request will update the entire page, or most of it, it makes better sense to do this as a normal round-trip with a page refresh. In short, use Ajax only where it enhances the operation of the application or the user experience.

the browser. The process is entirely *synchronous*—one event must complete before the next can start. Because an Ajax request is asynchronous, once the request is sent off to the server, control is immediately restored to the user, who can continue working while that request is being fulfilled. When the requested data is delivered to the browser from the server, a preassigned *callback function* is automatically called and the data is then processed and displayed by JavaScript.

The J in Ajax is for JavaScript. JavaScript handles the entire Ajax transaction, and this chapter focuses on showing you the programming techniques to implement Ajax functionality in your Web site.

The second A in Ajax is simply And.

The X in Ajax stands for XML. In Jesse James Garrett's client proposal where he first used the term, XML was the data format that would be returned from the server. However, the term XML is somewhat misleading, because data can be returned in many formats, of which XML is one. For example, HTML, plain text, and JavaScript Object Notation (JSON) are all commonly requested data formats used in Ajax transactions. I'll show you how to work with these formats later in this chapter.

JSON is a data format based on the object literal construct you saw in Chapter 3. Because it is a very compact data format and can be evaluated by JavaScript as code, JSON is frequently replacing XML as the data format of choice for today's applications.

Before starting into the workings of Ajax, let's consider how communication between the browser and server is implemented.

Communication with the Server

The HyperText Transfer Protocol (HTTP) defines how transactions between the browser and server are handled. While this protocol is pretty complex, in the scope of this discussion, you only need to understand the POST and GET methods, which control how the browser makes requests to the server.

When I talk about the HTTP request method, I mean *method* as in "way of doing things," not as in "a function in an object."

THE GET METHOD

A server request begins with an action that causes the browser to make either a GET or POST request to the server.

A GET request, typically made when a link is clicked, is a URL with a query string, like this:

```
display_product_info.html?productID=45034A&colorpref=red
```

The query string (highlighted) is separated from the rest of the URL with a question mark. It consists of a number of name/value pairs separated by ampersands that are passed to the requested page. These name/value pairs serve the same purpose as the arguments passed to a function; they contain data that the requested page will use when processing the request.

The entire GET request string is visible in the browser's address bar, and it's tempting for users to modify the query string to see what they might get (a different user's account, perhaps?) This means it's important to only use GET when the user is requesting nonsensitive information—a particular news story, for example.

THE POST METHOD

A POST request is typically made when a form is submitted. If you look at the markup for a form, you'll notice that the method attribute is almost always POST. For each field of the form, the name attribute value and the data entered in that field are passed as the name/value pair. However, while the URL is visible in the browser address bar, the name/value pairs are sent behind the scenes to the browser and are not visible in the address bar.

As a rule of thumb, if you are sending data that will be recorded on the server, use POST. If you are simply requesting a page, use GET.

There is typically a limit (depending on browsers and proxy servers) of 1024 characters in a GET URL.

THE TRADITIONAL MODEL

Under what I'll call the traditional model—the only model prior to Ajax—the data is passed to the server via a POST or GET request and is then processed by the middleware (such as PHP, .NET, or Java). A new Web page is then generated and served back to the browser in response.

The downside of the traditional model is that no user activity can take place between the request being submitted and the new page being entirely rendered in the browser. Once that link is clicked or the form submitted, the user must wait for that new page to display.

Even though a slow response can result in frustration and random clicking on the part of the user, the synchronous nature of the traditional "click-and-wait" model is very familiar and comfortable to the user.

THE AJAX MODEL

When an Ajax request is made to the server, again using a POST or GET request, it is made via the browser's XHR (**XMLH**ttp**R**equest) object, which I will discuss in detail in a moment. The XHR object is the key to Ajax because it acts as an intermediary between the browser and the server. Actually initiating an Ajax request by calling the XHR object takes a matter of milliseconds, and then control is returned to the user while the XHR object fulfills the request, as shown in **Figure 5.1**. Because the request is now happening "in the background," the user can continue working as soon as the XHR object receives the request.

FIGURE 5.1 Unlike a traditional request where the user must wait until a new page is rendered in the browser, an Ajax request returns control to the user as soon as the request is made, without waiting for a response.

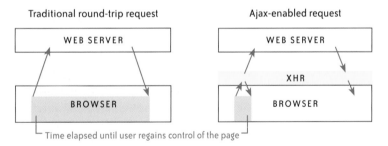

However, the most significant advantage of using Ajax it that you can request specific data, not just an entire page, as a response. For example, the user could add an item to a shopping cart and, instead of waiting while the server is updating the cart status, the user could do more shopping and add a second item. Once the server update is complete, the server could return just the text needed to update the onscreen cart display, and this text would then be added into the page using DOM scripting without a refresh of the page. With data able to flow into the browser in this way and the necessity for constant page refreshes removed, a Web site can be transformed into a responsive online application. This is why Ajax has created so much excitement in the Web development community.

The XMLHttpRequest Object

Ajax is made possible because of the browser's `XMLHttpRequest` (XHR) object. The XHR object can make requests to the server and receive data in response. It was developed as part of Microsoft's ActiveX strategy to enable its online mail products to communicate with a mail server. It was only recently made part of the official W3C standard, even though it has been well supported in all the major browsers for several years. Microsoft's implementation of the XHR object is different from the implementation in W3C browsers, so as with the event object you saw in Chapter 4, some cross-browser compatibility issues exist. Fortunately, the popularity of Ajax ensures that these issues have been thoroughly addressed by the many helper functions and frameworks that are available. You will rarely, if ever, have to concern yourself with the XHR object's differences between the browsers. However, even though these helper functions and frameworks exist, it is useful to understand how the XHR object works, so I'll now show you how to write an Ajax helper function that talks to the XHR object.

Note on Demo Ajax Function

While the `ajax_request.html` code I'll show in this section of the chapter works well in all modern browsers and serves the purpose of demonstrating the concepts of how an Ajax request is made, it is not industrial strength. It has no capability to reject really old browsers that don't have an XHR object. Also, there is no handling for the possibility of an HTTP status of 304 being returned, meaning that the document is already cached on the user's computer and the user will get that data instead of data from the server.

If you want a more robust Ajax function that you can use on a site you will be putting into production, it's best to use one of the many frameworks that offer Ajax capabilities. Or, if you don't want to use a framework, try `simpleXHR. js` written by *Scriptin's* technical editor Chris Heilmann—you'll find it in the Chapter 5 code folder. It overcomes the technical shortcomings associated with the demonstration Ajax function in this example but is rather more difficult to understand. However, as with other helper functions, you don't have to understand it to use it, and it accepts the same two arguments as the demonstration `ajax_request.html` example.

How to Use the XMLHttpRequest (XHR) Object

To use the XMLHttpRequest object, you must be able to communicate with it and then monitor its activity so you know when it has successfully acquired the requested data. The way you do this is to write a function that can communicate with the browser's XHR object and can handle all your application's Ajax requests.

This kind of function is known as a wrapper. A wrapper serves as an interface to a piece of usually complex functionality—in this case, the XHR object—and manages all communication with it. Your code will talk to the wrapper function, and the wrapper will be written to handle the complexities of managing the XHR object. When you call this wrapper function, you will simply pass it two arguments:

- *the name of the requested resource*—a filename that will provide the data you want from the server

- *the name of your callback function*—a function that will be called when the request completes. This function will receive the returned data and process it in some way according to your application's needs.

An XMLHttpRequest wrapper function greatly simplifies your life because it abstracts away from the rest of your code all the complexities of managing an Ajax transaction and the associated cross-browser differences. At any point where your code requires data from the server, you can just call this Ajax function, passing it the two required arguments. When the transaction is complete and the requested data is returned, the wrapper function will pass the data to the specified callback function—the function you write to process the returned data. Once the callback function is called, the process is complete.

You can see this completed ajaxRequest *function on page 144.*

I'll now show you, step by step, how to write this wrapper function (that I will name ajaxRequest), which will help you understand exactly how an Ajax transaction works. Of course, you don't actually have to write this function if you don't want to; you can find it in the Chapter 5 code examples. This function will perform the following steps:

1. Create a new instance of the XHR object.

2. Define a function to monitor the request's progress.

3. Send the request via the XHR instance.

4.   Check that the request was successful when the server responds.

5.   Pass the returned data to the assigned callback function so it can be used.

Let's look at each step.

1. CREATE A NEW INSTANCE OF THE XHR OBJECT

The first step in using the XHR object is to instantiate a new instance of it. In this example, I'll store it in a variable called ajaxObj. For a W3C browser, you would write

```
ajaxObj = new XMLHttpRequest();
```

and for a Microsoft browser, you would write

```
ajaxObj = new ActiveXObject("Microsoft.XMLHTTP")
```

You can write this as a one-step, cross-browser instantiation like this:

```
var ajaxObj = (window.ActiveXObject)
? new XMLHttpRequest()
:new ActiveXObject("Microsoft.XMLHTTP");
```

I have broken this into three lines for clarity, but it's the same ternary if *statement format of* (test) ? true stuff : false stuff *that I used for the cross-browser event object creation in Chapter 4.*

After you have instantiated the XHR object, you can then use its properties and methods to request and manage the movement of data between the browser and Web server.

2. DEFINE A FUNCTION TO MONITOR THE REQUEST

A crucial component of the XHR process is the server's communication with the browser. Without this feedback from the server, you would never know when the request has completed. At key points in the process, the server updates the XHR object's readystate property with a numerical value that defines the current state of the request.

The five possible values are:

   0 = uninitialized—the object exists but the open method has not been called

   1 = loading—the open method has been called but the send method has not

2 = loaded—the send method has been called and the request is in process

3 = interactive—the server is sending a response

4 = complete—the response has been sent

Your wrapper function can be notified each time this state changes by monitoring the onreadystatechange event handler, which as its name suggests is called each time the XHR object's readystate property is updated by the server.

Because the order of these responses is different between browsers, and because all you really need to know is when the request has completed, you simply want to monitor for a readystate property value of 4 each time the onreadystatechange event handler is triggered. You do this by assigning a function to the onreadystatechange event handler in which you can track the state of the request. You need to specify that function before making the request, because, as you can see from the descriptions of the values of the readystate property, the server starts sending back request state information even before the request is fully submitted.

Consequently, after instantiating the object—but before you do anything with it—you want to define the function that will process the onreadystatechange information.

The XHR object also tracks the three-digit HTTP status of the request. You are probably all too familiar with HTTP Status 404—Page Not Found, which you get when you request a URL that doesn't point to a valid resource. What you want your code to check for is status 200—success. Upon determining a status of 200, your object can safely assume the request data has arrived and pass whatever is in the response to the callback function. In the sequence of your code, once the readystate is 4, you check for the request's HTTP status (which is stored in the XHR object's status property). If the status is 200, the responseText property's value—the requested data—is passed to the callback function.

To do this, I simply assign an anonymous function that makes these checks to the onreadystatechange event handler each time the readystate changes. (This is a very similar concept to the onload event handler, because both are called by events that are not initiated by the user.)

```
myAjaxObj.onreadystatechange = function {

    if (ajaxObj.readyState == 4 && ajaxObj.status == 200) {

        cbFunc(ajaxObj.responseText);

    }

}
```

> if true, then the request has successfully completed

> pass the data to the callback function

With monitoring now in place for the request, you are all set to make the request for the data you want.

3. SEND THE REQUEST VIA THE XHR INSTANCE

The first decision you need to make when requesting data is the method to use to make the request—GET or POST.

Use the request method GET if you just want to get data from the server or POST if you want to update data on the server. I'll first show the GET request process.

Sending a request with GET. A GET request requires the use of two methods of the XHR object: open and send. The open method allows you to specify the kind of request method (GET or POST) you want to make, the name of the file you are requesting, and a Boolean value that defines whether you are making an asynchronous or synchronous request. Here is the format:

```
objName.open = (requestMethod, URL, asynchronous?)
```

If you set the third value to false, the application will stop running until the request is fulfilled, which defeats one of the key benefits of Ajax. Almost always you will set this third argument to true so that the user can continue working while the request is being fulfilled. There are additional optional parameters besides these, and you can learn more about them at www.w3.org/TR/XMLHttpRequest/ #xmlhttprequest.

The name of the file is simply a URL and, because I am using GET, can be extended with a query string of name/value pairs. A GET request might look like this:

```
myAjaxObj.open = ('GET', 'lookupUserInfo.php?username=ajaxScr
ipter&email=charles@scriptinwithajax.com'', true)
```

Now that your request is defined, you can send the request to the server

```
myAjaxObj.send(null)
```

When using GET, the data argument of the send method is always set to null; you don't need to include any data with the send. If you want to send information to further define your request, you can append a query string to the URL, as in the previous example where the query string states the user name in the record to be retrieved.

Sending a request with POST. A POST request, which is used when you want to update data on the server (such as a database record), requires two additional steps. First, you set the request method to POST. Second, you don't append a query string to the URL as you do with GET; any data that is part of the request is sent separately from the URL as the argument of the send method. To do this, the content type of the HTTP header must be set correctly using the XHR object's setRequestHeader method, so that this data is handled correctly when it arrives at the server.

The open and send steps shown earlier for GET would look like this for POST:

```
myAjaxObj.open = ('GET', 'updateUserInfo.php', true)

myAjaxObject.setRequestHeader('Content-Type', 'application/x-
  www-form-urlencoded'

myAjaxObj.send('oldEmail=charles@stylinwithcss.
  com&newEmail=charles@scriptinwithajax.com')
```

4. CHECK THAT THE REQUEST WAS SUCCESSFUL WHEN THE SERVER RESPONDS

Whether you use GET or POST to make your request, your Ajax function now keeps track of the request by monitoring the onreadystatechange event handler using the anonymous function assigned to it in the previous step. As shown earlier, once you get a readyState of 4 and status of 200, the request data has arrived.

5. PASS THE DATA TO THE ASSIGNED CALLBACK FUNCTION SO IT CAN BE USED

When the callback function is called, it is passed the responseText property value as its argument, which is the requested data, and the Ajax function's work is complete.

That's it. Here's what the complete function looks like:

parameters: the url of the data, the callback function

does browser support this property?

if so, determine which browser and create a new XHR object

if the ajaxObj object was successfully created…

set up function to run whenever readyState changes before making the request

if true, then the request data has arrived

pass the data to the callback function

open server connection– GET request, requested URL, asychronous set to true

send the request

CODE 5.1 ajax_request.html

```javascript
function ajaxRequest(url, cbFunc) {

    if (document.getElementById) {

        var ajaxObj = (window.ActiveXObject) ?
            new ActiveXObject("Microsoft.XMLHTTP") :
            new XMLHttpRequest();

    }

    if (ajaxObj) {

        ajaxObj.onreadystatechange = function() {

            if (ajaxObj.readyState == 4 && ajaxObj.status ==
                200) {

                cbFunc(ajaxObj.responseText);

            }

        }

        ajaxObj.open("GET", url, true);

        ajaxObj.send(null);

    }

}
```

Using the Ajax Function

I'll now use this Ajax function to request some text from a file called `basic_text.txt` on the server. The Ajax function will return the file's text as a string that I will display in the page. A simple file request like this requires no server-side middleware—the file simply has to be at the specified location on the server.

Here's some markup of a link that calls a function to request the data and an empty element into which I can add the requested text:

To keep this example simple, I am using an inline event handler on the element to trigger the function. In a real application, it would be better practice to set up an event listener on the element.

```html
<a href="basic_text.txt" onclick="readFile(); return
    false;">Get text</a>

<p id="display"></p>
```

makes the call to the Ajax function

CODE 5.2 ajax_request/ajax_request.html

```javascript
function readFile() {

    ajaxRequest('basic_text.txt',cbReadFile);

}
```

To help me always see the connection between the calling function and its associated callback function, I give both functions the same name except the callback handler's name begins with the letters cb; for example, myFunction and cbMyFunction.

called by callback from
Ajax function

The readFile function called by the link passes the Ajax function the two required arguments—the URL of the file and the name of the callback function that will display the data when it is returned. Note the name of the callback function is cbReadFile—so in this case, readFile() requests the data, and cbReadFile() handles the response.

Here's the callback handler.

```
function cbReadFile(theData) {
    var theDisplay = document.getElementById('display');
    theDisplay.innerHTML = theData;
}
```

This code simply writes the text into the element with the ID display.

Here's how this all looks onscreen to the user. **Figure 5.2** shows the link displayed in the page.

FIGURE 5.2 Clicking the link will initiate the Ajax request for the text file.

When the link is clicked, the Ajax request is made and the text is added into the empty paragraph tag, as shown in **Figure 5.3**.

FIGURE 5.3 The text from the requested file is displayed on the server.

Note that the text simply appears on the page. There is no page refresh and, except with a very slow Internet connection, an almost instantaneous response. The behind-the-scenes process is shown in **Figure 5.4**.

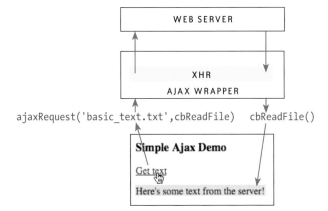

Using an Object Literal to Maintain State Through an Ajax Call

One problem with requiring two functions for an Ajax call—one to make the call and the other to handle the callback—is that you are passing control from one function to the other. However, because that control goes via the Ajax function, you can't at that time pass data from the calling function to the callback—one does not directly call the other. The variables that existed in the calling function are not accessible to the callback function. This is a problem of *maintaining state* in your application—where important values must persist for later reference.

I'll show you a simple example of this problem and then how to fix it using the two functions in the **Code 5.2**.

In this example, I'll get the user's name from a form field, so I can display a personalized welcome message. The form markup looks like this:

```
<form action="#" method="get">

    <label for="first_name">Enter your first name: </label>

    <input type="text" id="first_name">
```

I'm using onsubmit *as the event for the Submit button. Unlike* onclick, onsubmit *can also be triggered from the keyboard if the button has focus.*

```
<input type="Submit" onsubmit="readFile(); return false;"
value="Go!">

<p id="display"></p>

</form>
```

I've left the form action value as #—an anchor link, and not supplied a URL. I would usually, and more correctly, put a URL here to the server site script that would process the form if JavaScript were not available. I left out this step because I don't want to confuse the simple point of this demo.

Once I have the user's name, I'll fetch the welcome message from the server and add the user's name to it. I've modified the calling function to look like this:

```
function readFile() {

    var firstName = document.getElementById("name").value;

    ajaxRequest('basic_text.txt',cbReadFile);

}
```

get text from a form field and set the variable

makes the call to the Ajax function

Then I modify the corresponding callback function to look like this:

CODE 5.4 ajax_request/ajax_request_scope_problem.html (cont.)

```
function cbReadFile(theData) {

    var theDisplay = document.getElementById('display');

    theDisplay.innerHTML = "Hi, " + firstName + ". " + theData;

}
```

use the variable—DOESN'T WORK!

This code fails and the Firefox Error Console displays "Error: first-Name is not defined." This occurs because the variable firstName declared in the calling function has function-level scope and is therefore unavailable to the callback function. This issue can be overcome by refactoring the code as an object literal where both call and callback share the same scope (the object), like this:

```
ajaxFile = {

    readFile:function () {

        ajaxFile.firstName = (document.getElementById("first_name").value) || 'Visitor';
```

makes the call to the Ajax function

```
ajaxRequest('basic_text.txt',ajaxFile.cbReadFile);

},

cbReadFile:function (theData) {

var theDisplay = document.getElementById('display');

theDisplay.innerHTML = "Hi, " + ajaxFile.firstName + ". " +
    theData;

}

}
```

callback function to process response from Ajax function

CODE 5.5 ajax_request/ajax_request_obj_literal.html

Now the firstName variable declared in the calling function is available to the callback function because both share the ajaxFile object scope, as shown in **Figure 5.5**.

FIGURE 5.5 Because the calling and callback functions share the object literal's scope, the user's name declared in the calling function is available to the callback function.

Note that the highlighted line in **Code 5.5**, which gets the user's name from the field, is written as an OR structure. If the user leaves the field blank, the default name "Visitor" is used, as shown in **Figure 5.6**. Without this default text, a blank entry would result in "Hi, . Here's some text from the server."

FIGURE 5.6 By assigning the firstName variable using an OR structure, the default value "Visitor" is used when the name field is left blank.

Object literals are an effective way to keep variables in scope between functions without having to resort to the dangers of global variables.

Ajax and Data Formats

As mentioned earlier in this chapter, although the X of Ajax stands for XML, almost any kind of data can be served via the XHR object. The most common formats are HTML, JSON, XML, and plain text. The preceding example was a very simple demonstration of using plain text. More complex text formats, such as CSV (comma separated values) text files, can also be used and parsed out with JavaScript's String object methods.

However, because HTML, JSON, and XML are the most popular Ajax file formats, we'll take a look at each of them, starting with HTML.

Creating a Simple Catalog

A simple way to use Ajax is to store (or generate) data on the server as HTML fragments that can be added into a page. An HTML fragment, as its name suggests, is a term I use for an HTML file (or HTML that is generated by the middleware on your server) that is not a complete page but simply some HTML elements that are intended to be added to an existing page—they can't really "stand alone." I'll demonstrate using HTML fragments in a multipage catalog example.

In this example, I'll create a simple catalog that has an index page and three product pages. I'll again use my beloved guitars for content, as **Figure 5.7** illustrates.

In this three-column layout, only the content within the area with the blue border in the center column changes; the header, sidebars, footer, and the tabs in the center column are the same for every page. Consequently, I can use the same code file for these unchanging areas and just update the content area. I'll start by making the page work using just HTML and PHP, and then I'll layer on the Ajax functionality for JavaScript-empowered users.

FIGURE 5.7 The overview page of the guitar catalog example.

Using PHP Templates

In this section, I'll use a PHP template, which is a term for a PHP script that contains the common elements of the page. Although the PHP script requested will be the same one every time, it will include the correct piece of HTML for the content area according to the link the user clicks. The content area will automatically load with the Overview HTML fragment, which loads the page with all three guitars shown in Figure 5.7 when the page is first requested. Clicking the guitar names in the tabs will load an HTML fragment specific to that instrument.

I'll briefly explain the PHP functionality so you have an understanding of how to get the page working with a regular "round-trip" before enhancing it with Ajax.

The name of the PHP script is `guitar_ajax_demo.php`, and it is mostly made up of HTML. When requested, this PHP script will write out the HTML it contains and resolve some PHP statements into HTML that it will also write into the page. It will then serve this complete HTML page back to the browser.

THE PHP CODE

Here is the mix of HTML and PHP contained in the PHP script. When requested, the PHP script simply outputs an HTML page and sends it to the requesting browser. Any HTML within the script is added to the page output as is. Any code between the `<?php` and `?>` tags is PHP and will be replaced with the HTML to which it resolves. PHP is never sent to the browser, only the HTML that the PHP script generates.

Here is the PHP script edited down to just the relevant bits. The PHP, which will all be evaluated to HTML, is highlighted.

```
<div id="nav">

  <div id="nav_inner">

    <ul class="guitar_links">

      <li><a class="overview" href="guitar_catalog_ajax_
        html.php?request=overview">Overview</a></li>

      <li><a class="tiger" href="guitar_catalog_ajax_html.
        php?request=tiger">Tiger</a></li>

      <li><a class="jasmine" href="guitar_catalog_ajax_
        html.php?request=jasmine">Jasmine</a></li>

      <li><a class="sunny" href="guitar_catalog_ajax_html
        php?request=sunny">Sunny</a></li>

    </ul>

  </div>

</div>


<div id="content">

  <div id="content_inner" class="clearfix">
```

if the $_GET array's "request" variable is set, use its value, else use "overview"

clearfix class in CSS file makes element enclose child floated elements—see *Stylin' with CSS, Second Edition*, page 119 for details

```php
<?php ($_GET['request']) ? $guitarName=($_
    GET['request']) : $guitarName='overview'; ?>
<ul id="tabs" class="guitar_links clearfix rounded">
    <li class="rounded <?php if ($guitarName=='overview')
        {echo 'choice';} ?>"><a href="guitar_catalog_ajax_
        html.php?request=overview">Overview</a></li>

    <li class="rounded <?php if ($guitarName=='tiger')
        {echo 'choice';} ?>"><a href="guitar_catalog_ajax_
        html.php?request=tiger">Tiger</a></li>

    <li class="rounded <?php if ($guitarName=='jasmine')
        {echo 'choice';} ?>"><a href="guitar_catalog_ajax_
        html.php?request=jasmine">Jasmine</a></li>

    <li class="rounded <?php if ($guitarName=='sunny')
        {echo 'choice';} ?>"><a href="guitar_catalog_ajax_
        html.php?request=sunny">Sunny</a></li>
</ul>

<div id="guitar_display" class="clearfix">

<?php include 'html_frags/'. $guitarName .'_desc_frag.
    html'; ?>
```

the dynamic data is added here

```php
</div>

</div>

</div>
```

CODE 5.6 guitar_catalog.php

When the page is requested, the first piece of PHP code that runs is

```php
<?php ($_GET['request']) ? $guitarName=($_GET['request']) :
$guitarName='overview'; ?>
```

PHP's $_GET array contains the data from a URL query string, which are the optional sets of name/value pairs that follow a ? after the URL itself. This highlighted code checks to see if the query string has added a request property to the array: To be more precise, it checks if the request property is set. Because the initial request for the page has no query string and is simply

```
guitar_catalog_ajax_html.php
```

then ($_GET['request']) resolves to false and the $guitarName variable value defaults to overview. (Note the use of the ternary if statement.)

INCLUDING THE HTML FRAGMENT IN THE PAGE

The key piece of PHP is inside the guitar_display div (which is otherwise empty) in the content area of the page, which looks like this:

```
<div id="guitar_display">

<?php

include 'html_frags/'. $guitarName .'_desc_frag.html';

?>

</div>
```

Because $guitarName has defaulted to overview (as I showed earlier in the code), the highlighted PHP resolves to overview and PHP then interprets the line as

```
include 'html_frags/overview_desc_frag.html';
```

PHP then includes the HTML fragment that contains the markup for the Overview page in place of this code, and it is thereby added into the guitar_display div. The HTML fragment files for each guitar look like this:

```
<div id="picture_box" class="equal"> <img src="images/
   jasmine_200w.jpg" alt="Takamine Jasmine E40SC guitar" />
   </div>

<div id="info_box" class="equal">

   <div id="info_box_inner">

      <h4>Jasmine</h4>

      <ul>

         <li>Model: <strong>ES40C</strong></li>

         <li>Made by: <strong>Takamine</strong></li>

         <li>Year: <strong>1991</strong></li>

      </ul>

      <h5>About this guitar</h5>

      <p>Bright highs...(more text here).</p>
```

CODE 5.7 jasmine_desc_frag.html

```
<p>Comes fitted with...(more text here).</p>

    <p>The iMix controls...(more text here).</p>

    <p><a href="http://www.thewho.net/whotabs/equipment/
        guitar/equip-takamine.html#eg40sc">Pete Townsend
        likes Takamine Ex40 series guitars too!</a></p>

  </div>

</div>
```

Each HTML fragment file has been carefully named: The filenames are only slightly different for each file. Therefore, all I have to do is add the $guitarName value into the otherwise identical URL string to get the correct filename.

GENERATING THE LINKS

Because the URLs of the tabs all reference the current page, when a tab is clicked, the page will reload itself. Let's assume the user clicks the tab labeled Tiger, whose URL is

```
guitar_catalog_ajax_html.php?request=tiger
```

As the page is processed on the server, PHP again checks the $_GET array. Now the $guitarName variable—which takes its value from the query string—is set to tiger. The PHP statement within the guitar_display div resolves to

```
include 'html_frags/tiger_desc_frag.html';
```

PHP then includes the HTML fragment contained in the file right here in the page, and the information about the "Tiger" guitar is displayed. By using the value passed in the string from the link, PHP can generate the correct URL for the PHP include, as shown in **Figure 5.8**.

MAKING THE TABS HIGHLIGHT

The other aspect of the page controlled by PHP is the highlighting of the tabs along the top of the content area. See the sidebar "Stylin' the Tabs" for details on how these tabs are created. The "active" tab that relates to the currently displayed content is highlighted by adding the class choice to the appropriate tab's li. Adding this class to the correct tab is achieved by the following PHP on each link. Here's the code for the Overview tab.

```
<li class="<?php if ($guitarName==='overview'){echo
'choice';} ?>">
```

FIGURE 5.8 The "Tiger" guitar HTML fragment is now included in the page.

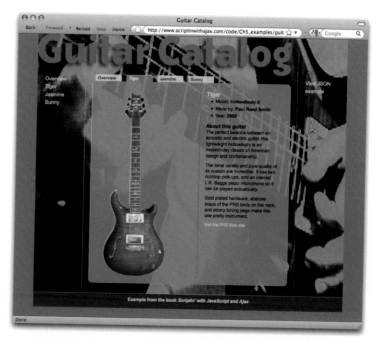

The highlighted PHP uses the $guitarName variable to determine whether to resolve itself to the class name or to nothing.

An Ajax-ready Page

The few pieces of PHP code in the previous sections create a dynamic page where the content area updates to reflect the link clicked by the user, and the tabs update to indicate the currently displayed page.

Stylin' the Tabs

The tabs across the top of the content in the catalog example are the primary way that users will select the content they want to view. However, they are not just for navigating but also for orientation. Appropriately styled tabs can tell the user: "You are here." This is achieved by having a special visual state for the tab that relates to the currently displayed content. Each tab in this design is simply a styled li element of an unordered list. By using relative positioning in the CSS, I am able to move the tabs so their bottom borders align with the top border of the guitar_display div. I then define a CSS class named choice, which when added to a tab (an li tag) will set the tab's background color and its bottom border color to match the color of the content area. This results in a strong visual association between the content and the related tab: The tab actually looks like it is part of the content area.

Because this tab styling is already set up in the CSS, I simply code the PHP so that the choice class is added to the li of a tab when it is clicked.

This little catalog is ripe for enhancement with Ajax because only a small part of the page needs to update each time, and yet currently, a complete new page must be generated and served for every request. So let's now layer on the Ajax so that only part of the page updates without any page refresh at all.

Adding Ajax Functionality to the Catalog

To add Ajax functionality to the catalog, I'll link two script files to the page in the `head` tag.

```
<script type="text/javascript" src="javascript/ajax_function.
js"></script>
```

```
<script type="text/javascript" src="../../js_lib/scriptin_
helpers.js"></script>
```

The `scriptin_helpers.js` *file is added so I can use one of its functions called* `cancelClick()`. *You will learn what this function does during this exercise.*

These scripts link the Ajax function script and the helper functions to the page, respectively. Now I don't have to add the functions contained in these directly in the page but can use them as if they were in the page. This helps to keep the main script short and less cluttered.

Except for linking the JavaScript files, I don't need to make any changes to this PHP page to "Ajax-ify" it.

ADDING EVENT LISTENERS

I can now start coding the JavaScript. In earlier examples, I added the JavaScript into the page with the HTML, but in a real-world project the JavaScript belongs in a separate linked file; I'll use a separate file here. I've linked a file called `guitar_ajax_html.js.` to the PHP file along with the `ajax_function.js` and `scriptin_helpers.js` files I previously added. This currently empty file will hold the Ajax-related JavaScript that loads the HTML fragments into the page and updates the tabs when the user clicks a link.

I have two sets of links that do the same thing on this page: the sidebar links and the tabs. I'll begin by writing an `onload` event that calls a function to add an identical event listener to the `ul` element of both sets of links: I can readily identify these `ul`s because each one has the `guitar_links` class. My strategy is that every link will call the same function—`linkClicked`. This function will get the guitar name from the query string of the URL that will then be used to assemble the URL, which requests the related HTML fragment.

I'll do all this in one big step here, since you've already seen how to implement event listeners several times.

```
guitarLinks={

  init:function(){

    guitarLinks.addListeners();

  },

  addListeners:function() {

    var theLists = document.getElementsByTagName('ul');

    for (i=0; i < theLists.length; i++) {

      if (theLists[i].className.search("guitar_links")!==-1)
      {

        addEvent(theLists[i], 'click', guitarLinks.
            linkClicked);

      }

    }

  },

  linkClicked:function(e) {

    alert ("link clicked");

    cancelClick(e);

  }

}

window.onload=guitarLinks.init;
```

get all the unordered lists

If the ul's class attribute contains "guitar_links"

then add an event listener to that ul

CODE 5.8 guitar_ajax.js

a temporary test to see if the function is called by the event

calls JS helper to cancel href click

There are just a couple of items in this code that you haven't seen before.

Because in one case I have more than one class on the ul tags (there is a clearfix class to force the ul to wrap the list elements—see the Aslett Clearing Method in the text_n_colors.css file, that I have also linked to the page.), I must do more than just check for a simple match on the class attribute: I use the search property of the String object (first highlighted line of **Code 5.5**) to search for the name of the class I'm looking for—guitar_links—anywhere within the class attribute's value. Even if there is more than one class, this code can still determine if the one I am looking for, or at least if the string "guitar_links," is present.

The second item I want to point out is a call to a new helper function (second highlighted line of **Code 5.5**) that's named `cancelClick`, which I call at the end of the `linkClicked` function. The `cancelClick` function is in the linked `scriptin_helper.js` file. Let me explain what this function does and why I need to call it here. Earlier, I showed you that if you call a function from a link, you might have code that looks like this:

```
<a href="somePage.html" onclick="someFunction(); return false;">A Link</a>
```

In this case, `return false` cancels the click that would normally trigger the `href`—without it, `somePage.html` would load after the `someFunction` completes. The `cancelClick` function does the same thing for event listeners: It stops the click going to the element after JavaScript has handled it. As a point of interest, it calls `e.preventDefault()` on W3C browsers and `window.event.returnValue = false;` on Windows browsers, which stops the `href` from being fired on the respective browsers. These cross-browser differences are conveniently abstracted away by the `cancelClick` function.

AJAX AND CANCELING CLICKS

The technique of canceling clicks to links after Ajax handles the request is key to providing progressive enhancement in your pages. Let's first consider the most likely case where JavaScript is supported by the browser, and Ajax is therefore enabled. If a user clicks a link that triggers an Ajax call to fetch data from the server, I don't want the click to also trigger the link's `href`, because this would then fetch the content a second time by refreshing the page on a round-trip. Instead, when the link is clicked, the JavaScript function runs, triggers the Ajax request, and then cancels the click to the link's `href`.

However, if JavaScript is not supported, the JavaScript does not run, and the link acts normally; the `href` is triggered, and the page request is fulfilled in the traditional round-trip manner. Once you understand this concept, you can make your pages work with or without JavaScript.

GETTING THE REQUESTED FILE

With event listeners now attached to the links triggering the `linkClicked` function, the next step is to have this function determine which link was clicked and initiate an Ajax call to get the appropriate HTML fragment file. I need to get the guitar name, which is the value of the name/value pair in the URL query string, and use it to assemble the URL.

determines the target of the click and calls readFile and setTab functions	`linkClicked:function(e) {`
set up cross-browser event obj names	`    var evt = e || window.event;`
	`    guitarLinks.evtTarget = evt.target || evt.srcElement`
get the entire URL e.g., guitar_cata-log_ajax_html.php?request=tiger	`    theURL=(guitarLinks.evtTarget.getAttribute('href'));`
split it into two array elements using the = sign as delimiter	`    theQuery=theURL.split("=")`
get the second element e.g., tiger	`    guitarLinks.guitarName=(theQuery[1]);`
call the readFile function	`    guitarLinks.readFile();`
call the set tabs function	`    guitarLinks.setTab()`
calls JS helper to cancel href click	`    cancelClick(e);`
	`},`
makes the call to the Ajax helper function	`readFile:function () {`
assembles filename using guitar name parameter	`    ajaxRequest('html_frags/'+ guitarLinks.guitarName +'_`
	`        desc_frag.html',guitarLinks.cbReadFile);`
	`}`
callback function	`cbReadFile:function (theData) {`
	`    var theDisplay = document.getElementById('guitar_`
	`        display');`
data is added to page	`    theDisplay.innerHTML = theData;`
	`}`

When the user clicks the link, I need the name of the guitar so I can use it in the name of the file I want to request. That name is at the end of the URL; here's how I get it. After adding the usual couple of lines of cross-browser event object code, I first get the target link's href value and put it in a variable called theURL (first highlighted line). For example, if the user had clicked the Tiger tab, the theURL value would be

`guitar_catalog_ajax_html.php?request=tiger`

I then use the split method of the string object to break the string into two array elements using the = as the delimiter. The second element of this array then holds the name of the guitar, and I store this in the guitarName variable. I can now call the readFile function (second highlighted line), which is almost identical to the readFile function in the first Ajax example earlier in this chapter. I don't need to pass guitarName to this function as an argument, because this variable is in scope for the readFile function: It's part of the same object literal. I simply use the guitarName variable when I assemble the URL to make the Ajax call. The callback function then displays the returned HTML fragment in the page.

HIGHLIGHTING THE TABS WITH JAVASCRIPT

At this point, although the tabs can be clicked and the correct content loads, the related tab does not highlight. I'll now show you how to do that.

As you saw when I made the pages work with PHP, a tab is highlighted by adding the choice class to it. PHP adds this class to the Overview tab when the page first loads, but because all subsequent content loading will now be done by JavaScript, JavaScript also needs to be able to manage the tabs.

This class must be added to the parent li of the appropriate a tag—the link that was clicked—and has to be removed from the tab that is currently highlighted. Here's how that's done.

```javascript
linkClicked:function(e) {

    var evt = e || window.event;

    guitarLinks.evtTarget = evt.target || evt.srcElement;

    guitarLinks.guitarName=(guitarLinks.evtTarget.
        className);

    guitarLinks.readFile();

    guitarLinks.setTab()

    cancelClick(e);

},

setTab:function() {

    var theTabBar=document.getElementById('tabs');

    var theItems=theTabBar.getElementsByTagName('li');

    var itemCount=theItems.length;

    for (i=0; i<itemCount; i++) {

        theItems[i].className="";

    }
```

call the setTab function

sets the tab bar highlight

gets the tab bar ul

get the li's

store the number of them

loop through the li's

clear any class names off the tabs

set the hilite on parent li of target link

```
guitarLinks.evtTarget.parentNode.className='choice';

guitarLinks.evtTarget.blur();

        },

// readFile function follows here
```

I've added a new function called setTab. In that function, I get the tab bar ul and then loop through each li, removing any classes as I go. Now all I need to do is highlight the tab that was clicked. I already have the event target—the a link that was clicked. I simply move up to its parent, the li, and add the choice class onto it. Note that I call the setTab function immediately after the Ajax call for the content, so that the tab updates while the request is being fulfilled.

An Accessible Catalog

In Chapter 1, I discussed three levels of accessibility: functional, styled, and enhanced. In the catalog exercise I just showed you, all three levels are available.

If the user has a modern browser and JavaScript is enabled, the user will see fully styled pages, and content will be updated via Ajax without page refreshes. This is the most enhanced user experience.

If JavaScript is not supported, the user will still view styled pages but the content will be delivered via round-trip page refreshes.

If neither JavaScript nor CSS are supported, the page will have the browser's default styling, but it will still function and the user will still be able to view the content.

You can observe these different levels by using the Firefox Web Developer Toolbar. First, use the page in a modern browser to experience the fully enhanced page. Second, use the toolbar to disable JavaScript, reload, and use the page again to see it fall back to the round-trip model. Third, disable the CSS and refresh again (also select Persist Features in the Options menu so the CSS remains disabled between refreshes). Now the page takes on a plain appearance but is still functional and useable.

If you view the source of the page during any of these tests, you will only see HTML. There is absolutely no CSS or JavaScript in the page's markup. Both the CSS and JavaScript are in external files and will add styling and behavior respectively to the page if these technologies are supported, but there will be no adverse effects and

Ajax is a problem for screen readers because they take a snapshot of the DOM when the page first loads and store it in a buffer (a block of memory) that is used to read the page. The problem is that if the page is updated with Ajax, the buffer's snapshot is then out of date. To learn how to update the buffer after each Ajax transaction in the most popular screen reader JAWS, see Gez Lemon's Juicy Studio site at http://juicystudio.com/article/ improving-ajax-applications-for- jaws-users.php.

no errors if they are not. As long as the user has an HTML capable device, this content will be accessible.

Working with JSON

JSON is a way of storing data in the same structure as the object literal format. It uses property/value pairs, (a map—see "Maps" sidebar), which are formatted like this:

```
{"property":"value", "property":"value", "property":"value"}
```

where values can be strings, arrays, or objects, making it a simple but very flexible format.

Here is how the HTML markup for one of the guitars that you saw earlier looks in JSON.

This JSON file could be one long line, but as you can see, I have formatted it to make it as readable as possible.

CODE 5.9 json/tiger.json

```
{

  "guitar_name":"Tiger",

  "model":"Hollowbody II",

  "manufacturer":"Paul Reed Smith",

  "year":"2008",

  "description": [

    "The perfect balance…",

    "The tonal variety and pure quality…",

    "Rich grained wood…"

  ],

  "link": {

    "url":"http://prsguitars.com/hollowbody2/index.html",

    "text":"About this guitar"

  },

  "image":

    {

      "url":"images/tiger_240w.jpg",

      "alt":"Paul Reed Smith Hollowbody 2 guitar"

    }

}
```

Maps

In JavaScript, sets of property/value pairs within a set of curly braces create a map. Maps, which are referred to as hash tables in languages like C++, are the basic data structure of JavaScript and you will often encounter the term map when you read about JavaScript; it simply means a set of property/value pairs. If you study **Code 5.9**, you will see it is simply a map, where the values are four strings, an array, and two maps.

As you can see, JSON is very lightweight compared to a tag format like HTML or XML. A JSON file can be one-third or less the file size of its XML equivalent.

Besides its simple and easy-to-understand format, the major benefit of data in JSON format is that it can be instantly transformed into a JavaScript object ready for use, as you are about to see. This is in strong contrast to XML where each element of the data must be parsed out of its tag and then added into generated HTML elements—a slow and tedious programming procedure.

These benefits are driving the adoption of JSON over the more established XML format in online applications. Many syndicators of content such as Yahoo! and Google now make their data feeds (RSS, for example) available in JSON as well as XML. In time, XML may be less widely used because data feeds are increasingly being consumed by JavaScript, and it is so much easier to do that with JSON.

EVALUATING JSON

JavaScript's eval method converts any string in JavaScript syntax, including JSON, into executable JavaScript. In JSON, eval creates an object from the data, which can then be accessed in the same way as the data in any JavaScript object. While this is convenient, it is also insecure, because malicious code can be passed in place of an expected file, evaluated as JavaScript, and then executed. Douglas Crockford, who devised the JSON format, has written a useful function called json.js that does the same job as eval but rejects any code that is not correctly formatted as JSON, making it almost impossible to pass malicious code through this function. While eval is a quick and easy way to turn JSON or any string data into JavaScript, it is much safer to evaluate JSON with the json.js function, as I do in the examples that follow.

The Guitar Catalog Using JSON

Because JSON is now a widely accepted data standard, let's look at how to deal with the guitar data as JSON instead of HTML. It is very simple to modify the guitar catalog to use JSON instead of the HTML fragments that I used in the previous example. Using the Ajax object I showed earlier in the chapter, you can fetch a JSON file from the server and have it delivered to a callback function in exactly the same way as I fetched text and HTML in the previous examples.

Once you have the JSON data, it's easy to convert it to a JavaScript object. Then you can use JavaScript to write out the required HTML elements, adding the JSON data from the object into them as you go, and add these assembled HTML elements into the page.

To use JSON as the data format, the only JavaScript I need to modify from the HTML example is the callback function and the requested filename.

After the JSON data is requested and arrives in the callback handler, the first step is to convert it to a JavaScript object using the `json.js` function.

receives the JSON from Ajax function	
convert the JSON data to a JavaScript object—using JSON object in json.js file (linked to page)	
the html var is set to the result of the guitarToHTML function	
display the generated HTML	
code continues in next code fragment	

```
cbReadFile:function (json) {

var jsonParsed = JSON.parse(json);

    var theDisplay = document.getElementById("guitar_
        display");

var html = guitarLinks.guitarToHTML(jsonParsed) ;

theDisplay.innerHTML= html;

    return;

},
```

CODE 5.10 part of guitars_ajax_jason.js

The two important steps (highlighted) are to convert the JSON returned from the Ajax call into a JavaScript object, and then pass this object to the `guitarToHTML` function, which will do the work of assembling page-ready markup.

```
guitarToHTML:function(json){

    var tags = '';

    tags = '<div id="picture_box" class="equal">\n';

    tags += '<img src=" ' + (json['image']['url']) +'"
        alt="'+(json['image']['alt'])+'"> </div>\n';

    tags += '<div id="info_box" class="equal">\n<div id="info_
        box_inner">\n';

    tags += '<h4>'+(json["guitar_name"])+'</h4>\n';

    tags += '<ul>\n';

    tags += '<li>Model: <strong>'+(json["model"])+'</strong></
        li>\n';

    tags += '<li>Made by: <strong>'+(json["manufacturer"])+'</
        strong></li>\n';

    tags += '<li>Year: <strong>'+(json["year"])+'</strong></
        li>\n';

    tags += '</ul>\n';

    tags += '<h5>About this guitar</h5>\n';

        var description =  json['description'];

    for(var i = 0; i < description.length; i++){

        tags += '<p>' + description[i] + '</p>\n';

        tags += '<p><a href='+(json['link']['url'])+'>' +
json['link']['text'] + '</a></p>\n';

        tags += '</div>\n</div>';

    }

    return tags;

    }

}
```

variable to hold the HTML elements as they are built

loop through the variable number of description text elements

if it's the first one, add the 'first' class to hide the left border on the column

I've highlighted one of the elements that evaluates to data from the JSON object:

```
(json['image']['url'])
```

This evaluates to

```
images/tiger_240w.jpg
```

because it reads the `url` property from the `image` property of the `json` object. Check the JSON code I showed in **Code 5.9** to see this data in the JSON file.

By concatenating these kinds of elements with strings of HTML (between the highlighted single quotes) like this:

```
'<img src="'+(json['image']['url'])+'" alt="'+(json['image']
['alt'])+'">\n';
```

the code produces a string of HTML like this:

```
<img src="images/tiger_240w.jpg" alt="Paul Reed Smith
Hollowbody 2 guitar">
```

Note the use of single quotes (highlighted) and double quotes right next to each other in this example. The single quotes delimit the strings, separating the strings that don't get evaluated from the JavaScript that does. However, the double quotes are *part* of the string: You can see them enclosing the attribute values in the evaluated version. It can be very tricky getting the placement of these single and double quotes exactly right, but remembering that they serve completely different purposes makes it easier. The fact that the object properties also use single quotes—a third use of quotation marks in this line—can add to the confusion, so you really need to keep track of what you are doing as you write code like this. View Generated Source with the Web Developer toolbar to visually check that the output is correctly formatted HTML.

Note also the \n within the last string of the line. This adds a line break into the source code to make it easier to read when you view the source code in the browser. Without line breaks, all the tags generated by the preceding code would appear in a single line. Doing this only formats the source code—it doesn't affect the onscreen appearance.

You can see that I am using a variable named `tags` to store each HTML element as I create it rather than writing it line by line into the page as I go. JavaScript is rather slow at adding to the DOM, and if you add a large number of elements individually, it can affect performance. Instead, I use the shorthand += operator to add the elements to the `tags` variable and then do a single write to the DOM when I have everything assembled in that variable. To help you understand the += operator, the code `tags+="hello"` is simply the shorter version of `tags=tags+"hello"`.

Once all of the required HTML elements are in the `tags` variable, I return this data to the callback function where it is stored in a variable called `html`. I then write the data to the element with the ID `guitar_display` like this:

```
var theDisplay = document.getElementById("guitar_display");

theDisplay.innerHTML=html;
```

Note that I do this by setting the element's `innerHTML` property, because the variable contains a string. This code would not work

```
theDisplay.appendChild(html);
```

because `html` does not reference an object.

While all this might seem like a lot of work to add a few lines of HTML for this example, in a real-world Web site application a JSON feed parser like this might handle dozens of identically formatted feeds for thousands of users for years to come. In a circumstance like that, it isn't such a bad investment of your time.

You will have to remind yourself of this fact frequently if you try to write a similar feed parser using XML. It is very time-consuming and tedious, so I've decided because of space limitations to just show you a brief example of how this is done. I have included a complete example of parsing this same data for the guitar catalog from an XML file called `guitar_ajax_xml.html` in the downloadable examples.

Using XML

An XML file looks a lot like HTML except the tags usually have names that describe their content. XML's purpose is to be a data exchange system so data can be moved between disparate systems. The X (Extensible) portion of the acronym refers to the fact that you can extend the language by creating your own tag names to accurately describe and structure your content.

Here's the equivalent XML for the previous JSON example.

```xml
<?xml version="1.0" encoding="utf-8"?>
<guitar>
    <guitar_name>Sunny</guitar_name>
    <model>Roland GR202</model>
    <manufacturer>Ibanez</manufacturer>
    <year>1983</year>
    <description>
        <title>About this guitar</title>
        <detail>This Stratocaster-like guitar…</detail>
        <detail>This setup was used…</detail>
        <link>http://www.joness.com/gr300/GR-100.htm</link>
    </description>
    <image>
        <url>../html_frags/images/sunny_240w.jpg</url>
        <alt>Ibanez Roland GR202 synth controller guitar</alt>
    </image>
</guitar>
```

CODE 5.11 xml_dom_parsing/sunny.xml

There are two approaches you can take to converting XML to HTML for use in your pages: parse it as an object and convert the XML elements to HTML elements or convert the XML to JSON and parse it out. Neither is easy, but I have provided you with some code in the download files as examples, including helper functions, to make it as simple as I can. Because I parsed the JSON as strings in the preceding example, I'll parse the XML as objects. Get ready for some fairly intense DOM scripting.

THE RESPONSEXML PROPERTY

When you request XML from the server, the XMLHttpRequest object stores the returned data in the responseXML property, not the responseText property where data from a request for text data, such as HTML or JSON, is stored. So when you request XML with Ajax, you need to pass your callback function the `responseXML` property of the `XMLHttpRequest` object. Doing this requires a simple modification to the Ajax object code: You simply change the property name `responseText` to `responseXML`.

| if true, then the request data has arrived |

```
if (ajaxObj.readyState == 4 && ajaxObj.status == 200) {
```

| pass the data to the callback function |

```
        cbFunc(ajaxObj.responseXML);
}
```

Then you can request an XML file in the same way that I showed you for text and JSON in earlier examples.

| CODE 5.12 xml_dom_parsing/ guitar_ajax_xml.html |

```
ajaxFile = {
```

| makes the call to the Ajax function |

```
  readFile:function () {

      ajaxRequest('sunny_cws.xml',ajaxFile.cbReadFile);

  },
```

| XML now in theData variable ready to parse |

```
  cbReadFile:function (theData) {

    // XML parsing code goes here, see next page

  }

}
```

Once you have the XML as an object in a variable, you can begin to parse out the data. You use exactly the same methods to parse XML as you do to manipulate the DOM—its tags are in the same kind of nested structure. The difference is that the top level of the DOM is `document`; the top level of the XML is the name of the parameter you use to receive the XML into your callback function—in this case, `theData` (highlighted).

In the next example, the HTML I create from the XML data will exactly match the HTML in the HTML fragment file `jasmine_desc_frag.html` that I used in the earlier example. Therefore, you might want to look at that file, or just refer to page 153 for the required outcome of this exercise.

As I mentioned, because the XML parsing code is long and complex, I will simply show you some of the key techniques for doing this and refer you to the code in Ch5_examples/XML_DOM_parsing/guitar_ajax_xml.html to see the full example.

OVERVIEW OF XML PARSING

The first step when parsing this XML is to create an array in which to store the HTML tags as I build them.

add each element to this array

```
var tagArray=[];
```

Now I can start building HTML elements that contain data from the XML. Here is the code to parse out a top level XML element and convert it into an HTML element—in this case, an h4 tag with the guitar name as its text.

```
var theEl=theData.getElementsByTagName('guitar_name')[0];

var theHtmlObj=xmlHelp.XMLTagAsHTMLTag('h4',theEl);
```

add obj to array

```
tagArray.push(theHtmlObj);
```

Now I have an HTML element in tagArray that looks like this:

```
<h4>Sunny</h4>
```

In the preceding code you can see the call to a helper function called XMLTagAsHTML (highlighted). I wrote this function to convert XML tags into HTML tags; this function, and another that I will use in this example called addTextInElement, are contained in an object literal called XMLhelp. The XMLTagAsHTML function looks like this:

function returns specified text of XML tag in the specified HTML element

extracts the text from the specified XML element

creates new element of specified type

adds the text into the element

CODE 5.13 xml_dom_parsing/guitar_ajax_xml.html (cont.)

```
XMLTagAsHTMLTag:function (elName,XMLTagObj) {

    theText=XMLTagObj.firstChild.nodeValue;

    newEl = document.createElement(elName);

    newEl.appendChild(document.createTextNode(theText));

    return newEl;

}
```

The code comments are fairly self-explanatory, but in short, this function extracts the text from the text node of the passed-in XML element object. It then creates an HTML element of type specified by the passed-in element name and adds the text into it. The brand-new element, newEl, is returned to the calling code. In the main block of code, I use the push array method to add the new element onto the end of tagArray. In this case, it's the array's first item, but I'll add others in the same manner as I create them. I use this helper function for virtually every tag in the XML file: It saves a lot of repetitious coding.

I next create an unordered list with the guitar's model, name, manu-
facturer, and year as list items. Here's how I do that.

the container for the list items

```
var theList=document.createElement('ul');
```

create an li with text in it

```
var listItem=xmlHelp.addTextInElement('li', 'Model: ');
```

get the XML tag with the data

```
var theEl=theData.getElementsByTagName('model')[0];
```

create a strong tag with the
element's text in it

```
var theHtmlObj=xmlHelp.XMLTagAsHTMLTag('strong',theEl);
```

add the strong tag into the li tag
after the li's text

```
listItem.appendChild(theHtmlObj);
```

```
listItem1=theList.appendChild(listItem);
```

add list item into the ul

The code results in the variable theList containing

```
<ul>
    <li>Model: <strong>Roland GR202</strong></li>
</ul>
```

CODE 5.14 xml_dom_parsing/
guitar_ajax_xml.html (cont.)

In the preceding code is a call to a helper function, addTextIn
Element (highlighted); that function looks like this:

returns an obj node–use
appendChild(node) to insert

```
addTextInElement:function (elName,textRef) {
```

creates new element

```
    newEl = document.createElement(elName);
```

adds text into new element

```
    newEl.appendChild(document.createTextNode(textRef));
```

```
    return newEl;
}
```

I pass this function an element name and a string of text (that
you will note in this case ends with a space), and the function
returns a newly created HTML element of the specified type with
the text inside it. After the highlighted function call is made,
listItem contains

```
<li>Model: </li>
```

Next, I need to add a strong tag containing the guitar model name
into this element, right between the space at the end of the text and
the closing </li>. To do this, I extract the model name text from the
XML element, and then call the XMLTagAsHTMLTag function, passing
the required arguments: the element to be created and the text to be
added. The function returns

```
<strong>Roland GR202</strong>
```

I then simply append this element as a child into the li element
that's in the theList variable; it is conveniently appended right after

the text that is already in that element. The variable called `list-Item1` now contains

```
<li>Model: <strong>Roland GR202</strong></li>
```

I repeat this process for the other two list items I need to create, adding them into variables called `listItem2` and `listItem3`. Then I add the three of them into the `ul` element I created earlier, like this:

CODE 5.15 xml_dom_parsing/
guitar_ajax_xml.html (cont.)

```
theList.appendChild(listItem1);

theList.appendChild(listItem2);

theList.appendChild(listItem3);

tagArray.push(theList);
```

Finally, I add the completed `ul` with its three child `li` elements into the tag array (highlighted) ready to be added to the page. The finished list looks like this:

```
<ul>

    <li>Model: <strong>Roland GR202</strong></li>

    <li>Made by: <strong>Ibanez</strong></li>

    <li>Year: <strong>1983</strong></li>

</ul>
```

I think this is enough to give you a flavor of what's involved in parsing XML. It's certainly an exercise in patience and attention to detail.

If you need to use XML in a project, the complete code example `guitar_ajax_xml.html` that I provide as part of the download code for this chapter will be a useful guide for you. My advice, if you have the choice, is to use JSON for third-party data feeds. Within your own site, code your middleware—such as PHP or .NET—to generate HTML on the server side using the data from your data sources, such as a database. Then use Ajax to bring it into the browser and add it directly into an element in the page using `elementName.innerHTML(theHTML)`.

The Author Carousel project in Chapter 7 shows how to use Ajax to call a PHP script that reads a file, generates HTML from its data, and returns HTML to the Ajax request.

Using Sajax—the Simple Ajax Framework

Many Ajax frameworks are available. I'll now show you one of the simplest. In Chapter 1, I created a PHP page with a form that validated an email address. Now I'll show you how to enhance it with

Ajax, so that the email address can be validated without submitting the form. You may remember that I broke out the function that validated the email address so that I could later call that function with Ajax without running the rest of the PHP code. That is what I'll do now.

Calling a function on the server is more complex than simply requesting a file, which is what I have done so far. To call the validation function, I'll use a framework called Sajax (Simple Ajax). It has a very interesting capability: It can run server-side functions as if they were on your local computer, as well as do the standard request for file data. Sajax comes in several versions including PHP, Ruby, Python, Perl, Cold Fusion, and others.

The Sajax framework is a small JavaScript file that you link to your page. Then all you have to do is add a few lines of Sajax-related server-side code (PHP in this case) to your page and list in that code the names of the functions you want to access. You can then call those functions at any time. Whatever they return appears in your stated callback handler in the same manner as the files I requested earlier.

You may want to refer to `simple_form_step2.php` on page 15 as I show you the modifications you need to make to enable an Ajax call to the email validation function. I'll just show enough of that original Chapter 1 file to allow you to see where the additional code goes.

Here is how the start of the file looks with the Sajax-related pieces in place.

```php
<?php

include "php_includes/form_functions.php";

include "sajax/Sajax.php";

if ($_POST) {

    $email = $_POST['email'];

    $valid = verifyEmail($email);


    if ($valid) {

        writeToFile($email);

        $msg= 'Thanks for signing up! Please visit our <a
            href="members.php"> members only area.</a>';

    } else {
```

this code runs only if the form was submitted—specifically, if there is anything from the form in the POST array

move the email address from the POST array to a variable

calls the verifyEmail function— $valid is set to 1 if email is valid, 0 if not

if the email passed validation

pass email to writeToFile function to record it in a text file

the email is invalid, so tell the user

the $msg will get written into the markup as PHP generates the page

```
        $msg = 'Please type a valid email address.';
    }
```

end if POST

```
    }
    // code required to instantiate Sajax
        $sajax_request_type = "GET";
        sajax_init();
```

add comma-delimited names of functions to be called by Sajax here

```
        sajax_export("verifyEmail");
        sajax_handle_client_request();
    ?>
    <script>
    <?
```

adds Sajax-related JavaScript into page

```
        sajax_show_javascript();
    ?>
    validation = {
        validateEmail:function (button_click) {
            document.getElementById("msg").innerHTML = "sending…";
```

get text from field

```
            theEmail=document.getElementById("email").value;
```

send text and callback name to verifyEmail PHP function via Sajax—note x_ to indicate call goes via Sajax

```
            x_verifyEmail(theEmail,validation.validateEmail_cb);
        },
```

appropriate message is added to page

```
        validateEmail_cb:function (valid) {
            if (valid) {
            var msg = 'Valid email address'
            } else {
            var msg='Please type a valid email address';
```

CODE 5.16 sajax_demo/simple_form_ajax.php

```
            }
            document.getElementById("msg").innerHTML = msg +" - data
                tested via Ajax";
        },
    }
    </script>
```

Notice that if you compare this code with the Chapter 1 code on page 15, the PHP is unchanged. If JavaScript is not present, the form will still be processed with a regular round-trip.

Also notice that for testing purposes, the text "data tested via Ajax" is tacked onto the generated message in the last line of the callback handler. If that text appears in the page, you know the Ajax works and the page did not make a round-trip.

HOW TO USE THE SAJAX FRAMEWORK

The Sajax-related code is highlighted in the preceding code block. The Sajax framework file is first added to the page with an include, right after the include that adds the validation function, which is also in a separate file. Then after the PHP shown in Chapter 1 are four additional lines that set up the Sajax functionality. These must be copied verbatim into any page that uses Sajax. The line that is worth noting here is sajax_export, which is a function whose arguments are the names of the PHP functions to be accessed with Sajax. In this case, I need to access only one function—validateEmail, but I could add as many PHP function names as I wished, separated by commas. Then within the script tag is a PHP function called sajax_show_javascript, which adds some Sajax-related JavaScript into the page. Every Sajax-enabled page requires these elements. Once they are in place, I simply request the function I want to run.

To do this, I create a JavaScript function validateEmail to make the Ajax call and, as always with Ajax interactions, I also create the corresponding callback function, in this case called cbValidateEmail. I have grouped these two related functions within an object literal called validation. The important line here is the one that makes the Ajax request

```
x_verifyEmail(theEmail,validation.validateEmail_cb);
```

Note that the PHP function I want to call is called verifyEmail, so the name I must use is x_verifyEmail (highlighted). I have to prepend x_ to the function name so that Sajax recognizes that it must handle the request. You can see that there are also two arguments I pass: the email address that I want the function to validate and the callback handler that Sajax will call after the request has been fulfilled. I can add as many comma-separated arguments for Sajax to pass to the PHP function as I wish, but the last argument must be the name of the callback function.

Finally, to set the whole process in motion, I add an inline event handler to the field (normally, I'd do this more correctly with an

Because you have to first trigger a JavaScript function that in turn triggers the Ajax call to the PHP function, you will often end up, as I do here, with two very similar function names. In this case, the JavaScript function is named validateEmail, *and it calls the PHP function on the server named* verifymail. *You could give them both the same name, since one is JavaScript and one is PHP, but I find that too confusing.*

event listener, but I want to remain focused on the Sajax code here.) that triggers the validateEmail function, which in turn calls the verifyEmail PHP function on the server when the field is blurred.

```
<input id="email" name="email" type="text" size="24"
value="<?php echo $email;?>" onblur="validation.
validateEmail()" />
```

Now when I click away from the field, the Sajax call passes the email address to the PHP function validateEmail on the server, which looks like this:

checks for a well-formed email address—i.e., in format someTextAndNumbers@ someTextAndNumbers.2-6 characters

returns 1 (TRUE) if email well formatted

```
function verifyEmail ($testString) {
    return (eregi("^([[:alnum:]]|_|\.|-)+@
        ([[:alnum:]]|\.|-)+(\.)([a-z]{2,6})$", $testString));
}
```

The email address gets matched against this regular expression pattern, and back comes 1 or 0 to the callback function, depending on whether the email matches the pattern or not. Based on this true/false response, the appropriate message is added to the page. See **Figures 5.9** and **5.10**.

FIGURE 5.9 The Ajax callback function generates an error message when the PHP function on the server determines the email is invalid.

FIGURE 5.10 The callback handler generates a message confirming that the email address is valid.

This is a basic example of Sajax in action, but Sajax is a great little framework that does one thing—accessing server functions from the browser—really well. It's easy to take an example like this and modify it for your own purposes. The capability to run server-side functions opens a world of possibilities—such as validating forms on the client and again on the server when the form is submitted (as you must for security reasons) using the same set of validation functions. This reduces the amount of code you need to write and means you only have to maintain this code in one place.

Perhaps the most exiting possibility that a framework like Sajax offers is that you can query a database using server-side functions without round-tripping the page. For example, if users of your site have to choose a unique user name during the registration process, you can call a server-side function that checks the database for the existence of that name as soon as the user finishes typing a name choice and clicks away from the field.

Summary

This chapter gave you an introduction to Ajax and the different formats of data that it enables you to bring into the browser. In the next chapter, I'll explore more advanced coding techniques and look at other frameworks that provide sophisticated interactions for the user interface.

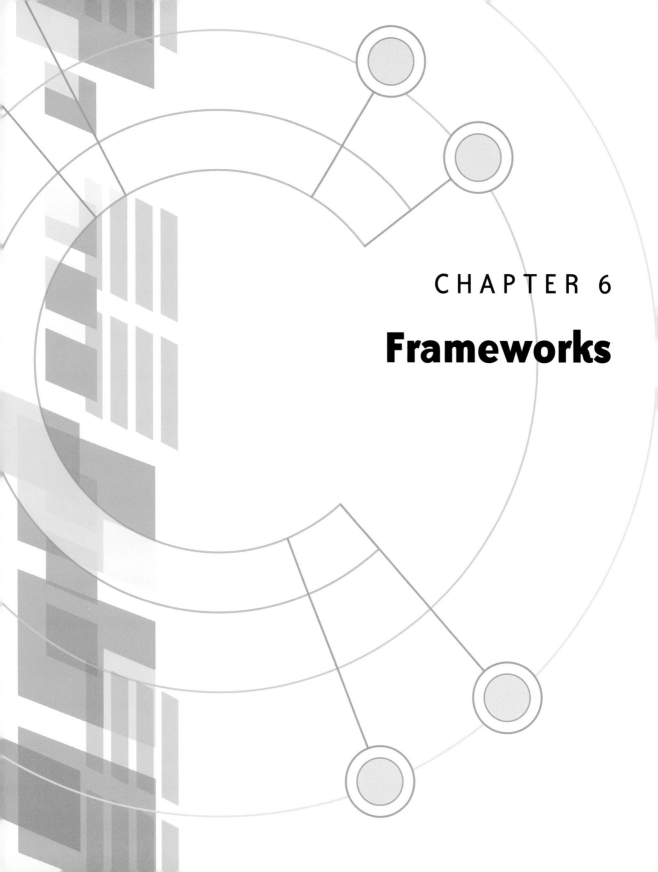

CHAPTER 6

Frameworks

IN THIS CHAPTER, I DISCUSS JAVASCRIPT FRAME-WORKS, also known as libraries, and how they can speed the development process. There are both technical and business considerations in deciding if a framework is necessary and if so which one to use. In a single chapter, I can only give you a taste of how each of the frameworks I demonstrate works, but you will see some simple but practical examples that can help you understand the benefits that frameworks offer, and determine which framework is right for your needs.

About Frameworks

Danny Douglas compares the features of a number of the popular frameworks in this article on his Web site at www.danny-douglass.com/post/2008/04/Comparing-Popular-JavaScript-Frameworks.aspx.

A framework is a collection of tightly integrated helper functions that abstract away many of JavaScript's complexities and help you build your application quickly. Most are free and are often developed by the Open Source community. Some, most notably jQuery and Prototype, are a single library file of core functionality that can extended by a large number of plug-ins built by developers all over the world that provide almost every capability your application might need. However, it's important to test any plug-in that you want to use to ensure that it can really do what you want and doesn't interact adversely with other areas of your code. Then there are frameworks, like Yahoo! User Interface (YUI), that are built on a large base of core functionality, which is extended with numerous specialized modules. The great advantage of YUI is that the modules are all developed by the same team and designed to work together.

Advantages of Frameworks

Using a framework can provide many benefits. A framework typically does the following:

- **Makes common programming tasks easy.** A couple of examples of basic capabilities offered by frameworks include:

  - Selecting DOM elements more economically by eliminating the need to repeatedly type `document.getElementById`

  - Easily adding and removing element classes

- **Simplifies Ajax implementation.** Most libraries provide a simplified method of making Ajax requests, with built-in error and slow-response handling. They also include special Ajax features like automatic timed requests that you might use in an application, such as chat, where the browser needs to be synched frequently with data on the server.

- **Provides interface component libraries.** Coding interface components, aka widgets, especially those such as tree menus and accordions that also have an animation aspect to them, can be time-consuming and present significant cross-browser incompatibilities. Both the Prototype and jQuery libraries offer add-on libraries of interface components—such as Scriptaculous and jQuery UI respectively—that enable you to invoke complex interface components rapidly from basic HTML

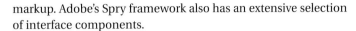

Learn about advanced object-oriented programming techniques at www.digital-web.com/articles/objectifying_javascript. This article builds on concepts such as object literals and the use of new in constructor functions. Also, follow the links at the bottom of the article to more articles on object-oriented JavaScript.

markup. Adobe's Spry framework also has an extensive selection of interface components.

- **Eliminates cross-browser issues.** Framework developers invest a lot of time ensuring that their code works correctly across a wide variety of browsers. You can think of a framework as a large-scale Façade design pattern implementation—you talk to the framework and it deals with the browser differences. This benefit alone makes a compelling case for using a framework.

Considerations When Using a Framework

Frameworks are hyped as the solution to many programming issues, and indeed they are. However, you need to remember that a framework is a specialized layer of code that runs on top of JavaScript. This means that before you decide to use a framework for your next project, you should consider the following points.

YOU QUICKLY GET LOCKED IN

Once you start to build an application, and its functionality depends on a particular framework, it's not easy to back out. If your chosen framework is not supported in the future, you may have a tough time reengineering your site. Part of the reason I picked these four frameworks is that they are well supported and widely adopted.

IT'S ANOTHER LANGUAGE TO LEARN

While frameworks follow JavaScript-like syntax, part of the attraction of frameworks is that they provide simplified coding (for example, jQuery's $ namespace—more on namespaces next) and enhanced capabilities (for example, Prototype's excellent implementation of classes, aka polymorphism).

For a checklist of questions you might want to consider before deciding on a particular framework, see Brian Reindel's blog article at http://blog.reindel.com/2007/10/30/how-to-choose-a-javascript-framework.

With these features come new programming techniques that must be mastered, and using jQuery's powerful chaining capability, which I will also show in this chapter, is a good example. This need for framework-specific knowledge doesn't just affect you: If you want to hire an extra programmer for your team, that person needs to know both JavaScript and the framework you are using. Creating a test project to hone your skills and investigating the availability of programmers who know your framework of choice can be time well spent.

Most of the considerations I list here are business issues. However, there is a related technical issue that I want to cover before I start showing some examples of frameworks in action, and that issue is namespacing.

Namespacing

A namespace is a container that provides scope context for items within it. Let me explain what that means and why it matters to you.

You may remember that earlier I stated that JavaScript only has two kinds of scope for variables—global, meaning accessible from everywhere, and function/object level, meaning only accessible from within the function or object where they are declared.

If you create a function like this

not within an object literal

```
function myFunction { some code };
```

or a variable like this

within a function but var is not stated

```
myVariable="Hello";
```

both these entities are now in the global namespace: They share the same scope, which in this case means accessible by the entire codebase.

Programming languages use namespaces to avoid conflicts with similarly named libraries and functions. If, during development, a team member uses a function name that you have already used, some hard-to-debug problems could be introduced.

Let's say you write a function that adds an option to a select box after retrieving the options from your database via an Ajax request. This function has parameters for the select box element and the value and text for the option, which will add each option as you pass the data to it, like this

```
function addOption(element, value, txt){

   var option = new Option(txt, value);

   element.options[element.options.length] = option;

}
```

This addOption function would by default be defined globally, or more specifically, within the global namespace.

What if a third-party library that you are using also happens to define an addOption function within the global scope? Suddenly, those menus in the forms that the library is rendering for you don't work any longer. This is because when there are two functions in the same namespace with the same name, whichever function loads last is the one that's used for all scripts. It's very easy to accidentally override the functionality of the library by defining a function in global scope with the same name, especially if a number of people are working on a project and creating arbitrary function names as they go.

Namespacing fixes this problem by scoping functions within constructs that avoid naming conflicts. You achieve namespacing in JavaScript by placing the functions within an object literal.

```javascript
var thirdPartyLib = {

    addOption : function(elementName, value, txt){

        var selectBox = document.
            getElementById(elementName);

        var option = new Option(txt, value);

        selectBox.options[selectBox.options.length] =
            option;

    }

}


var CWS = {

    addOption : function(element, value, txt){

        var option = new Option(txt, value);

        element.options[element.options.length] =
            option;

    }

}
```

You then invoke the functions with the fully qualified name, like this:

this is the function call you want to make to your function	`CWS.addOption(document.getElementById("theSelect"), "Lennon", "All you need is love");`
example function call within the third-party library	`thirdPartyLib.addOption("theSelect", "McCartney", "Let it be");`

As you can see from this example, both functions can now safely use the same function name because the functions' container—the namespace—prevents conflicts with the other identically named function.

Function names like `addClass` or `removeElement` are very common and are potential namespace problems. Rather than dream up absolutely ridiculous names that aren't likely to be found anywhere else, such as `aCleverLittleFunctionThatAddsTwoNumbersTogether`, all you need to do is namespace your scripts.

The object literals I have used in earlier chapters provide this benefit, but understanding namespacing gives you additional insight into the best ways to organize and strengthen your code.

Pseudo-global Variables

For further discussion of namespacing, read Robert Nyman's blog article at http://robertnyman. com/2008/10/29/javascript-namespacing-an-alternative-to-javascript-inheritance.

Generally, for the reasons I've illustrated, it's good practice to avoid having variables and functions in the global namespace, but if you must, minimize your footprint to the smallest number of references possible. Frameworks generally need to be in the global namespace to offer the widest access from your code, and minimize their impact there with a single large object that contains their entire functionality. An alternative, if you actually do want to create variables that can be available to your entire application, is that you can use this same namespacing technique to create pseudo-global variables. You can treat them as global variables, although they are not really in the global namespace but in one of your own making. To remind yourself and others who work on your code why you are doing this, create a namespace that is clearly used for this purpose, so that it's obvious. The convention of capitalizing the variable name helps in this regard, as in this style:

```
var APPGLOBALS = {

    'property1': 'value',

    'property2': appGlobalFunction:function { return: true; }

}
```

When it comes to JavaScript, Douglas Crockford is the Supreme Being. The page at www.scripttags. com/tag/crockford/namespace provides a link to YUI architect Eric Miraglia's explanation of Crockford's Module pattern. This article, while perhaps complex, is a natural continuation of this chapter's rather superficial look at namespacing. This Web page (note that the URL is actually a tag search rather than a link to a specific page) also contains links to a wealth of other JavaScript-related information, including videos of Crockford's lectures on JavaScript—which are essential viewing.

Then, of course, you can reference a property like this:

`APPGLOBALS.property1`

Understanding and using namespacing is good defensive programming that increases the robustness of your code.

Let's now look at some frameworks. It would be impossible to show all the available frameworks, so I've picked four of the larger and well-known ones that I have used on different projects to give you a good grounding in how they work and how they differ.

The four frameworks are jQuery, the Yahoo! User Interface (YUI), Prototype, and Adobe Spry. The overall goal of each framework is to provide consistent and predictable functionality that's easy to use. Each framework goes about the solution in similar yet subtly different ways.

In each case, the framework is a file or a number of JavaScript files that each have to be linked to your page using a `script` tag. You can see in the source of each example the files required to implement the interaction illustrated.

I'll give you a nice easy introduction to these four frameworks by showing how each one implements Ajax.

Downloading the Frameworks

The following list contains the sites where you can download the code for the four frameworks I illustrate in the chapter. I also include these libraries in the downloads so that the examples actually work but I advise you to obtain copies from these sites to ensure that you are working with the latest versions:

- **YUI.** http://developer.yahoo.com/yui

- **Prototype.** http://www.prototypejs.org

For Prototype-based UI components, you also need Scriptaculous

- **Scriptaculous.** http://script.aculo.us

- **jQuery.** http://jquery.com

For some useful jQuery-based UI components, you also need jQuery UI

- **jQuery UI.** http://jqueryui.com

- **Adobe Spry.** http://labs.adobe.com/technologies/spry/home.html

Ajax Implementation in Four Frameworks

As you will see, Ajax coding is a lot easier with a framework than trying to write an Ajax wrapper that can cope with all the different browsers it might encounter. In the four frameworks I'll show here, and most others, cross-browser issues are abstracted away and you don't have to think about them.

I'll start with what is now probably the most popular framework, jQuery. To put the framework in context, I'll start with a look at some key jQuery concepts.

jQuery Namespace

The jQuery framework can be downloaded from jquery.com. This library can be extended with the jQuery user interface components framework, which can be downloaded at http://jqueryui.com.

jQuery's entire framework is abstracted behind the $ symbol, which is the global instance variable that contains the actual jQuery object. As an example of this, and of jQuery's economic style, let's compare using regular JavaScript and jQuery to get elements in your page. So far you have been using this idiom:

```
var element = document.getElementById('myDiv');
```

With jQuery, that is reduced to:

```
var element = $('#myDiv');
```

Note that the argument, `#myDiv`, is a CSS expression that identifies an element by ID—jQuery references elements with the same syntax as CSS selectors. No longer having to repeatedly type `document.getElementById()` is a small but very convenient benefit of using jQuery.

CHAINING

Prototype also uses $ as its namespace. If you are using both frameworks for some reason, you can use the alternate `jQuery` namespace, as in `jQuery("#myDiv")`.

A very interesting aspect of jQuery is a technique called chaining, where you can string a number of actions together on one line instead of writing a separate line for each. Every jQuery command starts with the $ factory function, which is written $(). A CSS selector in quotes goes inside the parentheses, for example, $("ul#nav > li"). This selects all the `li` elements that are children of the `ul` with the ID `nav`. The fun begins when I tack on what I want to have happen to these elements, like this:

```
$("ul#nav > li").addClass('menulink')
```

Now each of the selected `lis` has the class of `menulink`. This chaining capability can make complex code short and simple to write (and read), and is part of the reason for jQuery's wide adoption by the development community.

JQUERY AND AJAX

In the following Ajax examples, I'll execute a simple Ajax GET request with these four frameworks. In each example, I'll request the contents of a text file named "loremIpsum.html" from the server and put the returned text into a `div` element named "content." I'll start with jQuery.

For Ajax transactions, jQuery provides a `get` method, which takes a URL as the only required argument, followed by an optional callback function. This optional argument is a map (property/value pairs) that specifies the data to send to the server and the type of data (XML, HTML, JSON, etc.) to be returned to the browser.

I'm using the optional callback argument to replace the contents of the `div` with the data returned from the server, as illustrated in **Figures 6.1** and **6.2**. Note that the three other frameworks illustrated produce visually identical results to these two figures.

ready is an event fired by jQuery after the DOM loads	`$(document).ready( function(){`
use Ajax to get the text of the file	`$.get("loremIpsum.html",`
and use this callback function when the Ajax call is complete	`function(data){`
get the div by its ID and use the jQuery provided function to set the data as the innerHTML property	`$("#content").html(data);`
	`}`
	`);`
CODE 6.1 ajax_jquery.html	`});`

jQuery's Ready Event

You saw in earlier examples that the `onload` function has some shortcomings in that it doesn't fire until the entire page has loaded. This includes images and other embedded elements that might continue to load for some time after the DOM has loaded. This means forms and links could already be firing events from user actions before the `onload` event has initialized the associated listeners for these events. To overcome this problem, jQuery offers the `$(document).ready` event that fires as soon as the DOM is loaded. This is illustrated in the section "jQuery and Ajax" in this chapter. It's an important feature that is found in other frameworks also, where the method may be named `contentReady`, `onAvailable`, or the like, but the idea is the same; you can put your JavaScript to work as soon as the DOM is loaded.

FIGURE 6.1 The page has a button and a text element.

FIGURE 6.2 When the button is clicked, the page is updated with text from the server. Each of the three subsequent framework Ajax examples produces the same visual result.

Here's an example of passing a function as a parameter, in this case, a parameter of the $.get method. Instead of the callback triggering a function as you saw in the previous chapter, the callback *is* a function and it just runs itself when the request is complete. This technique generally works best when the callback function is short, as is this example, and is only called by one request. If you find that you are writing the same or a very similar function for other requests, break out the function separately and set the callback of each request to call that function.

Prototype

The Prototype framework uses a more object-oriented approach where you instantiate JavaScript objects. Its Ajax object has a request method you instantiate with a URL and options.

In this example, I instantiate the Ajax.Request object with the URL and a map (property name/value pairs) containing parameters for the HTTP request method, and function definitions for event handlers.

```
new Ajax.Request('loremIpsum.html',

{

    method:'get',
```

CODE 6.2 accordion_prototype.
html

```
    onSuccess: function(request){

    $("content1").innerHTML = request.responseText;

    },

    onFailure: function(){ alert('Something went wrong...')

    }

});
```

As you saw in the Ajax example with the guitars in Chapter 4, updating the contents of a specific div is a common Ajax-related task, so the Prototype framework provides an object named "Updater" for that purpose. If you just want to make an Ajax query and simply stick the result into a div, here's a very simple way to do that: The Updater constructor takes a div ID and a URL as arguments along with the generic parameters map. The specified div's contents will be replaced with the content of the Ajax response.

```
new Ajax.Updater("content2", "loremIpsum.html", {method:
'get'});
```

This is a great example of a framework making a common task very simple. Note that you would also want to add an onFailure function as shown in Figure 6.2 to handle any problems.

Yahoo! User Interface (YUI)

The YUI framework is probably the most comprehensive of all. I think of it more as an interface development platform on which large online applications can be built; it's best for where high levels of robustness and accessibility are required. The downside is that it's more complex and verbose in its code requirements, and best suited to large enterprise-scale projects where that robustness is truly needed.

The YUI framework is namespaced within the YAHOO package and provides a Connect module containing Ajax functionality. The asyncRequest method takes a URL as an argument along with a parameters map containing event handlers similar to Prototype's. Upon completion, the ayscRequest automatically calls one of two functions, success or failure, depending on the request's outcome.

```
var request = YAHOO.util.Connect.asyncRequest("GET",
    "loremIpsum.html",

    {
```

CODE 6.3 ajax_yui.html

```
success:function(request){

    YAHOO.util.Dom.get("content").innerHTML = request.
        responseText;

},

failure: function(request){ alert("something went
    wrong..."); }

  }

);
```

Adobe Spry

Like YUI, Adobe's Spry framework leans more toward robustness and completeness than the "keep it light, simple, and fast" approach of jQuery and Prototype. The interface widgets and particularly the form validation module are very strong in Spry. If you have a lot of forms on your site and need to carefully validate that data as it comes in, you should take a close look at Spry. The effects animation is also very smooth in Spry. Run the jQuery and Spry accordion code examples that I show later in the chapter to see what I mean.

Adobe's Spry framework offers similar Ajax functionality, namespacing, and arguments to YUI. Spry's loadURL function requires the HTTP type (get or post), a URL, a Boolean flag to define if the call is asynchronous or synchronous, and a callback function. The Spry framework, also like YUI, offers a utility method for getting a reference to a DOM element and setting the innerHTML property.

```
var request = Spry.Utils.loadURL("GET", "loremIpsum.html",
    true,

    function(spryRequest){

        Spry.Utils.setInnerHTML("content", spryRequest.
            xhRequest.responseText);

    }

);
```

CODE 6.4 ajax_spry.html

Now let's use three of these frameworks to look at a few Rich Interface Application (RIA) components, commonly known as widgets. I'll feature YUI in some detail in Chapter 7, so you will see more on YUI then.

RIA Components

See the Adobe Spry effects demo at http://labs.adobe.com/technologies/spry/demos/effects/index.html for examples of grow, shake, slide, and many other interface animation effects.

RIAs are defined by the improved user interactions that they offer over the basic HTML interface components. First, they offer enhancements to a basic HTML interaction: search fields can be improved by AutoComplete functionality, tables by sorting and paging capabilities, and forms by easily adding validate-as-you-go user feedback. Second, some interactions are "new" in as much as they cannot be achieved at any level simply with HTML—drag-and-drop and animation are two examples.

Animations, such as grow, shake, and slide, when used appropriately, can help the user better understand workflows or the state of the data, especially when Ajax interactions are changing the content without refreshing the page.

As with Ajax, frameworks make implementation of RIAs much easier, and in this section, I'll show how some of the most popular interactions are implemented in these frameworks. First, let's look at Accordion.

Accordion with jQuery and Spry

An accordion is a set of sliding panels where one is always open. Clicking a panel heading reveals the associated content, as shown in **Figures 6.3** and **6.4**. This can conserve screen real estate while showing the user that other content is available.

FIGURE 6.3 Here the user is about to click the YUI heading.

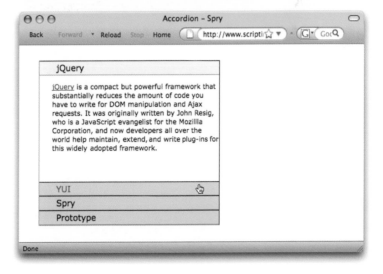

FIGURE 6.4 When the YUI heading is clicked, it slides upward to reveal its content.

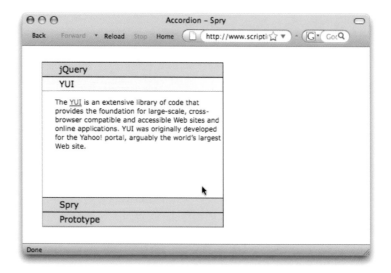

Another aspect of an accordion, which is a valuable aspect of this component, is the playful feel that the user gets when she clicks and a panel slides open to reveal new content. Engaging the user in the interface is a great first step to engaging that user in the content. If you run the code example, you will find that once you slide open one panel, the desire to open all the others is almost irresistible. Of course, playful interactions should support and not be a substitute for meaningful content.

ACCORDION WITH JQUERY

Here's how to create an accordion with jQuery. This example is illustrated in Figures 6.3 and 6.4.

```
<div id="Accordion1" class="accordion">

    <h3>one</h3>

    <p>Lorem ipsum…</p>

    <h3>two</h3>

    <p>Donec eget est…</p>

    <h3>three</h3>

    <p>Vivamus accumsan…p>

    <h3>four</h3>

    <p>Pellentesque eget…</p>

</div>
```

Working with jQuery UI Components

All the jQuery examples in this section are based on the jQuery UI library, which extends the basic jQuery library. Therefore, you must have the jQuery library, the jQuery UI library, and the jQuery UI library style sheet linked to the page to make these examples work. After you have downloaded jQuery and jQuery UI from www.jquery.com and www.jqueryui.com respectively, you must then add the following code in the head of your page.

```
<link href="jquery/jquery-ui.css" rel="stylesheet" type="text/css" />

<script src="jquery/jquery-1.3.2.js" type="text/javascript"></script>

<script src="jquery/jquery-ui-1.7.2.min.js" type="text/javascript">
```

You may need to adjust the path names to these files, depending on where they are located on your server. The preceding path names assume the jQuery files are in a folder called jquery at the same level as the HTML page.

Also, another way to link one of the widely used Ajax frameworks to your Web page is to use a Content Delivery Network, such as Google or Yahoo. This means, for example, that you may link to the version of jQuery on the Google servers instead of yours, like this:

```
<script type="text/javascript" src="http://ajax.googleapis.com/ajax/libs/
jquery/1.2.6/jquery.min.js"></script>
```

You can also use the google.load() method as described at the Google Ajax Libraries Application Programming Interface (API) page at http://code.google.com/apis/ajaxlibs/documentation. You may then want to follow the API Playground link on that page to http://code.google.com/apis/ajax/playground/?exp=libraries#jquery for practical examples of the Ajax and other Google APIs.

You can style the accordion using any two HTML tags, not just h3 and p.

CODE 6.5 accordion_jquery.html

Each h3 heading is styled in the jQuery style sheet as a bar with the heading text, and the paragraph is styled with a border and holds the content. The paragraph boxes are collapsed to zero height by jQuery, except for the first one, which is open by default when the page loads. The script to make the accordion work is very simple.

```
<script type="text/javascript">

$("#Accordion1").accordion({ header: "h3" });

</script>
```

All you need to do is define which element is the header (in this case, the h3) and the next element in the markup (in this case, the p tag) is treated as the collapsing content area. jQuery does a good job of providing very simple implementations of popular features. The thinking behind many jQuery features is *how simple can we make this—even if we limit the user's choices*. In this case, the limitation is requiring the collapsing element to follow the clickable head in the markup. Of course, a few more lines and you could write this from scratch so you could use a different element or be able to add other elements between the head and the collapsing element if you needed to. If you can live with the rules of the markup, however, it's very simple to get this and many other interactions into your page.

If you want more than one panel open at once, you actually don't want to use the accordion effect. Instead, use this code fragment provided on the jQuery UI site to open any closed panel and close any open panel.

```
jQuery(document).ready(function(){

    $('.accordion .head').click(function() {

        $(this).next().toggle('slow');

        return false;

    }).next().hide();

});
```

ACCORDION WITH SPRY

Let's now compare the jQuery Accordion implementation with that of Spry. There is slightly more HTML markup (only two panels shown here), although the visual result is virtually identical to Figures 6.3 and 6.4.

```
<div id="basicAccordion" class="Accordion">

<div class="AccordionPanel">

        <div class="AccordionPanelTab">YUI</div>

        <div class="AccordionPanelContent">

            <p>YUI is is an extensive library…</p>
```

More on Chaining in jQuery

I mentioned jQuery's chaining capability earlier and now you'll see it in action. Let's take this fragment of code from the jQuery Accordion example.

```
$('.accordion .head').click(function()
```

Here the `click` event handler is chained onto `$('.accordion .head')`, which is the "get" of the element with the `.head` class within the element with the `accordion` class. Many methods can be chained together in this way into a single line that would, in regular JavaScript code, each require its own line. The reason that this works is that each part of the chain, for example, `$('.accordion .head')`, returns the jQuery object created, so effectively the next part of the chain reads `obj.click (function)`. Each piece of the chain resolves to an object that provides a reference for the next piece. This enables jQuery code to be very compact and concise.

Working with Spry Components

After you have downloaded the Spry framework from http://labs.adobe.com/technologies/spry/home.html, you must then add the following code in the head of your page:

```
<script src="spry/SpryAccordion.js" type="text/javascript"></script>
```

This is the only file required for the Spry Accordion. You will need to adjust the path names to this file, depending on where it's located on your server.

```
                                    </div>
                                </div>
                            <div class="AccordionPanel">
                                <div class="AccordionPanelTab">Prototype</div>
                                <div class="AccordionPanelContent">
                                    <pPrototype and jQuery are similar in that…</p>
                                </div>
                            </div>
                        </div>
```

While the markup is a little more verbose, the JavaScript is only a single line.

CODE 6.6 accordion_spry.html

```
var basicAccordion = new Spry.Widget.
Accordion("basicAccordion");
```

You then have only to create an accordion instance with the appropriate ID. The additional HTML markup has the benefit of allowing you to choose which element is the sliding panel; it doesn't necessarily have to be the first one after the panel header—as with the provided jQuery implementation—but simply the one that has the AccordionPanelContent class.

Highlight with Prototype and Spry

While it's good for a user's experience to use Ajax to add or update a small piece of content without refreshing the page, there's the possibility that the user won't even notice the change. Obviously, you have to ensure that if your code changes the page content, the user is aware of it. The now widely accepted solution, established by 37signals in its Backpack and Basecamp applications, is to briefly highlight the background of the changed area. The classic visual implementation of this effect is that the new content element first appears with a background of bright yellow, and then the color fades away over a few seconds.

All four of the frameworks I show in this chapter have an out-of-the-box implementation of this effect, and here I'll illustrate how to use the ones in Prototype and Spry. In both cases, I'll fetch a small piece of text with Ajax, using the same code you saw in the earlier Ajax section, and then highlight the text as it is added to the page.

HIGHLIGHT WITH PROTOTYPE

Adding a highlight with Prototype is very simple.

```
new Ajax.Request('ajax_request_text.html',

  {

  method:'get',

  onSuccess: function(request){

     $("content").innerHTML = request.responseText;

     new Effect.Highlight("content");

  },

  onFailure: function(request){ alert('Something went
     wrong…') }

});
```

CODE 6.7 highlight_prototype.html Prototype/Scriptaculous files used for this effect:
prototype-1.6.0.3.js
scriptaculous.js
effects.js

Only the highlighted line of code is needed for this effect, but the effect only makes sense by first adding some text to the page from an Ajax request; the code illustrates how to put these two things together. See **Figure 6.5**.

FIGURE 6.5 The text is momentarily highlighted after being loaded into the page from an Ajax request.

HIGHLIGHT WITH SPRY

To illustrate highlighting in Spry, I'll again extend the earlier Ajax example.

```
var request = Spry.Utils.loadURL("GET", "ajax_request_text.
  html", true,

  function(spryRequest){

    Spry.Utils.setInnerHTML("content", spryRequest.
      xhRequest.responseText);

    var thehighlight = new Spry.Effect.Highlight('content',
      {from:'#66aaff', to:'#ffffff'});

    thehighlight.start();

  }

);
```

CODE 6.8 highlight_spry.html
Spry files used for this effect:
SpryData.js
SpryEffects.js
SpryDOMUtils.js

Spry requires just two lines of code for the highlight: one to instantiate the `Highlight` object and another to call the `start` method on it. Once you've instantiated this effect on a specific element, you can call `start` repeatedly without reinstantiating the object.

Drag-and-drop with Prototype and jQuery

I've mentioned drag-and-drop a few times as a good example of an RIA interaction, so now let's see how easy it is to implement drag-and-drop with both Prototype and jQuery. Here I'll show the basics of the implementation.

The basic notion of drag-and-drop is that elements can be dragged using the mouse from their source location to a target location. If the dragged element is released over the target element, it is removed from the source location and added to the target location. If the dragged element is released anywhere else, it remains in the source location. See **Figures 6.6** and **6.7**.

FIGURE 6.6 An item is dragged from the list on the left…

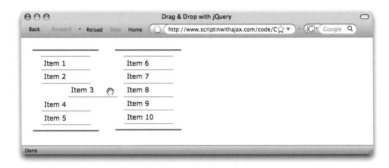

FIGURE 6.7 …and dropped into the list on the right, which automatically creates space to accommodate it.

I'll demonstrate this concept with two lists and show how the elements can be sorted within the two lists and also dragged between them. In both frameworks, the development team has abstracted away the complexity of this interaction, meaning the code you have to write is trivial.

DRAG-AND-DROP WITH PROTOTYPE

To implement drag-and-drop with Prototype, you just need simple, semantic markup like this:

```
<div>
    <ul id="list1">
        <li id="item1">Item 1</li>
        <li id="item2">Item 2</li>
        // etc.
    </ul>
</div>
<div>
```

CODE 6.9 dragdrop_prototype. html
Files used for this effect include: prototype-1.6.0.3.js
scriptaculous.js

```
<ul id="list2">

    <li id="item6">Item 6</li>

    <li id="item7">Item 7</li>

    // etc.

</ul>

</div>
```

Then all you need to do is this:

```
Sortable.create("list1", { dropOnEmpty:true,
    containment:["list1", "list2"]});

Sortable.create("list2", { dropOnEmpty:true,
    containment:["list1", "list2"]});
```

This code makes both lists sortable, meaning the items can be dragged into any order, and each list can accept elements from the other. Each element's dropOnEmpty Boolean property is set to true, allowing new items to be dropped on it from another element, even when it's empty. In other words, even when a list's items have all been dropped in another location and it is then an empty list, it can still receive new items. The property containment contains a map of value/pair that defines the related elements to which the drag-and-drop is limited—in this case, the two lists.

DRAG-AND-DROP WITH JQUERY

The markup for the same effect with jQuery is

```
<div>

    <ul id="list1" class="connectedSortable">

        <li id="item1">Item 1</li>

        <li id="item2">Item 2</li>

        // etc.

    </ul>

</div>

<div>
```

CODE 6.10 dragdrop_jquery.html
Files used for this effect include:
jquery-ui.css
jquery-1.3.2.js
jquery-ui-1.7.2.min.js
(In both drag-and-drop examples,
I also added a few simple inline
CSS styles to pretty up the lists.)

```
<ul id="list2" class="connectedSortable">

  <li id="item6">Item 6</li>

  <li id="item7">Item 7</li>

  // etc.

</ul>

</div>
```

The code is, unbelievably, even shorter than Prototype's.

```
$(function(){

  $("#list1, #list2").sortable({

    connectWith: ".connectedSortable"

  });

});
```

Note that there's a class on the ul element that is used in the con-nectWith property to cross-reference the two lists so elements can be dragged between them.

Tabs with jQuery and Spry

Tabs run along the top of a content area and allow users to select from a limited number of content sections, typically four to six. The metaphor is tabs in a ring binder or a box of recipe cards that provide divisions of major groups of content. This concept is illustrated in **Figures 6.8** and **6.9.**

FIGURE 6.8 When the page loads, Tab 1 is selected by default.

FIGURE 6.9 Different content loads when another tab is clicked.

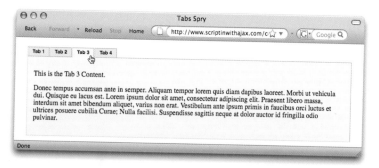

TABS WITH JQUERY

The required markup for the tabs using jQuery is a set of links organized within an unordered list. The href of each of these links points to its associated content div. The lists and content are in turn contained within a div with an ID—in this case, named demo.

CODE 6.11 tabs_jquery.html

```
<div id="demo">

  <ul>

    <li><a href="#tab1"><em>Tab One Label</em></a></li>

    <li><a href="#tab2"><em>Tab Two Label</em></a></li>

    <li><a href="#tab3"><em>Tab Three Label</em></a></li>

  </ul>

  <div>

    <div id="tab1">

      <p>Tab One Content</p>

    </div>

    <div id="tab2">

      <p>Tab Two Content</p>

    </div>

    <div id="tab3">

      <p>Tab Three Content</p>

    </div>

  </div>

</div>
```

Learn about the Breadcrumbs design pattern at: http://developer.yahoo.com/ypatterns/pattern.php?pattern=breadcrumbs.

The code, again, is very simple.

```
<script type="text/javascript">
  $(function() {
    $("#demo").tabs();
  });
</script>
```

You simply invoke the tabs method on the div that contains the tabs and the content.

TABS WITH SPRY

The markup in Spry is similar in organization to jQuery except with Spry every element requires a class. Even though it is more code, it provides some flexibility in adding other elements—perhaps breadcrumbs at the top of the content area—within the markup specific to the tabs and the associated content.

CODE 6.12 tabs_spry.html

```
<div class="TabbedPanels" id="TabbedPanels1">
  <ul class="TabbedPanelsTabGroup">
    <li class="TabbedPanelsTab">Tab 1</li>
    <li class="TabbedPanelsTab">Tab 2</li>
    <li class="TabbedPanelsTab">Tab 3</li>
    <li class="TabbedPanelsTab">Tab 4</li>
  </ul>
  <div class="TabbedPanelsContentGroup">
    <div class="TabbedPanelsContent">Tab 1 Content</div>
    <div class="TabbedPanelsContent">Tab 2 Content</div>
    <div class="TabbedPanelsContent">Tab 3 Content</div>
    <div class="TabbedPanelsContent">Tab 4 Content</div>
  </div>
</div>
```

The JavaScript required is absolutely minimal—a single line.

```
var TabbedPanels1 = new Spry.Widget.
TabbedPanels("TabbedPanels1");
```

Summary

In this chapter, I've shown some examples of four popular frameworks. There are many other excellent frameworks that I could have chosen. I can only recommend that you explore the examples and documentation on each framework's respective Web site and start to build with them to discover which one is right for you.

I've only shown the most basic implementation of the various interactions I've illustrated in this chapter rather than real-world uses. For example, in reality, if the user sorts a list using drag-and-drop, your code then needs to be able to determine the new order and provide appropriate responses.

To show you more real-world use of frameworks and coding techniques, in the next and final chapter, as I did in *Stylin' with CSS* (New Riders, 2008) and *Codin' for the Web* (New Riders, 2007), I'll pull together many of the ideas you have seen so far in this book into two simple but fully functional RIAs.

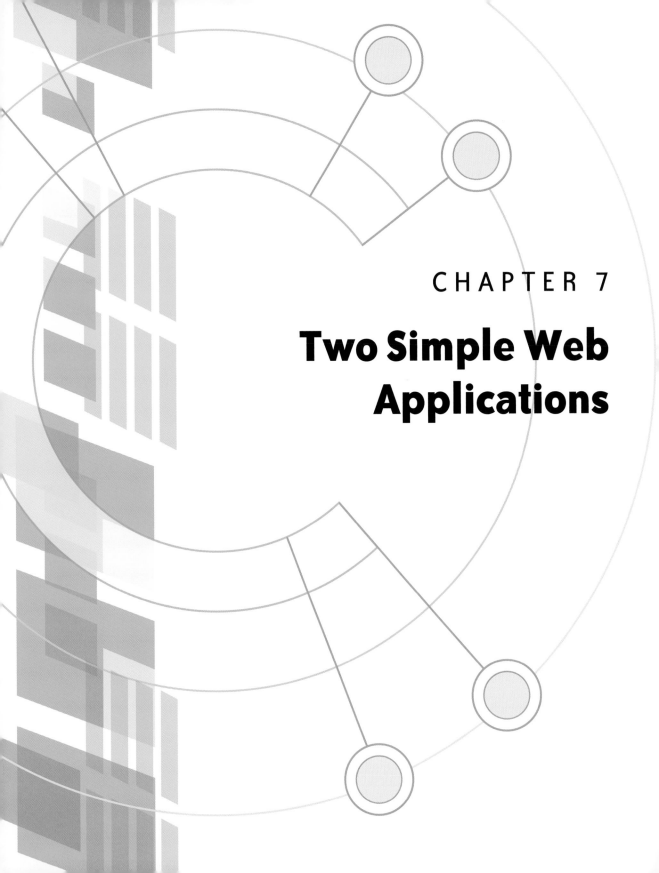

CHAPTER 7

Two Simple Web Applications

THIS FINAL CHAPTER FEATURES TWO SIMPLE APPLICATIONS that bring together many of the ideas and techniques that you saw in the earlier chapters. The previous examples were written in a way that made them as simple to understand as possible. In this chapter, where the code was developed for me by Austin Markus and Chris Heilmann, two respected professional programmers, we take a more pragmatic approach and write the code as it would be developed in business projects. This chapter's examples differ from real applications in the scope of their feature sets, which have been kept to an absolute minimum while still illustrating the concepts I want to show. To maintain the consistency of voice throughout the chapter, I'll continue to write "I now do this or that..."—but understand that this includes the voices of the contributing programmers.

The first project is a very visual interface that uses a selection of jQuery components, whereas the second is more data driven and built on the Yahoo! User Interface (YUI) library.

About the Projects

Unlike the preceding examples, both projects illustrated in this chapter combine a number of interactions and processes. Both offer progressive enhancement and work acceptably even if JavaScript is not present.

Technically, both projects use PHP for the server-side coding and use file-based data sources such as JSON and CSV (comma separated value) files. This means that you can run them with just a server that supports PHP, although in reality both could be improved by the addition of a database. I have deliberately avoided the use of databases for these examples because I want to keep things simple to ensure that as many readers as possible can get the demo code running.

Both projects also use a mix of HTML, CSS, and JavaScript on the front-end, and while their feature sets are not extensive, both are usable applications that are coded to professional standards.

For this reason, if you are relatively new to Web development, these projects may seem a little daunting, but the downloadable code is heavily commented throughout. Taking the time to study these examples can help you improve your knowledge, better understand how applications are assembled, and write code that is concise, robust, and extensible in the future.

It's not my intention to go into detail on every line of code in these projects, but rather to discuss their features, the strategies for building them, and the areas of the code that are of particular interest. Before you start reading this chapter, I suggest you go to the *Scriptin'* Web site and play with the demos. Then, as you read, open the related scripts for each project in a code editor. I have listed code filenames in the margin as I discuss them so you can see the parts of the code as I refer to them in their broader context.

Most of all, I hope you will take these projects and modify them for your own needs. This is absolutely the best way to build your skills and become familiar with the demonstrated techniques.

An Image Carousel

The first project is called Author Carousel and provides image-based access to information about a number of fellow New Riders' authors and their books. The interface is composed of a row of 11 photos. Only three are visible at one time, but the user can scroll horizontally through all the images in any of three ways: by clicking left and right arrows onscreen, using the left and right keyboard arrows, or using the scroll wheel of the mouse, as illustrated in **Figure 7.1**.

FIGURE 7.1 A carousel is a compact component that can contain a large number of images.

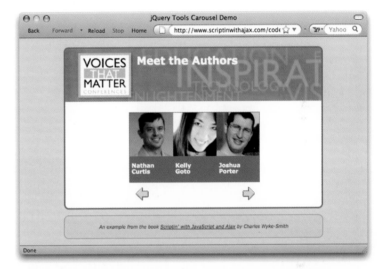

Learn more about the Carousel design pattern at the Yahoo! Design Pattern Library at http://developer. yahoo.com/ypatterns/pattern. php?pattern=carousel.

Carousels, named after the trays that hold slides on slide projectors (remember them?), have become very popular on the Web. Carousels either slide side to side or rotate their images in a circle. The one I'll show slides side to side. Carousels are intuitive and fun to use, allow many items to be viewed rapidly, and occupy very little space in relation to the content they can contain. They also provide a visual rather than textual interface, which is especially appropriate for applications such as shopping and of course photo sites.

In this project, a second design pattern, Overlay, is integrated with the carousel. If the user clicks on an item in the carousel (in this case, an item comprises the author's picture and the area containing the author's name below it), an overlay with information about that author appears, as shown in **Figure 7.2**.

The overlay can be closed by clicking its close box, pressing Escape, or clicking anywhere outside of it.

FIGURE 7.2 The overlay zooms out of the clicked image and displays over the carousel.

The Overlay design pattern is modal; that is, once the overlay opens, the user can only interact with the content of the overlay and can only regain access to the rest of the page by closing it. Be sure this is the desired interaction before using overlays in your work. If you just want to show information when the user rolls over an element and remove that information when the user rolls off it, then you need the Tooltip pattern.

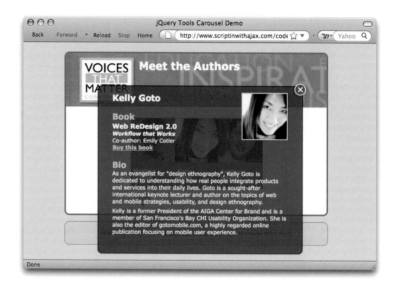

A Location Finder with AutoComplete

The second project, named Location Finder, is search-based. Many sites offer a search feature, and it's very helpful if the field into which the user types her search has AutoComplete. As you have probably noticed, when you search on Google, the AutoComplete Control adds a drop-down menu containing possible matches to the entered text as soon as you start to type. This happens because the browser is passing the entered string to the server via Ajax each time you release a key, and matching results are being returned for display.

AutoComplete has two important advantages for the user. First, the user may not need to type the entire search phrase. If the desired search term appears in the drop-down menu after a few characters are entered, the user can simply select the choice without typing it in full. Second, as Google Search illustrates, with additional programming the control can offer useful matches that expand on what the user typed or offer corrections for mistyped words. An acceptable alternative can then be offered instead of a search that yields disappointing results.

In the case of the Location Finder project you will see in this chapter, the user is able to find the locations of Yahoo! offices around the world. Just typing a single character will display a list of matches, and as the user types more the search becomes more refined. If the user types "Fra", for example, suggestions will include the offices in San Francisco and Paris, France, as shown in **Figure 7.3**.

FIGURE 7.3 Typing the letters "Fra" in the search field returns results France and San Francisco as results in the drop-down menu.

Once the user selects an office, the address and a map are displayed, as shown in **Figure 7.4**. The map is loaded using a query to the Yahoo! Maps API.

FIGURE 7.4 Selecting Paris from the drop-down menu displays the full details of the location and map.

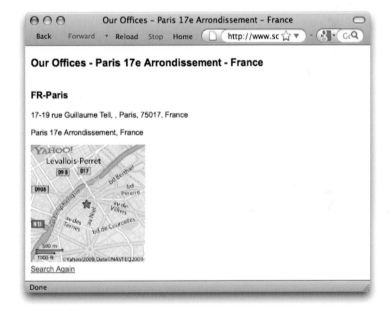

It's a simple example of a "mash-up" where the page's data comes from different sources, not just a single server. Let's look at these two applications in more detail, starting with the Carousel example.

Building the Author Carousel

The business objective of Author Carousel project is to display information about the Voices That Matter authors in an engaging and easy-to-access way. In any project, once that business need

If the project had larger scale, I would have created an online form for the authors to enter their data and then developed some code to write that information into a database.

has been determined and the project gets a go-ahead, one of the first questions is, "Where will the data come from?" In this case, I received the author data in a spreadsheet from the publisher and simply created a JSON file format to represent it.

Because this is a demonstration and there was only data on 11 authors, I first created a JSON file that represented the data for one author. I then copied and renamed it for each author, and cut and pasted the data into the JSON files from the spreadsheet.

Here's what one of the JSON files for this project looks like:

CODE 7.1 json/goto.json (you can see all the JSON files in this folder)

```
{
    "first_name":"Kelly",
    "last_name":"Goto",
    "photo":
        {
        "url":"images/headshot/goto100.jpg",
        "alt":"Kelly Goto"
        },
    "book":
        {
        "title":"Web ReDesign 2.0",
        "description":"Workflow that Works",
        "co-author":"Emily Cotler",
"buy_link":"http://www.peachpit.com/store/product.
    aspx?isbn=0321534921"
        },
    "bio":
        [
            {"para":"As an evangelist for…(text removed here)…
                usability, and design ethnography."},
            {"para":"Kelly is…(text removed here)…editor of
                gotomobile.com…(text removed here). "}
        ]
}
```

As you can see, the values of the properties of this file are simple text strings in the case of the author name properties, name/value pairs in the case of the image and book properties, and an array for the bio property. The reason I use an array for the bio information is that the number of paragraphs changes from author to author, so I need to be able to get a length count on these elements and then write out as many as I find. Now that I have the data in a useable format, I'll move on to getting the basic interface working.

I decided to build this project in jQuery, not only because it is simple to write and very widely used, but also because an excellent implementation of the core functionality required for the carousel is available in a jQuery add-on library called jQuery Tools.

jQuery Tools is similar in concept to jQuery UI in that it runs on top of jQuery and, at less than 6K of code minified, offers considerable functionality for its size. In jQuery Tools, the carousel is known as Scrollable, and there is an excellent demo at http://flowplayer.org/tools/demos/scrollable/visual.html.

You can find the jQuery Tools library at http://flowplayer.org/tools/index.html.

Styling the Carousel

I'll start explaining the code by showing you the key markup for the carousel elements.

```
<div class="scrollable">

  <div id="thumbs" class="">

    <div class="thumbContainer">

      <a href="?index=0" class="linkToSite" rel="0">

        <img class="person_pic" alt="Dan Brown"
          src="images/headshot/brown100.jpg">

      </a>

      <h3 class="person_name">

      <a href="?index=0" class="linkToSite" rel="0">
        Dan Brown</a>

      </h3>

    </div>

    <div class="thumbContainer">

      // next carousel item goes in here

    </div>
```

a carousel item

CODE 7.2 Generated source code of index.php

end carousel item

Tips on Integrating Online Examples into Your Work

If you are a newcomer to JavaScript and frameworks, it's often easiest to take a demo like the jQuery Tools site's Carousel example as the foundation of your page and modify it to look like the other pages in your site rather than trying to add the framework's functionality into an existing page. In other words, the first step toward building your own carousel is to take that demo, or the one that I have provided in the download files for this book, and get it working on your server. Once you've done that, you can start modifying it with your own content and styling it to your desired look.

In the case of the jQuery Tool's Carousel demo, here is what you would do:

1. Go to http://flowplayer.org/tools/demos/scrollable/visual.htm and View Source using the browser's View menu (don't View Generated Source using the Web Developer toolbar in this case—you want to get the original source code before the JavaScript code modifies it). Copy and paste the source code into a new blank HTML file. Copy the file onto your server. You will be pleased to find that is all you have to do to get the demo running. The reason this is so easy is that all the scripts and images are served from the Flowplayer.org servers; you can see the URLs in the source code. However, you do not want to use these URLs in your final version: Flowplayer.org is only serving all this content for a limited time as it establishes the product, and it's simply not wise to rely on any third party for linked content except through an established content distribution network (CDN) such as Google or Yahoo!.

2. The next rather tedious step is to start grabbing the served content and moving it onto your own server so you can link to your own copies, modifying the URLs appropriately as you go. You have to work through the markup and get the content associated with each link, script, or image tag.

    The first file in the demo markup is the jQuery Tools library, which also contains the base jQuery library. You can download this file from the jQuery Tools downloads. Put it in a folder called jQuery. Now you can modify the link to it to read something like (in the case of my site) http://www.scriptinwithajax.com/code/Ch7_examples/vtm_carousel_small/jquery/jquery.tools.min.js.

3. Because other elements like the CSS and graphics are not available for download, you need to get a little more creative. Simply cut and paste the URL of the required element into the address bar of the browser and load it. Next, in the case of text such as CSS, just copy and paste it into a file and save it, or in the case of a graphic, right-click on it (Control-click on Mac) and use the menu's Save As command to save it to an appropriate folder. Then modify the path in the code to reflect the new location. (Of course, if you use the example I provide, this work has been done for you.)

    Some of the graphic elements are available for download on the jQuery Tools site, but it's not worth copying down the content images for the carousel because you'll be changing them out for your own, so you would leave them linked to the demo site for now. Often, I simply create a graphic placeholder, usually just a colored rectangle, of the right size to use until I have my own images ready.

4. After you have all the graphic and code elements on your server and have updated all paths so everything is functional again, back up the project folder so you can pick up again from here if things fall apart (and sometimes they do—it even happened to me once!). Then you can start modifying the demo file to your own needs.

```
         <!-- 9 more carousel items here

    </div>

</div>
```

I'll now show you how this markup is styled to create the onscreen carousel.

The two primary HTML elements of the carousel (highlighted) are `div.scrollable` and `div#thumbs`. In the CSS, the width of `div.scrollable` is set to 300 pixels, exactly wide enough to display three carousel items; the width of its child element `div#thumbs` is always just wide enough to contain all the carousel items. You'll see how the width of `div#thumbs` is determined in a moment.

The CSS for this project is contained in two files: `carousel.css`, *which has all the CSS except the rules specific to the overlay. The overlay rules are in* `overlay.css`.

If you look at the CSS file `carousel.css`, you will observe that `div.scrollable` is the positioning context for `div#thumbs`; the former's position property is set to `relative`, and the latter's position property is set to `absolute`. This means that when the user scrolls the carousel, `div#thumbs` moves with respect to `div.scrollable`. The individual items within `div#thumbs`, each in a div called `div.thumbContainer`, move as one unit. This relationship is illustrated in **Figure 7.5**.

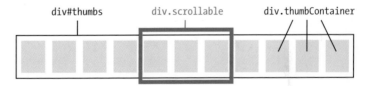

FIGURE 7.5 The `div.scrollable` element acts as a mask through which a part of the strip of images is viewed. The `div.thumbContainer` divs are spaced apart in this diagram for clarity, but in reality there is no horizontal space between them.

The result of this CSS styling is that `div.scrollable` becomes a mask behind which `div#thumbs` slides from left to right, and in this way only three items are visible at any given time. To better understand what is happening, temporarily remove the CSS style `position:relative` from `div.scrollable` to see `div#thumbs` pop out of the `div.scrollable` mask. It will then position itself relative to the default positioning context `body`, and you will see the entire strip of all 11 items.

The name "thumbs" is shorthand for "thumbnails," which is a term for a set of small images such as the ones in the carousel.

An interesting aspect of the CSS comes from the fact that `div#thumbs` must be given a width that is great enough to enclose all the `div.thumbContainer` items. In the jQuery Tools demo, I noticed that the width had been set at 10000 ems, presumably by someone who assumed that this would accommodate any potential content. I decided to be more precise and set the `#thumbs` element width to the exact required width. I did this by placing this rule in a style tag in the `index.php` page:

```
#thumbs {

  width: <?php print (count($JSONFileNameArray)*100).
    'px';?>;

}
```

This code takes the number of files in the JSON folder (each file causes one `.thumbContainer` item to be generated), multiplies it by 100—the width of each `.thumbContainer` element—and sets the width of `#thumbs` to that value. This is a great example of when you might want to occasionally add a style into the markup instead of into the linked style sheet. The CSS rule can now include the PHP `$JSONFileNameArray` variable, which is then used to calculate the width property of the `#thumbs` div. When author data files are added (or removed), the `#thumbs` div adjusts to the correct new width.

Managing the Scrollbar

As you will have discovered if you have played with the online demo, the carousel can be scrolled in three ways: by clicking the arrow controls, clicking on an image that is not in the center, or by pressing the keyboard arrows. These controls won't work if JavaScript is not enabled, so to ensure that everyone will be able to access the content, I first build the carousel with a regular horizontal scrollbar, as shown in **Figure 7.6**. I ensure the scrollbar shows by initially setting the CSS of the horizontal overflow of `div.scrollable` to `auto`, like this:

```
div.scrollable {overflow-x:auto;}
```

Actually, because the very wide `div#thumbs` is wider than its fixed-width parent `.scrollable`, `div.scrollable` is already in a state of overflow, and automatically displays a scrollbar unless there are so few images they are all visible at once. I really set this CSS style to remind me that it is showing, and to make absolutely certain that the scrollbar shows—if it's not there, the carousel cannot be used without JavaScript. Now the user can scroll the images with a regular scrollbar if JavaScript is not available.

Overflow is actually quite a complex aspect of CSS. It is well worth understanding its nuances because it comes into play in determining not only what happens to content that is too big for its container, but also is a neat way of forcing elements to enclose floated child elements. You can learn more at the CSS Tricks site at http://css-tricks.com/the-css-overflow-property.

FIGURE 7.6 The scrollbar displays when JavaScript is unavailable, so the user can view all the elements in the carousel.

To get the carousel built to this point, I used some hard-coded HTML markup to add a few items to the carousel. This allowed me to get the interface working and also to refine the markup and style it with CSS, before I began writing the PHP code to generate the markup dynamically from the author data in the JSON files.

This scrollbar will be hidden when JavaScript is active by having jQuery set this `overflow-x` property to `hidden`.

The PHP Backend

Now that the interface is usable without JavaScript, I need to write some PHP to get the carousel's functionality—generating the content for the carousel and displaying the author's info when the user clicks an image—to work without JavaScript, too. Then I'll layer on the JavaScript interactions. PHP has three important roles in this project:

This example requires PHP5 because it uses PHP5's new and improved file reading capabilities.

1. It reads the JSON files from the server.

2. It writes out the required HTML elements for each item (author photo and name) of the carousel using the JSON data and then serves up the initial page.

3. When the user clicks on an item and the request for the overlay data is made by Ajax, the PHP script will simply serve the requested JSON data to the browser where it will be processed by the Ajax callback function and displayed in the overlay.

    If the request is not made via Ajax, because JavaScript is not available, PHP writes the JSON into HTML elements and serves a new page as a regular round-trip. In this case, the selected author's information will be displayed in a div below the carousel. You'll see how PHP determines whether or not the request was made via Ajax later in the chapter. Let's first look at the PHP that generates the initial page in more detail.

READING THE JSON DATA

Using files stored on the server is a simple way to provide data to an Ajax-enabled page. In this example, PHP will scan the folder to determine the number of files, read them, and then add the required information into the page. PHP needs what's called a fully qualified path to do this. A fully qualified path for a file lists every folder from the Web server root all the way down to the folder containing the file in question; in this case a folder called json. Such a path might look like this:

CODE 7.3 vtm_carousel/index.php

```
/root/html/code/examples/vtm_carousel/json
```

Let's see what it takes to build a fully qualified path to the JSON files.

the name of the script

```
$JSONFolderName='json';
```

Unix folder separator–use "\" for Windows

```
$sep='/';
```

the name of the folder where the JSON files live

```
$basename="index.php";
```

These three lines are hard-coded variables:

1. The name of the folder containing the JSON files

2. The correct path element delimiter symbol. This symbol is the slash that goes between the elements of the file path name, as in json/filename.json. The reason this needs to be stored in a variable is that it is either a backslash / or a forward slash \ depending on whether the PHP server is running on Linux or Windows, respectively. So note that when you see the variable $sep, it contains a slash.

3. The name of the file that contains the PHP script. The folder with the JSON file is located at the same level as the PHP script, so I will first ascertain the name of the folder containing the script, and then append the name of the JSON folder onto it.

    ```
    $JSONPath=dirname($_SERVER['SCRIPT_FILENAME']).$sep.$JSON
    FolderName;
    ```

Now that I have the path to where the files are stored, I can pass that path to a function that will build a list of the names of those files in an array. This array can then be used to supply the correct data when the user clicks an element of the carousel.

```
$JSONFileNameArray=makeJSONFileNameArray($JSONPath);
```

Here's the function that gets called:

```
function makeJSONFileNameArray($JSONPath){
```

Many sites use basename($_SERVER['PHP_SELF']); to obtain the name of the PHP script; by obtaining the filename this way, if the script's filename later changes, the code will not break. However, this is a security hazard because it is vulnerable to XSS (cross-site scripting) attacks. See the MC2 Design site at www.mc2design.com/blog/php_self-safe-alternatives for information on XSS attacks and how to prevent them.

scandir reads the filenames from the folder–PHP5 ONLY

```php
$JSONFileNameArray=scandir($JSONPath);
```

get rid of the . and .. paths–current dir and dir above current, respectively

```php
unset($JSONFileNameArray[array_search('.',
    $JSONFileNameArray)]);

unset($JSONFileNameArray[array_search('..',
    $JSONFileNameArray)]);
```

reenumerate the array so you start at 0, not 2

```php
$JSONFileNameArray=array_values($JSONFileNameArray);

return $JSONFileNameArray;
```

CODE 7.4 vtm_carousel/index.php (cont.)

```php
}
```

In this function, I use the PHP5 `scandir` method to put the names of all files in the target folder into an array. Next, I delete the files that start with one or two dots (which are references to the current folder and the folder above). Two empty elements remain, so I reenumerate the array to eliminate them, and return the array of filenames.

WRITING OUT THE HTML

Now I can write the items—the authors' photos and names—into the carousel markup by iterating over the list of files. Inside the `thumbs` div, I write a div called `thumb_container` that contains the markup for each author's information.

```html
<div class="scrollable">
```

the container for the sliding "thumbs" div

```html
  <div id="thumbs" class="">
    <?php
```

loop through the files

```php
    foreach ($JSONFileNameArray as $index => $fileName){
```

read each file

```php
    $authorInfo=readJSONFile($JSONPath.$sep.$fileName);
```

write out the HTML elements of each author's image and name for the carousel

```php
print '
```

the image and text container for each author element

```html
      <div class="thumbContainer">
```

the href provides the index number on a round-trip, the rel attribute provides the index ref for an Ajax request

```html
        <a href="?index='.$index.'" class="linkToSite"
           rel="'.$index.'">

        <img class="person_pic" alt="'.$authorInfo['photo']
           ['alt'].'" src="'.$authorInfo['photo']['url'].'" />

        </a>

        <h3 class="person_name">

        <a href="?index='.$index.'" class="linkToSite"
           rel="'.$index.'">
```

CODE 7.5 vtm_carousel/index.php (cont.)

```
                          '.$authorInfo['first_name'].' '.$authorInfo['last_
                             name'].'</a>

            </h3>

                </div>

                ';

                }?>

            </div>

        </div>
```

I then iterate over the `$JSONFileNameArray`. For each filename in the array, I read the JSON file (first highlight) by calling the `readJSON-File` function, which looks like this:

```
function readJSONFile($JSONfileNameAndPath){

    $fileHandle = fopen($JSONfileNameAndPath, "r");

    $JSONData = fread($fileHandle, filesize
        ($JSONfileNameAndPath));

    fclose($fileHandle);

    return json_decode($JSONData, TRUE);
```

CODE 7.6 vtm_carousel/index.php (cont.)

I then write the author's name, image, and the current numerical index of the array (thereby adding a reference to the author's JSON file) into the markup template that follows, and this is added to the PHP output. After looping through all the files, each `thumb_container` div contains something like this:

```
<div class="thumbContainer">

    <div class="thumb_inner">

            <a href="?index=2" class="linkToSite" rel="2">
                <img class="person_pic" alt="Curt Cloninger"
                src="images/headshot/cloninger100.jpg"></a>

            <h3 class="person_name">

            <a href="?index=2" class="linkToSite" rel="2">
                Curt Cloninger</a>

            </h3>

        </div>

    </div>
```

CODE 7.7 vtm_carousel/index.php (cont.)

I've highlighted an interesting and key part of the previous block of PHP code, which is the link around the image that makes it clickable.

```
href="?index='.$index.'"
```

The output, (assuming we are writing out the third file in the `$authorInfo` array) looks like this:

```
href="?index=2"
```

What happens here is that `'.$index.'` (highlighted) resolves to the numerical index of the `$authorInfo` array for the file that is currently being read. The URL begins with a question mark, meaning a query string; because there is no page name preceding this query string, the current page is implied—in this case, it's the equivalent of

```
href="index.php?index=2"
```

When an item is clicked, it will pass this query string reference back to the server with the request, so the related file can be retrieved. Note that I also add the numerical value of the array into the `rel` attribute of the links. I'll use this reference when we retrieve the JSON using Ajax, which I will show later.

The code shown so far simply displays the page in the browser. Now I'll show you the code that runs when the user clicks on an image that serves up the detailed information about the selected author.

The reason that I wrote the numerical value of the array into the `href` *instead of the filename is because using the filename is insecure. Filenames in query strings can be easily replaced with malicious code that then gets passed into the script and possibly executed. By using a number instead of a text string, I can test for a number and reject anything else.*

RESPONDING TO A CLICK

When an author's image or an author's name text (which also has a similar link wrapped around it) is clicked, the `index.php` page loads again, only this time the reference to that author's JSON file is passed with the request in the query string. The query string might look like this:

```
?index=4
```

All that's now needed is some PHP code to get the correct file and use its data to write out the complete information about that particular author. That code looks like this:

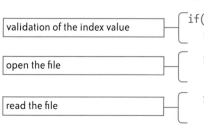

```
if(ctype_digit($_GET['index'])&&($_GET['index']>=0 &&
    $_GET['index']<=count($JSONFileNameArray))){

    $fileHandle = fopen($JSONPath.$sep.$JSONFileNameArray
        [$_GET['index']], "r");

    $JSONData = fread($fileHandle, filesize($JSONPath.$sep.
        $JSONFileNameArray[$_GET['index']]));
```

| validation of the index value |
| open the file |
| read the file |

close the file

was the request made by Ajax?

if so, return the content to the Ajax request and stop the script

not an Ajax request, so build requested content using PHP

```php
fclose($fileHandle);

if(($_GET['ajax']=='true')){

    die($JSONData);

} else {

    $dataArray=json_decode($JSONData, TRUE);

    $overlayHTML = '';

    $overlayHTML .= '<div id="author_info">';

    $overlayHTML .= '<img src=" ' . ($dataArray['photo']
        ['url']) .'" alt="'.($dataArray['photo']['alt']).'">
        </img>'."\n";

    $overlayHTML .= '<h1>';
```

note space at end of line—appears between first and last name

```php
    $overlayHTML .= '<span>'.($dataArray["first_name"]).
        '</span> ';

    $overlayHTML .= '<span>'.($dataArray["last_name"]).
        '</span>';

    $overlayHTML .= '</h1>'."\n";

    $overlayHTML .= '<h2>Book</h2>';

    $overlayHTML .= '<h3>' . $dataArray['book']['title'].
        '</h3>'."\n";
```

CODE 7.8 vtm_carousel/index.php (cont.)

```php
    $overlayHTML .= '<p class="description"><strong><em>'
        . $dataArray['book']['description'] . '</em>
        </strong></p>'."\n";

        if ($dataArray['book']['co-author']) {

            $overlayHTML .= '<p class="description">
                Co-author: ' . $dataArray['book']
                ['co-author'] . '</p>'."\n";

        }

    $overlayHTML .= '<p class="description"><a href="' .
        $dataArray['book']['buy_link'] . '" target=
        "_blank">';

    $overlayHTML .= 'Buy this book</a></p>'."\n";

    $overlayHTML .= '<h2>Bio</h2>';

    $bio = $dataArray['bio'];
```

```
        foreach($bio as $bioPara){

            $overlayHTML .= '<p class="bio">' . $bioPara['para']
                . '</p>'."\n";

        }

        $overlayHTML.= '</div>';

    }

}
```

When the page request is submitted, the numerical value is stored in the $_GET array with the property name of index. In the first line of the preceding code

```
if(ctype_digit($_GET['index'])&&($_GET['index']>=0 && $_GET['
index']<=count($JSONFileNameArray)))
```

you can see I then do three tests to check that index contains the right kind of data: Is it a number?; is it a number greater than 0?; is it a number equal to or less than the number of files in the folder? If not, we don't proceed. This test prevents malicious code from getting passed in through the query string.

The next step is to concatenate the folder path (which I assembled previously) with the appropriate slash and the filename that corresponds to the index value passed from the query string.

This gives me the full path of the file, which I store in the $JSONdata variable.

```
$JSONData = fread($fileHandle,    filesize($JSONPath.$sep.
$JSONFileNameArray[$_GET['index']]));
```

The highlighted part of the previous code block is an if statement—it begins with

```
if(($_GET['ajax']==='true')){
```

This statement detects if the request was made by an Ajax request or a regular page request. When there is an Ajax request (we'll look at that part of the code in detail next), I will pass a query string with the name/value pair ajax=true in it. Each time a request is made, PHP will test for the presence of an element named ajax in the $_GET array to determine if the request was made by Ajax, or is a regular page request that must be served by PHP.

In anticipation of an Ajax request, I test here for a $_GET array property name of ajax. If it's present, then the die method is called: This method will simply pass the data in the `json` variable back to the requesting Ajax call, and as its name suggests, stop the script.

If the `ajax` property is not set, it's a regular page request, and PHP must supply the data in a new page. In such a case, the `else` part of the `if` statement runs. This creates a number of HTML elements in a variable called `overlayHTML`, adding the appropriate JSON data into each one.

This variable contains the same HTML elements that would be displayed in the overlay if Ajax was handling the request. However, if PHP generates the HTML (because JavaScript is not present), these HTML elements won't appear in the overlay but instead in a div that will be displayed below the carousel—the overlay can't work without JavaScript.

The way I use PHP to assemble the HTML elements here is similar to the way I used JavaScript to assemble the HTML elements when using JSON in the guitar example in Chapter 5. The only real difference is that in PHP a `.` (period), not a `+`, is used to concatenate the HTML and the JSON data when assembling the HTML elements.

As I mentioned, without JavaScript I can't use the overlay to display the HTML elements generated by PHP, so I need to add a div into the markup that I use for this purpose. Farther down the PHP script, in the HTML markup, you will see the line

```
if ($overlayHTML) {print '<div id="overlay_content_noJS">'
.$overlayHTML . '</div>';}
```

where I test for the existence of the `overlayHTML` variable. This variable only exists if I wrote out the HTML with PHP, so if it's present, I need to add a div—with the contents of the `overlayHTML` variable inside it—into the page after the carousel markup. You can see how this looks in **Figure 7.7**.

You can see the code to this point in the file index_php_only.php.

I now have a page that works with just HTML and PHP. Let's look at the Ajax implementation next.

Layering on the JavaScript

The first step to adding the JavaScript that enables the fully functional carousel, complete with its Ajax-powered overlay, is to link the required jQuery files. This is done by adding the following script tags into the head of the document:

FIGURE 7.7 When JavaScript is not available, the content is displayed below the carousel.

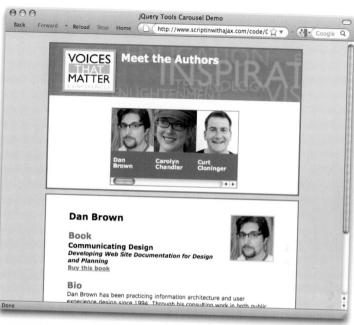

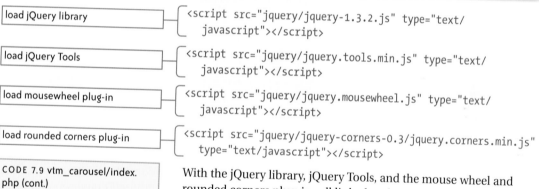

load jQuery library

```
<script src="jquery/jquery-1.3.2.js" type="text/
    javascript"></script>
```

load jQuery Tools

```
<script src="jquery/jquery.tools.min.js" type="text/
    javascript"></script>
```

load mousewheel plug-in

```
<script src="jquery/jquery.mousewheel.js" type="text/
    javascript"></script>
```

load rounded corners plug-in

```
<script src="jquery/jquery-corners-0.3/jquery.corners.min.js"
    type="text/javascript"></script>
```

CODE 7.9 vtm_carousel/index.
php (cont.)

With the jQuery library, jQuery Tools, and the mouse wheel and rounded corners plug-ins all linked to the page, you're all set to take a rather basic PHP application into the modern age. Let's start with something easy and add rounded corners to the header and the main content area.

ROUNDED CORNERS

In my book *Stylin' with CSS, Second Edition*, I illustrated how to use a helper function called Nifty Corners to create rounded corners on elements. Most modern Web sites use rounded corners on elements with borders because they help to break up the boxy look of the regular rectangular border. Besides, rounded corners just look cool and help give any page a stylish look.

Download the Rounded Corners plug-in and view the documentation at DaveTurnbull's site at www.atblabs.com/jquery.corners.html.

Today, I use the jQuery Rounded Corner plug-in written by Dave Turnbull, because it offers better support for margins and padding on the rounded element. It's simple to use, works reliably across a variety of browsers, and requires only the addition of one class to any element that you want to display with rounded corners.

I linked the Rounded Corner plug-in to the page earlier, so now I just need a little jQuery to tell the plug-in the class name that I will use for elements that need rounded corners. I first add the rounded class to each element that I want to have rounded corners, like this:

```
<div id="people_display"  class="rounded clearfix">
```

jQuery adds the rounded corners with a single line of code that runs when the DOM is loaded.

CODE 7.10 vtm_carousel/index. php (cont.)

function called when DOM is ready.

adds rounded corners with 12 pixel radius to all elements with "rounded" class

```
$(document).ready(function(){

    $('.rounded').corners('12px');

}
```

Now both the main content div and footer div have rounded corners, as you can see in **Figure 7.8**.

FIGURE 7.8 As soon as the DOM is loaded, jQuery adds the rounded corners.

In Figure 7.8, the scrollbar is still visible. In the next step, I'll remove it and add some navigation options that are more user friendly.

Implementing the Carousel Interactions

In the PHP-only version, I needed a scrollbar on the carousel so the user could move through the content.

The clearfix class that is also on this element invokes the Aslett Clearing technique that forces this div to enclose floated elements, not the default behavior. You can see the clearfix code in the carousel.css *file and read about it on page 119 of my book* Stylin' with CSS, Second Edition.

In the JavaScript-powered version, the user will be able to move the carousel using a variety of navigation options, so the scrollbar can be removed.

If JavaScript is present, I'll have it hide the scrollbar at the same time as I invoke the rounded corners.

CODE 7.11 vtm_carousel/index. php (cont.)

hides the scrollbar–not needed if JS is available

```
$(document).ready(function(){

    $('.rounded').corners('12px');

    $("div.scrollable").css("overflow-x","hidden");
```

This highlighted code simply overrides the related settings in the style sheet.

IMPLEMENTING THE SCROLLING FUNCTIONALITY

The carousel will have a number of interactions associated with it; scrolling will be possible by using the mouse wheel, onscreen arrows, or clicking. Clicking on any image will move it to the center position if it's not there already and pop up the overlay with the author's description in it. The first step is getting the carousel to scroll.

the number of visible thumbs–you must alter the widths of the container in the css if you change this

the container for the scrolling elements

the class added when the mouse hovers

```
$("div.scrollable").scrollable({

    size: 3,

    items: '#thumbs',

    hoverClass: 'hover'

});
```

CODE 7.12 vtm_carousel/index. php (cont.)

In this code that invokes the jQuery Tools Scrollable component, I get the containing element for the scrollable elements—the div with the class `scrollable`—and assign the scrollable method to it. I also pass this object a configuration object with three properties. These properties define:

- The size of the visible part of the carousel in terms of number of images that are visible at any given moment. This information lets the Scrollable component keep track of the position of the carousel so a clicked item can be brought to the center. It also allows the component to calculate "paging" moves; that is, moving the carousel to the next set of three images. Paging is functionality that I have not enabled in this project, but it's simple to implement—check the jQuery Tools documentation for details.

- The nested element, which is a div with the ID `thumbs`, that contains all the individual items of the carousel.

•. The class that will be added to a scrollable item when the mouse moves over it so CSS rules can be invoked to highlight it. You can see this in action when you move the mouse over an author's name and the background changes color.

IMPLEMENTING THE MOUSE WHEEL FUNCTIONALITY

Enabling the user to scroll the carousel from the mouse wheel (and even my Mac has one these days!) allows very fast movement of the carousel, which is useful if it contains a large number of elements. With jQuery Tools, mouse wheel functionality for the carousel is simple to implement. As long as I use the class name `scrollable` for the carousel's main containing div (as I do here), I can simply add the jQuery mouse wheel plug-in to my page with a `script` tag as I did earlier, and the mouse wheel then scrolls the carousel (if you also have the mouse over the carousel) without any further coding. This is because control of a div named `scrollable` via the `mousewheel.js` code is already built into the jQuery Tools Scrollable component.

IMPLEMENTING THE NAVIGATION ARROW BUTTONS

Two arrows below the carousel also enable the user to scroll. The navigation arrows markup is simply two links with the classes `prev` and `next`, respectively. The size, position, and background graphics—the arrow icons—are all controlled from the CSS in the style sheet called `carousel.css`. I'll make two comments on these navigation arrows.

The first comment is about the way the rollover effect, which turns the arrows from blue to a tan color when the mouse moves over it, is implemented using a technique called image spriting—see the sidebar, "About Image Sprites." Both states (sprites) of each arrow, normal and hovered, are in one file, as shown in **Figure 7.9**.

The graphic in Figure 7.9 is used as the background for the left arrow's a link. The link's height and width are exactly the same as one of the arrows, so the other arrow doesn't show onscreen. The CSS `:hover` setting for the links simply moves the hovered link's graphic up 35 pixels when the user mouses over it, bringing the hovered state of the graphic into view.

FIGURE 7.9 Both visual states of the left arrow control are on one graphic.

The checkerboard background of this Adobe Fireworks screenshot indicates the transparent areas of the graphic.

CODE 7.13 vtm_carousel/index. php (cont.)

```
div#carousel_wrapper a.prev:hover, div#carousel_wrapper
    a.next:hover{

    background-position:0px -35px;

}
```

Visually, the arrow simply changes color. When the mouse moves off the arrow, the initial position is restored; visually, the arrow simply returns to its original color.

Displaying one of the sprites simply requires sizing an HTML element to the size of the sprites to be displayed, and then adding the image file as a background image with CSS. You must also set the x and y `background-position` coordinates of the image so that the desired sprite shows through. Once an image file is cached on the user's machine, there is no delay waiting for rollover state graphics to download when the user mouses over a graphical button. The CSS hover coordinates simply reposition the image file so the "hover state" sprite is positioned behind the HTML element. Of course, setting the coordinates of the sprites can be done with JavaScript too, which offers some interesting animation possibilities.

My second comment is about the automatic control of the display of the arrows. Notice that when the page first loads, the left arrow is not displayed. This is because the carousel is initially fully scrolled

About Image Sprites

The technique of downloading a single graphic containing several images and displaying them individually by placing them behind a masking element is known as "image spriting." This is now a very popular technique for implementing rollovers, because numerous image "sprites"—a term used for the small graphics used for button backgrounds and icons—can be placed in one image file. Downloading all these graphics in one file decreases the number of HTTP requests to the server, resulting in improved performance of your site.

Learn about the application of this and other Web site performance enhancing techniques by watching Nicole Sullivan's video *Design Fast Websites* at www.yuiblog.com/blog/2008/12/23/video-sullivan.

You can upload sprites images to SpriteGen at http://spritegen.website-performance.org and you will get back a large graphic with all the sprites laid out on it at coordinate intervals you can specify. Sweet.

to the left so the user could not scroll left if he wanted to. As soon he scrolls to the right, the left arrow appears, because left scrolling is now possible. In the same way, the right arrow is also removed when the carousel is fully scrolled to the right. This user-friendly behavior is implemented automatically by jQuery Tools. All you have to do is simply follow the naming convention for the links by giving them a class of prev and next, respectively, to invoke this functionality.

Implementing the Overlay

In the PHP-only version of the carousel that I showed in the first part of this project, you saw that a click on an image resulted in the related information being added into a div farther down the page. With JavaScript enabled, the information can be presented in an overlay that displays on top of the carousel. This makes for a much more visually pleasing and user-friendly presentation, and eliminates the possibility that the user will have to scroll to read the information.

ASSOCIATING THE OVERLAY WITH A MOUSE CLICK

The overlay functionality is provided by another jQuery Tools' component called Overlay. I already have the jQuery Tools library added to the page, so it's just a matter of invoking the overlay's behavior.

```
var api = $("div.overlay").overlay({oneInstance: false, api:
    true, onClose:function () {

        $('#author_info').remove();

    }
});
```

CODE 7.14 vtm_carousel/index. php (cont.)

Like the code that invoked the scrolling, this code specifies the element that will be used as the overlay—a div with the class overlay. However, the difference here is that the overlay method in this case takes a configuration object of name/value pairs that affect how the overlay functions. In this object, I set three properties of the Overlay component:

1. Multiple instances of the overlay are allowed (even though I am only using one in this example).

2. The overlay method will return a reference to the jQuery Tools API so I can call its methods.

3. The onClose method will call a function that will remove the overlay's contents when the overlay is closed, so that content

does not accumulate in the div between requests. Without this, every selected author's information would remain in the div.

With the overlay behavior primed and ready, I now need to have the overlay display when an image is clicked.

add event listeners to the thumb-
nail containers and assign event
function

get the index of the author from the
link's rel attribute

```
$('.thumbContainer').bind("click", function(){

    var authorIndex=$(this).children('div.thumb_inner').
        children('a').attr('rel');

    $.getJSON("?index="+authorIndex+"&ajax=true",
        function(JSONData){

        // code to display the JSON data goes here

}
```

CODE 7.15 vtm_carousel/index.
php (cont.)

Instead of attaching event listeners to every element in each item's container to detect a click, I use event delegation and let the click bubble up to the containing element thumb_container. The first line of the preceding code attaches a click event listener to each #thumbContainer element (the div that wraps around each author's image and name area in the carousel) and assigns an anonymous function that will run when a container is clicked.

This function gets the container's link and reads its rel attribute value. This is the index number for this author's location in the JSON array. You may remember that PHP wrote this number into each link's rel attribute when building the initial page. Because jQuery correctly binds the this keyword to the element that receives an event, (something JavaScript can have problems with), I am able to use this as a reference to the clicked element instead of having to dig into the event object to determine which element got the click.

Normally, a jQuery method returns a reference to the jQuery object; that's what makes jQuery's chaining capability possible. By invoking the jQuery Tools component's API, a reference to that API is returned instead and I can then call any of its methods. Listings of the methods of each component's API can be found on the respective components demo pages that are listed at www.flowplayer.org/tools.

Once I have the numerical value of the rel attribute—the all-important reference to the clicked person's data—I make an Ajax call to the server, passing the index value in a name/value pair named index in the same way as I did before when JavaScript was not present. This Ajax call triggers the same script (the PHP script index.php) that originally loaded the page.

However, because I also pass a second name/value pair—ajax=true—with the request, the PHP behavior is different. In the if statement that I added after the code that reads the JSON file, PHP will detect the presence of the ajax element in the $_GET array. Here's that bit of code again:

was the request made by Ajax?

if so, return the content to the Ajax request and stop the script

not an Ajax request, so build requested content using PHP

CODE 7.16 vtm_carousel/index. php (cont.)

```php
if(($_GET['ajax']=='true')){

    die($JSONData);

}else{

    // code here to build HTML elements with PHP

}
```

Because an element named `ajax` is now present in the `$_GET` array, PHP no longer writes out the JSON and returns an HTML page. Because the request was made by Ajax, PHP simply returns the requested file's JSON data to the browser and terminates the script (highlighted code). This `if` statement is the key to making this page accessible to users who do not have JavaScript enabled in their browser.

Parsing the JSON with JavaScript

With the JSON now returned to the browser, it's time to build the required HTML. Because I want to show you as much JavaScript as possible, instead of just returning the fully constituted HTML from the PHP script (which I could do by moving the if statement in the preceding code to the end of the PHP code that writes out the HTML and returning the HTML instead of the JSON), I'll bring the JSON into the browser. Now I can show how to build the HTML with JavaScript, too. In reality, it's a little redundant, but it's a useful exercise that builds on the parsing of the JSON you saw in the earlier guitar exercise. Here's the entire code that detects the user click, gets the JSON via an Ajax call (first highlighted code below), and then builds the HTML elements.

```javascript
$('.thumbContainer').bind("click", function(){

    var authorIndex=$(this).children('div.thumb_inner').
        children('a').attr('rel');

    $.getJSON("?index="+authorIndex+"&ajax=true",
    function(JSONData){
```

initialize variable with empty string

```javascript
        tags = ' ';

        tags += '<div id="author_info">';

        tags += '<img src=" ' + (JSONData['photo']['url']) +'"
            alt="'+(JSONData['photo']['alt'])+'"> </img>\n';

        tags += '<h1>';
```

```
            tags += '<span>'+(JSONData["first_name"])+'</span> ';

            tags += '<span>'+(JSONData["last_name"])+'</span>';

            tags += '</h1>\n';

            tags += '<h2>Book</h2>';

            tags += '<h3>' + JSONData['book']['title'] + '</h3>\n';

            tags += '<p class="description"><strong><em>' +
                JSONData['book']['description'] + '</em></strong>
                </p>\n';

            if (JSONData['book']['co-author']) {

                tags += '<p class="description">Co-author: ' +
                    JSONData['book']['co-author'] + '</p>\n';

            }

            tags += '<p class="description"><a href="' +
                JSONData['book']['buy_link'] + '" target="_blank">';

            tags += 'Buy this book</a></p>\n';

        tags += '<h2>Bio</h2>';

            var bio = JSONData['bio'];

            for(var i = 0; i < bio.length; i++){

                tags += '<p class="bio">' + bio[i]['para'] +
                    '</p>\n';

            }

            tags += '</div>';

            // insert the assembled html into the page after the
                overlay's close box div

            $(".close").after(tags);

            });

        api.load();

        return false;

        });

    });
```

CODE 7.17 vtm_carousel/index.
php (cont.)

pop up the overlay

It was very easy to create this parsing code by simply taking the corresponding PHP code and replacing the PHP . delimiters with JavaScript + delimiters.

As you can see, after requesting the JSON file, which is automatically evaluated into JavaScript by jQuery as part of the `getJSON` method, I can immediately start to write out a list of HTML tags. I start by opening a div called `author_info`, so I can have a hook to style the elements it will contain. As I write out each tag, I include the appropriate data from the JSON file. Notice in the second highlighted piece of code that I put the `bio` property value—an array—into a variable. Because the number of elements in this array might vary, I then use the array's length property to loop through it as many times as there are elements in the array and write each element's data into a paragraph tag.

Once I have all the elements in the `tags` variable, I get the div with the `close` class. The Overlay component automatically adds a div with this class as the first element inside the specified overlay container div when it is initialized. The purpose of this `close` div is to hold a graphic that the user can click to close the overlay—more on this in a moment. After getting this element, I can use the jQuery `after` method to add the new HTML elements immediately after it inside the overlay container div.

Finally, I use the Overlay API (last highlight), which I have already referenced in the `api` variable, to open the overlay using its `load` method. The overlay then animates out from the clicked picture, and the information about the requested author is displayed, as shown in **Figure 7.10**. I then return `false` to prevent the `href` of the link from triggering a regular page request.

FIGURE 7.10 The overlay displays the requested information.

The Ajax request, the building of the HTML from the JSON, and the opening of the overlay usually happens in a matter of a second or two, even though it's taken several pages here to describe how it works.

Clicking the close button, pressing Escape, or clicking outside of the overlay causes the overlay to close, so the user can make another choice. Again, as long as the close button graphic is within (or the background element of) an element with the class close, this functionality is automatically provided by the Overlay component.

This covers the key functionality of the Author Carousel project. Now I'll show you the AutoComplete example that uses the YUI framework and Yahoo! Maps.

AutoComplete and Maps with the Yahoo! API

Without a doubt the most comprehensive JavaScript library in existence is the Yahoo! User Interface (YUI), which is a layered framework of components for just about every task that your interface might need to handle. At its foundation is the YUI Global Core, which is required for all components, the DOM collection for managing the DOM, and the Event utility, which simplifies the management of events. On top of this foundation, you can run a wide variety of interface widgets—from data tables and calendars to sliders and a text editor—and a variety of utilities for animation, cookie management, and much more. There are also development tools to help you as you write your application and a set of CSS tools to help you lay out and style your pages.

Learn more about YUI at http:// developer.yahoo.com/yui. Scroll down this page to the Get Started section, which has a wealth of information to help you get YUI working in your projects.

In this project, I will use the AutoComplete widget to enhance a search form to help users find Yahoo! offices around the world. AutoComplete is well suited to a multi-element data set like this, where the user might know only the street, city, or country where the office is located. By typing any of these bits of information, the AutoComplete can search the data and provide suggestions to help the user make the right choice.

You will also see how to use the Yahoo! Loader utility, which automatically loads the correct supporting files for each YUI widget, and the Yahoo! Maps API, which will display a map of the selected location.

The Location Data

In this project, the data for the Yahoo! office locations is stored in a CSV (comma separated values) file, also often referred to as a flat file. Each record looks like this:

CN-Shanghai,"Room 2936 Lippo Plaza,No. 222 Huai Hai Zhong Road,Shanghai,200021,China",City,31.2477092743,121.472618103,21 51849,Shanghai,China

The values in each record are

> office name
>
> the mailing address (a string with sub-elements)
>
> the WOEID (WhereOnEarth ID) type (suburb, city, etc)
>
> the WOEID
>
> the longitude
>
> the latitude
>
> city name
>
> country name

CODE 7.18 locations.csv

This data will be used to supply matches for the AutoComplete display and for the full display of search results, including use of the longitude and latitude data to display a map of the selected location.

The Project Template—index.php

An interesting aspect of this project is that although there are three pages that can be displayed, they are all generated from a single PHP "template" script that acts as a container to load other scripts. This project has a script to read the JSON files, another to display the search form, and another to display the search results; all are included in the `index.php` page as needed. As you will see, the logic coded within the template page determines the condition under which a particular script is included.

This kind of modular page strategy enables key functionality to be added into pages as needed and logically divides the codebase into discrete and easily managed blocks. If a certain aspect of the design changes—perhaps a database will be used instead of JSON files—all that's required is to update that one script that reads in the data and then every page that includes that script is updated too. You

If you want to quickly find the exact longitude and latitude coordinates of a street address, visit GPSVisualizer at www.gpsvisualizer.com/geocoding.html. To integrate this capability into an application, use the Yahoo! Maps API at developer.yahoo.com/maps.

can compare such a write-once, use-many approach to the use of functions, which can be called from many places within the code. In short, if a section of code must be present in many pages, write it in its own script and include it in each page that needs it. Headers, footers, and navigation elements that appear in every page are also obvious "include" candidates. The benefits of such an approach are clear even from a small project like this and are an essential design strategy for building larger applications.

I'll start by showing you the code for this template—the index.php script—whose logic determines when to include the other scripts.

```php
<?php

    include('getlocations.php');

?>
```

include a script that reads the location data from the CSV file

```php
<?php

    if(!isset($_GET['showlocation'])){

        $header = 'Our Offices - find a location';

    }
    if(isset($_GET['location'])){

    $header =  'Our Offices - pick a location';

    }
    if(isset($_GET['showlocation'])){

        $header = 'Our Offices - '.$current['city'].' - '
            .$current['country'];

    }

?>
```

true if the page is first loading, so show the search form—note the ! NOT operator

true if the form was submitted on a regular round trip so the form reloads with the search results list below

if true, the search results detail is displayed

```html
<!DOCTYPE HTML PUBLIC "-//W3C//DTD HTML 4.01//EN"

"http://www.w3.org/TR/html4/strict.dtd">

<html>

<head>

    <meta http-equiv="Content-Type" content="text/html;
        charset=UTF-8">

    <title><?php echo $header;?></title>
```

adds Yahoo! style sheet

```html
<link rel="stylesheet" href="http://yui.yahooapis.
    com/2.7.0/build/reset-fonts-grids/reset-fonts-grids.css"
    type="text/css">

<link rel="stylesheet" href="http://yui.yahooapis.
    com/2.7.0/build/base/base.css" type="text/css">

<style type="text/css" media="screen">
```

highlights text in the AutoComplete results

```css
    .highlight {color:#069;}
```

```html
</style>

</head>

<body class="yui-skin-sam" >

<div id="doc" class="yui-t7">

    <div id="hd" role="banner"><h1><?php echo $header;?>
        </h1></div>

    <div id="bd" role="main">
```

true if the page is first loading, so show the search form– note the ! NOT operator

```php
<?php

    if(!isset($_GET['showlocation'])){

        include('searchform.php');
```

if true, the form was submitted on a regular round-trip so the form reloads with the search results list below

```php
    }

    if(isset($_GET['location'])){

        include('searchresults.php');
```

if true, the search results detail is displayed

```php
    }

    if(isset($_GET['showlocation'])){

        include('locationdetails.php');

    }

?>
```

```html
    </div>
```

CODE 7.19 autocompete_n_maps/ index.php

```html
<p><em>An example from the book <a href="http://www.
    scriptinwithajax.com">Scriptin' with JavaScript and Ajax
    </a> by Charles Wyke-Smith</em></p>

</div>

</div>
```

```
</body>

</html>
```

Figure 7.11 illustrates how the highlighted block in the preceding code controls the logic of the program flow.

FIGURE 7.11 The presence or absence of certain elements in the $_GET array determines which files are included in the index.php "template" page.

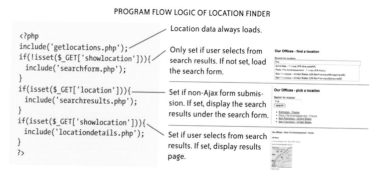

PROGRAM FLOW LOGIC OF LOCATION FINDER

```
<?php
include('getlocations.php');
if(!isset($_GET['showlocation'])){
  include('searchform.php');
}
if(isset($_GET['location'])){
  include('searchresults.php');
}
if(isset($_GET['showlocation'])){
  include('locationdetails.php');
}
?>
```

Location data always loads.

Only set if user selects from search results. If not set, load the search form.

Set if non-Ajax form submission. If set, display the search results under the search form.

Set if user selects from search results. If set, display results page.

THE LOCATIONS DATA—GETLOCATIONS.PHP

Here is the included code for reading the CSV file that contains the locations:

this array holds each location record as an element–this data is used when displaying the search results

```php
$locations = array();
```

this array holds the name of each location–this data is used in the AutoComplete drop-down list results

```php
$locationnames = array();

ini_set("auto_detect_line_endings", 1);

$current_row = 1;
```

open the file

```php
$handle = fopen("locations.csv","r");
```

get CSV data

```php
while(($data = fgetcsv($handle,10000,","))!== false){

  $number_of_fields = count($data);
```

get header row

```php
  if($current_row == 1){

    for($c=0; $c < $number_of_fields; $c++){

      $header_array[$c] = $data[$c];

    }
```

get data rows

```php
  } else {

    for($c=0; $c < $number_of_fields; $c++){

      $data_array[$header_array[$c]] = $data[$c];

    }
```

here we assemble a simple string of office name, city, and country to display in the AutoComplete

```
$locations[] = $data_array;

$locationnames[] = $data_array['Office'] . ' - ' .

    $data_array['city'] . ' - ' .

    $data_array['country'];
```

CODE 7.20 autocompete_n_maps/ getlocations.php

```
    }

    $current_row++;
```

close the file

```
    }

fclose($handle);
```

This code first reads the file from disk and then iterates the records and creates an array called $locationnames that contains the name, city, and country of each office. This is the data that will be used to produce results for the AutoComplete Control.

Because this getlocations.php script is included at the very top of the template script, any PHP script that is included farther down can access the locations and loacationnames variables.

After loading the data from the CSV file, the code checks the $_GET array to determine the correct text to put in the page's title tag; remember, the index.php template script generates all the pages the user sees so it has to manage all aspects of the page content.

The first time the index.php is requested, the $_GET array will contain nothing. However, each time the script is called again, as a result of the user clicking an onscreen element within the generated HTML page, the $_GET array will contain an element named either location or showlocation.

Let's only consider the case where the page first loads for now. In this case, the first test in the index.php file

note the ! NOT operator

```
if(!isset($_GET['showlocation'])){

    $header = 'Our Offices - find a location';

}
```

resolves to true—the $_GET array contains nothing (there is no query string appended to the URL). This test therefore determines showlocation is not set, and the $header variable is set to "Our Offices - find a location".

Next in the code is the HTML document DOCTYPE and head elements, which just get written into the page as is. The PHP in the `title` tag (first highlight in **Code 7.4**) writes the $header variable into the tag and gives the page its correct title.

Then, I add the YUI style sheets that take care of styling the components—this saves a lot of tedious CSS work. The style sheet called `reset-fonts-grids.css` contains CSS that does three things: It removes all the browser's default styles, gives pleasing proportional font sizes to all HTML text elements, and provides access to a huge array of CSS layouts. The style sheet `base.css` provides a consistent style foundation for all HTML across all the A-grade browsers, as defined by Yahoo!.

In short, whichever browser you are using, the styles applied by its internal CSS style sheet are "neutralized," and new styles that have been carefully designed for aesthetics and cross-browser consistency are applied in their place.

Except for one style that I decided to add to highlight the matching letters in the AutoComplete, I didn't have to write any CSS for this project. Its styling comes entirely from these two YUI style sheets. However, I've kept the markup in this project to the absolute minimum; the pleasing overall effect provided by these style sheets is more apparent when working on a larger document with a variety of HTML elements.

After writing the $header data again into an `h1` tag as the page heading, all that's left to do is load one of the page content scripts for the content I want to display. There is a block of `if` statements that determines which scripts get loaded. Again, because the initial URL is simply `index.php` without any query string appended and the `$_GET` array is therefore empty, the first of the tests

Learn more about Yahoo!'s notion of graded browsers at http://developer.yahoo.com/yui/articles/gbs/.

note the ! NOT operator in this test condition

```php
if(!isset($_GET['showlocation'])){

    include('searchform.php');

}
```

resolves to true and the search form is loaded.

The Search Form Script—searchform.php

Here's the code in the `searchform.php` file that gets added to the `index.php` template page when the page first loads:

```html
<form action="index.php" method="get" accept-charset="utf-8">

    <div>

        <label for="location">Search for location:</label>
```

```
                    <div><input type="text" id="location" name="location">
                    <div id="autocomplete"></div></div>
                    <input type="submit" id="submit" value="search">
                </div>
            </form>
```

<table>
<tr><td>use the YUI loader to load all the required components to support the AutoComplete Control</td></tr>
</table>

```
<script type="text/javascript" src="http://yui.yahooapis.
    com/2.7.0/build/yuiloader/yuiloader-min.js"></script
<script type="text/javascript">
(function(){
    var loader = new YAHOO.util.YUILoader({
        base:'',
        require:['autocomplete'],
        loadOptional:false,
        combine:true,
        filter:'MIN',
        allowRollup:true,
        onSuccess:function(){
```

<table>
<tr><td>the AutoComplete Control has successfully loaded</td></tr>
<tr><td>encode the location data array into JSON ready for the AutoComplete Control to use</td></tr>
<tr><td>define the datasource for the AutoComplete</td></tr>
<tr><td>instantiate the AutoComplete, telling it which field the entered data comes from, where to write out the results, and what datasource to use</td></tr>
<tr><td>matches query to any word in a record, not just first word in record</td></tr>
<tr><td>format each result as it is found</td></tr>
</table>

```
            var locations = <?php echo json_
                encode($locationnames);?>;

            var datasource = new YAHOO.util.
                LocalDataSource(locations);

            var autocomplete = new YAHOO.widget.AutoComplete
                ('location', 'autocomplete',datasource);

            autocomplete.queryMatchContains = true;
        autocomplete.formatResult = function(resultitem,query){
            var parts = resultitem[0].split(' - ');

            var out  = parts[1] + ' - ' + parts[2] + ' (' +
                parts[0] + ')';

            return out.replace(query,'<strong class=
                "highlight">'+query+'</strong>');
        };
```

when user makes selection, immediately load page with full result set (overrides default behavior of adding user's selection into search field)

```
                         autocomplete.itemSelectEvent.subscribe
                            (function(type,args){
                              var office = args[2][0].split(' - ');
                              window.location = 'index.php?showlocation=' +
                                 office[0];
                          });
                       }
                    });
                    loader.insert();
                  })();
</script>
```

CODE 7.21 autocompete_n_maps/ searchform.php

This code is where the AutoComplete Control is initialized and ready for use. Let's break it down: First, the form is loaded.

THE AUTOCOMPLETE FORM MARKUP

This form is essentially a single field form with a label and a Submit button, but with an important addition. There is a div that is wrapped around the text field input that also contains a div called autocomplete. The AutoComplete Control will use this autocomplete div to display the drop-down list of results. More specifically, when there are results to display, the autocomplete div is absolutely positioned along the bottom edge of the text field into which the user is typing, and is populated with an unordered list containing the results.

USING THE YUI LOADER

As I mentioned at the beginning of this project, YUI controls such as AutoComplete sit on top of some base components that are shared by many components in the YUI library. The order in which all these components load is critical to their operation, and some widgets require a number of components to be loaded before they can function. Fortunately, the YUI Loader prevents you from having to worry about what's needed when in order to support a particular widget. Just tell the Loader the name of the widget you want to use, and it knows how to find and load the required supporting components directly from Yahoo!'s content distribution network. This is also a performance boost because users around the world will get the files from the geographically closest Yahoo! server. So, before initializing

The YUI Loader manages and optimizes the loading of YUI components in a variety of ways through its API. Learn more at http://developer.yahoo.com/yui/yuiloader.

the AutoComplete Control, I tell the Loader to load the required components in a syntax like this:

```
var loader = new YAHOO.util.YUILoader ( { map of
properties } )
```

The Loader object constructor can be customized with a map of properties that is passed in as an argument when it's instantiated. The most important of these properties in this case is `require:['autocomplete']`, which tells the loader to load the AutoComplete Control and all its supporting components. In the map, I also define an `onSuccess` function. As you might imagine from its name, this function is triggered by the Loader's `success` event that fires once the required components are loaded. I use this event to start the next step—initializing the AutoComplete Control—confident that everything I need to make it work is loaded.

INITIALIZING THE AUTOCOMPLETE CONTROL

The AutoComplete Control likes its data in JSON, so I have PHP write the location data that it is holding in a variable called `$locationnames` into the page as a string of JSON right here inside the JavaScript code:

```
var locations = <?php echo json_encode($locationnames);?>;
```

Of course, PHP does this work on the server before the page is sent to the browser. Then, when the browser runs the JavaScript, the JSON string is already written into the page in place of the highlighted PHP. If you View Generated Source using the Web Developer toolbar, you can see all the location data within this block of code.

Now that I have the JSON location data in the `locations` variable, I use this variable to define the data source object for the AutoComplete Control.

```
var datasource = new YAHOO.util.LocalDataSource(locations);
```

Now I can instantiate a new AutoComplete instance. The three required arguments are the ID of the text field into which the user will be typing, the ID of the element that will display the results, and the data source object.

```
var autocomplete = new YAHOO.widget.AutoComplete('location',
'autocomplete',datasource);
```

I've now done what's needed to make the AutoComplete Control work, but I have a few small customizations I want to make to its default behavior.

CUSTOMIZING THE AUTOCOMPLETE CONTROL'S DEFAULT BEHAVIOR

By default, the AutoComplete Control only supplies matches based on an exact match between what the user is typing and the first letters of one of the results. In other words, if the user types Ma, there would be a match on Madrid but not on San Mateo. Because the user might be searching by office, city, or country name, I want to loosen up this behavior and match anywhere within the search results, which I do like this:

```
autocomplete.queryMatchContains = true;
```

With the `queryMatchContains` property set to `true`, as long as the user string is contained somewhere in the location information, a result will be displayed. Now typing Ma returns both Madrid and San Mateo.

However, this change now means the results don't relate directly to the query: If the user types D, the first result would be *AU-Docklands - Melbourne - Australia* (see **Figure 7.12**) because there's now a match on Docklands.

FIGURE 7.12 Because the "looser" search returns any result with a letter D in it, the first five results don't start with the letter the user typed.

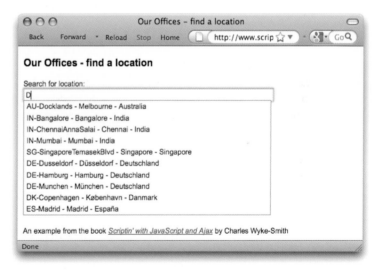

Because of this potentially confusing behavior, I want to highlight the matching letter(s) in the result so the user understands why that result is displaying. The AutoComplete's API has a `formatResult` method that allows you to define a function through which each result string is processed before being added to the results display so that you can tweak its appearance.

```
autocomplete.formatResult = function(resultitem,query){

   var parts = resultitem[0].split(' - ');

   var out  = parts[1] + ' - ' + parts[2] + ' (' + parts[0]
      + ')';

   return out.replace(query,'<strong class=
      "highlight">'+query+'</strong>');

};
```

If you highlight text with color, also bold it as I have done here or add some other noncolor dimension for emphasis, so that color-blind users can differentiate these characters.

In this function, I wrap a `strong` tag with the class `highlight` around the part of the result that matches the user's query string (highlighted). The `strong` tag bolds this part of the result, and for additional clarity, I use the class to invoke a CSS style to colorize it as well. (I also use this opportunity to organize each result's elements into a more logical order.) As **Figure 7.13** shows, the reason these results are offered is now much clearer.

FIGURE 7.13 The bold and colored highlights, and the improved sorting of the list, make the results relate better to the users search.

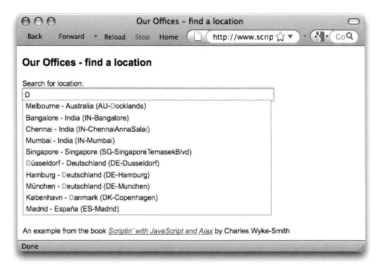

Another default behavior is that selecting a result simply writes it into the text field, and the user has to then submit the form using the Submit button. In this project, I want the selection of a result to immediately take the user to the full information relating to that result.

```
autocomplete.itemSelectEvent.subscribe(function(type,args){

      var office = args[2][0].split(' - ');

      window.location = 'index.php?showlocation=' + office[0];

   });
```

Here I assign a listener function to the `itemSelectEvent` so that the `location` method of the Window object is invoked and requests the `index.php` script again. Selecting a result from the AutoComplete Control (and I'll again use the Madrid office as an example here) now requests the `index.php` script and passes a query string with the name/value pair. The last line of the preceding code resolves to:

```
window.location = 'index.php?showlocation=ES-Madrid'
```

This request of the index page triggers the next step, displaying the information and map of the selected office.

DISPLAYING THE LOCATION INFORMATION— SHOWLOCATION.PHP

Let's see what happens when the `index.php` script runs after the user has made a selection (in this case, the Madrid office) from the results drop-down list. Now the `$_GET` array, which stores the query string data, contains

```
showlocation="ES-Madrid"
```

Earlier in this example, I showed the first part of the PHP-only script called `getlocations.php` that manages the reading and parsing of the CSV file data. This script is included unconditionally (the `include` is not wrapped in an `if` statement) at the very top of the `index.php` script. The rest of the code in that file now comes into play.

```
if(isset($_GET['showlocation'])){

    $location_html = filter_input(INPUT_GET, 'showlocation',

        FILTER_SANITIZE_SPECIAL_CHARS);

    foreach($locations as $loc){

        if($loc['Office']==$location_html){

            $current = $loc;

            break;

        }

    }

}
```

true when the user makes a selection from the AutoComplete

filter out XSS attacks

find the matching location in the $locations array and put its data in the $current variable.

CODE 7.22 autocomplete_n_ maps/getlocations.php

This code displays the location information and map, which is served from Yahoo! using the Yahoo! Maps API, as shown in **Figure 7.14**.

This code tests if there is an element named `showlocations` in the `$_GET` array. At this point, there is, so the value of that variable is then sanitized by the `filter_input` method. This method removes any characters that would only be present in injected code, such as { or <, so it can be safely used by the script. This step is important because this value came directly from a form field and therefore should be treated with suspicion. The sanitized data is then stored in a variable called `location_html`.

In the `for` loop that follows, this variable is then compared with the office name of each location's record in the `$locations` array. When a match is found, that entire record is copied into a variable called `$current` and the process stops. Now all the information for the selected office is in the `$current` variable ready to display.

FIGURE 7.14 When a search result is selected, the information and map for the selected location are displayed.

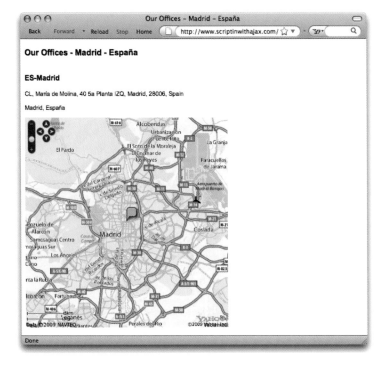

Farther down in the `index.php` script, the presence of the `showloca-tion` element in the `$_GET` array also causes this code to run.

```
if(isset($_GET['showlocation'])){?>

    <?php include('locationdetails.php');?>

<?php }
```

The PHP script `locationdetails.php` then loads and is evaluated. Here's the code in that script:

write out the office, address, and city from the $current array

```php
<h2><?php echo $current['Office'];?></h2>

<p><?php echo $current['Address'];?></p>

<p><?php echo $current['city'].', '.$current['country'];?>
  </p>
```

```html
<div id="map"></div>

<script src="http://yui.yahooapis.com/2.7.0/build/utilities/
  utilities.js"></script>

<script type="text/javascript" src="http://l.yimg.com/d/lib/
  map/js/api/ymapapi_3_8_2_3.js"></script>

<style type="text/css" media="screen">
```

CODE 7.23 autocompete_n_maps/ index.php

```css
#map{

width:450px;

height:450px;

}

#map table,#map td{

border:none;padding:0;

}
</style>
```

```html
<script type="text/javascript">
```

get your own ID to replace this one at https://developer.yahoo.com/ wsregapp

```javascript
var YMAPPID = 'UKjUlvvIkY5ZOCNOZOY9ThFW7luJ8EgWjxg-';
```

get the element that will display the map

```javascript
var map = new YMap(document.getElementById('map'));
```

add zoom and pan controls

```javascript
map.addZoomLong();

map.addPanControl();
```

set central point for map using location data

```javascript
var point = new YGeoPoint(

<?php echo $current['lat'];?>,

<?php echo $current['long'];?>

);
```

set a marker at the point

```javascript
var newMarker = new YMarker(point);
```

show the name of the office when users hover over the marker

```javascript
newMarker.addAutoExpand(<?php echo $current['office'];?>);
```

| add marker to the map | `map.addOverlay(newMarker);` |
| show the map | `map.drawZoomAndCenter(point,7);` |

```
</script>
```

Learn all about the Yahoo! Maps API at developer.yahoo.com/maps.

In the first three lines of this code, the information about the selected office—its name, address, and city—are written into the page. Next, a map of the location is loaded as a 450 pixel square graphic. You can see from the margin notes what each line of code does in providing the correct view and controls on the map.

Note that to use Yahoo! Maps in your own projects, you need a special ID that you include in the request for the map. You can see the one that I generated especially for this project in the code. You can obtain your own ID by registering your project at https://developer.yahoo.com/wsregapp.

Implementing Search Without JavaScript— searchresults.php

You must provide an alternative way to present search results in case the user does not have JavaScript enabled, as the Auto-Complete Control will not function. In such a case, the user will simply type a search string into the form and click the Search button to submit the form. (The Search button is hidden when JavaScript is active.) Because the `name` attribute on the text field is `location`, this causes the query string `location=userEnteredText` to be passed to the script and stored in the `$_GET` array.

In the `index.php` file are the following `if` statements:

You don't have to have the longitude/latitude information to display the map using the Yahoo! Maps API. You can simply pass in the street address.

```
if(!isset($_GET['showlocation'])){

include('searchform.php');

}

if(isset($_GET['location'])){

include('searchresults.php');

}
```

Both these tests evaluate to true, so both `searchform.php` and `searchresults.php` are included in the page. Of course, `searchform.php` is the search form that the user just used to submit the request. The inclusion of the file `searchresults.php` causes the search results to be displayed directly below it, as shown in **Figure 7.15**. Here's the code for that file:

```php
<?php
echo '<ul>';
$location_html = filter_input(INPUT_GET, 'location',
FILTER_SANITIZE_SPECIAL_CHARS);
$needle = '/'.$location_html.'/msi';
$found = false;
foreach($locations as $loc){
if(preg_match($needle,$loc['city']) or
preg_match($needle,$loc['country']) or
preg_match($needle,$loc['Address'])){
echo '<li><a href="index.php?showlocation='.$loc['Office'].
'">'.$loc['city'].' - '.$loc['country'].'</a></li>';
$found = true;
   }
}
if($found == false){
echo '<li>Could not find any location with that name.</li>';
}
echo '</ul>';
?>
```

don't forget to filter inputs!

loop through all locations and test if the city, the country, or the address contains the search term–if so, add a list item with links for each match

open an unordered list

In this code, I first open an unordered list. Then I check the input to ensure that no code-like characters such as { and < are getting through. Then I compare the user-entered string with each office location's name, city, and country. If there is a match, I add a list item with a link inside it. Each link's href links to the results page and includes the office name in its query string so the correct information will load on the results page when the link is clicked. The city name and country name of that office are written into the text for the link so the user can see the location that was found. You can see the results for a search on "Fra" in **Figure 7.15**.

FIGURE 7.15 When JavaScript is off, search results are displayed below the form after it is submitted instead of in the AutoComplete drop-down list as the user types.

It's user friendly to retain the text the user entered in the form. This allows the user to modify what was typed and try to submit the form again. Making a form retain its contents between submissions is called making the form "sticky." To do this, I just set the form's value attribute to the value of the submitted data like this:

```
<input type="text" id="location" name="location" value="<?php
echo ($_GET['location']); ?>">
```

If the user clicks a link, the results page with the location's information and map are displayed in the same way as if the user had selected from the AutoComplete menu, as shown in Figure 7.14.

AutoComplete provides a very simple and positive user experience that belies the complexity of the coding and the data requirements that support it. Using the YUI AutoComplete Control makes a complex task somewhat easier, but as you can see, a fair amount of work is involved. I hope the code I provided for this example will simplify the task of creating your own implementation of this classic Web 2.0 control. At this point, we reach the end of this project and this book.

Summary

The projects in this chapter clearly demonstrated that JavaScript is an additional layer that enhances the foundation of a Web page—a foundation that is created through languages such as PHP on the server, and HTML and CSS in the browser.

The Author Carousel project showed the concept of building links containing a small part of a data set that could later be clicked to request the full data set; the clickable photos of each author enables the user to request all the available information about that author. In making this happen, you saw how PHP was used to create a script that read the data records from JSON files, and built a Web page on the server. As each link in the page was being built, references to the data source (the index numbers of the file array) were embedded in it. When the user clicked a link requesting the full data set, those references were accessed and passed back to the server, and the correct data was located and sent to the browser.

The Yahoo! AutoComplete project showed how to build a number of pages from a template page and how to build and later detect query strings in the URL so that the server could understand the user actions and provide appropriate responses. You also saw how third-party content, in this case Yahoo! Maps, can be accessed through an API and be integrated seamlessly into the page.

In both projects, JavaScript enhanced the user experience in two important ways: by improving communication between the browser and server, and by providing intuitive and easy-to-use interactions.

I hope that this book has helped you understand how JavaScript works and how to write it. Most of all, I hope that you now have the knowledge and confidence to start using JavaScript in the creation of the next generation of online user experiences.

APPENDIX A

Environment

These appendixes are listings of the most important JavaScript objects. I have divided them into four groups: Environment (browser related), Data (data related), Document (DOM related), and Interaction (mouse and keyboard related).

For details on the featured methods, properties, and attributes and examples of their uses, visit: http://w3schools.com/jsref/default.asp or https://developer.mozilla.org/en/Core_JavaScript_1.5_Reference

These appendixes do not list the lower level document objects, such as form and anchor. Details on these objects can also be found at the sites listed above. The author gratefully acknowledges W3Schools (www.w3schools.com), an award-winning e-learning site, for permission to reproduce these tables.

WINDOW OBJECT

The Window object is the top level object in the JavaScript hierarchy.

WINDOW OBJECT METHODS

METHOD	DESCRIPTION	IE	F	O
alert()	Displays an alert box with a message and an OK button	4	1	9
blur()	Removes focus from the current window	4	1	9
clearInterval()	Cancels a timeout set with setInterval()	4	1	9
clearTimeout()	Cancels a timeout set with setTimeout()	4	1	9
close()	Closes the current window	4	1	9
confirm()	Displays a dialog box with a message and an OK and a Cancel button	4	1	9
createPopup()	Creates a pop-up window	4	No	No
focus()	Sets focus to the current window	4	1	9
moveBy()	Moves a window relative to its current position	4	1	9
moveTo()	Moves a window to the specified position	4	1	9
open()	Opens a new browser window	4	1	9
print()	Prints the contents of the current window	5	1	9
prompt()	Displays a dialog box that prompts the user for input	4	1	9
resizeBy()	Resizes a window by the specified pixels	4	1	9
resizeTo()	Resizes a window to the specified width and height	4	1.5	9
scrollBy()	Scrolls the content by the specified number of pixels	4	1	9
scrollTo()	Scrolls the content to the specified coordinates	4	1	9
setInterval()	Evaluates an expression at specified intervals	4	1	9
setTimeout()	Evaluates an expression after a specified number of milliseconds	4	1	9

IE: Internet Explorer, F: Firefox, O: Opera. Table shows earliest versions of these browsers that support each item.

WINDOW OBJECT COLLECTIONS

COLLECTION	DESCRIPTION	IE	F	O
frames[]	Returns all named frames in the window	4	1	9

WINDOW OBJECT PROPERTIES

PROPERTY	DESCRIPTION	IE	F	O
closed	Returns whether or not a window has been closed	4	1	9
defaultStatus	Sets or returns the default text in the statusbar of the window	4	No	9
document	See Document object	4	1	9
history	See History object	4	1	9
length	Sets or returns the number of frames in the window	4	1	9
location	See Location object	4	1	9
name	Sets or returns the name of the window	4	1	9
opener	Returns a reference to the window that created the window	4	1	9
outerHeight	Sets or returns the outer height of a window	No	1	No
outerWidth	Sets or returns the outer width of a window	No	1	No
pageXOffset	Sets or returns the X position of the current page in relation to the upper left corner of a window's display area	No	No	No
pageYOffset	Sets or returns the Y position of the current page in relation to the upper left corner of a window's display area	No	No	No
parent	Returns the parent window	4	1	9
personalbar	Sets whether or not the browser's personal bar (or directories bar) should be visible			
scrollbars	Sets whether or not the scrollbars should be visible			
self	Returns a reference to the current window	4	1	9
status	Sets the text in the statusbar of a window	4	No	9
statusbar	Sets whether or not the browser's statusbar should be visible			
toolbar	Sets whether or not the browser's tool bar is visible or not (can only be set before the window is opened and you must have UniversalBrowserWrite privilege)			
top	Returns the topmost ancestor window	4	1	9

IE: Internet Explorer, F: Firefox, O: Opera.

HISTORY OBJECT

The History object is automatically created by the JavaScript runtime engine and consists of an array of URLs that the user has visited within a browser window. The History object is part of the Window object and is accessed through the window.history property.

HISTORY OBJECT PROPERTIES

PROPERTY	DESCRIPTION	IE	F	O
length	Returns the number of elements in the history list	4	1	9

HISTORY OBJECT METHODS

METHOD	DESCRIPTION	IE	F	O
back()	Loads the previous URL in the history list	4	1	9
forward()	Loads the next URL in the history list	4	1	9
go()	Loads a specific page in the history list	4	1	9

LOCATION OBJECT

The Location object is automatically created by the JavaScript runtime engine and contains information about the current URL. Example: Send a user to a new location. The Location object is part of the Window object and is accessed through the window.location property.

LOCATION OBJECT PROPERTIES

PROPERTY	DESCRIPTION	IE	F	O
hash	Sets or returns the URL from the hash sign (#)	4	1	9
host	Sets or returns the hostname and port number of the current URL	4	1	9
hostname	Sets or returns the hostname of the current URL	4	1	9
href	Sets or returns the entire URL	4	1	9
pathname	Sets or returns the path of the current URL	4	1	9
port	Sets or returns the port number of the current URL	4	1	9
protocol	Sets or returns the protocol of the current URL	4	1	9
search	Sets or returns the URL from the question mark (?)	4	1	9

LOCATION OBJECT METHODS

METHOD	DESCRIPTION	IE	F	O
assign()	Loads a new document	4	1	9
reload()	Reloads the current document	4	1	9
replace()	Replaces the current document with a new one	4	1	9

IE: Internet Explorer, F: Firefox, O: Opera.

NAVIGATOR OBJECT

The Navigator object is automatically created by the JavaScript runtime engine and contains information about the client browser.

NAVIGATOR OBJECT COLLECTIONS

COLLECTION	DESCRIPTION	IE	F	O
plugins[]	Returns a reference to all embedded objects in the document	4	1	9

NAVIGATOR OBJECT PROPERTIES

PROPERTY	DESCRIPTION	IE	F	O
appCodeName	Returns the code name of the browser	4	1	9
appMinorVersion	Returns the minor version of the browser	4	No	No
appName	Returns the name of the browser	4	1	9
appVersion	Returns the platform and version of the browser	4	1	9
browserLanguage	Returns the current browser language	4	No	9
cookieEnabled	Returns a Boolean value that specifies whether cookies are enabled in the browser	4	1	9
cpuClass	Returns the CPU class of the browser's system	4	No	No
onLine	Returns a Boolean value that specifies whether the system is in offline mode	4	No	No
platform	Returns the operating system platform	4	1	9
systemLanguage	Returns the default language used by the OS	4	No	No
userAgent	Returns the value of the user-agent header sent by the client to the server	4	1	9
userLanguage	Returns the OS' natural language setting	4	No	9

NAVIGATOR OBJECT METHODS

METHOD	DESCRIPTION	IE	F	O
javaEnabled()	Specifies whether or not the browser has Java enabled	4	1	9
taintEnabled()	Specifies whether or not the browser has data tainting enabled	4	1	9

IE: Internet Explorer, F: Firefox, O: Opera.

JAVASCRIPT FUNCTION REFERENCE

The top-level properties and functions can be used on all of the built-in JavaScript objects.

TOP-LEVEL FUNCTIONS

FUNCTION	DESCRIPTION	FF	IE
decodeURI()	Decodes an encoded URI	1	5.5
decodeURIComponent()	Decodes an encoded URI component	1	5.5
encodeURI()	Encodes a string as a URI	1	5.5
encodeURIComponent()	Encodes a string as a URI component	1	5.5
escape()	Encodes a string	1	3
eval()	Evaluates a string and executes it as if it was script code	1	3
isFinite()	Checks if a value is a finite number	1	4
isNaN()	Checks if a value is not a number	1	3
Number()	Converts an object's value to a number	1	
parseFloat()	Parses a string and returns a floating point number	1	3
parseInt()	Parses a string and returns an integer	1	3
String()	Converts an object's value to a string	1	
unescape()	Decodes a string encoded by escape()	1	3

TOP-LEVEL PROPERTIES

PROPERTY	DESCRIPTION	FF	IE
Infinity	A numeric value that represents positive or negative infinity	1	4
NaN	Indicates that a value is "Not a Number"	1	4
undefined	Indicates that a variable has not been assigned a value	1	5.5

FF: Firefox, IE: Internet Explorer

APPENDIX B

Data

ARRAY OBJECT

The Array object is used to store multiple values in a single variable. Syntax for creating an Array object:

```
var myCars=new Array("Saab","Volvo","BMW")
```

To access and to set values inside an array, you must use the index numbers as follows:

* myCars[0] is the first element
* myCars[1] is the second element
* myCars[2] is the third element

ARRAY OBJECT PROPERTIES

PROPERTY	DESCRIPTION	FF	IE
constructor	Returns a reference to the array function that created the object	1	4
index	Returns zero based index of the match in the string	1	4
input	Returns original string against which regular expression was matched	1	4
length	Sets or returns the number of elements in an array	1	4
prototype	Allows you to add properties and methods to the object	1	4

ARRAY OBJECT METHODS

METHOD	DESCRIPTION	FF	IE
concat()	Joins two or more arrays and returns the result	1	4
join()	Puts all the elements of an array into a string. The elements are separated by a specified delimiter	1	4
pop()	Removes and returns the last element of an array	1	5.5
push()	Adds one or more elements to the end of an array and returns the new length	1	5.5
reverse()	Reverses the order of the elements in an array	1	4
shift()	Removes and returns the first element of an array	1	5.5
slice()	Returns selected elements from an existing array	1	4
sort()	Sorts the elements of an array	1	4
splice()	Removes and adds new elements to an array	1	5.5
toSource()	Represents the source code of an object	1	-
toString()	Converts an array to a string and returns the result	1	4
unshift()	Adds one or more elements to the beginning of an array and returns the new length	1	6
valueOf()	Returns the primitive value of an Array object	1	4

FF: Firefox, IE: Internet Explorer

BOOLEAN OBJECT

The Boolean object represents two values: "true" or "false." Syntax for creating a Boolean object:

```
var myBool=new Boolean(value)
```

Note: If the value parameter is omitted, or is 0, -0, null, "", false, undefined, or NaN, the object is set to false. Otherwise it is set to true (even with the string "false").

BOOLEAN OBJECT PROPERTIES

PROPERTY	DESCRIPTION	FF	IE
constructor	Returns a reference to the Boolean function that created the object	1	4
prototype	Allows you to add properties and methods to the object	1	4

BOOLEAN OBJECT METHODS

Method	Description	FF	IE
toSource()	Returns the source code of the object	1	-
toString()	Converts a Boolean value to a string and returns the result	1	4
valueOf()	Returns the primitive value of a Boolean object	1	4

FF: Firefox, IE: Internet Explorer

DATE OBJECT

The Date object is used to work with dates and times. Syntax for creating a Date object:

```
var myDate=new Date()
```

Note: The Date object will automatically hold the current date and time as its initial value!

DATE OBJECT PROPERTIES

PROPERTY	DESCRIPTION	FF	IE
constructor	Returns a reference to the Date function that created the object	1	4
prototype	Allows you to add properties and methods to the object	1	4

DATE OBJECT METHODS

METHOD	DESCRIPTION	FF	IE
Date()	Returns today's date and time	1	3
getDate()	Returns the day of the month from a Date object (from 1-31)	1	3
getDay()	Returns the day of the week from a Date object (from 0-6)	1	3
getFullYear()	Returns the year, as a four-digit number, from a Date object	1	4
getHours()	Returns the hour of a Date object (from 0-23)	1	3
getMilliseconds()	Returns the milliseconds of a Date object (from 0-999)	1	4
getMinutes()	Returns the minutes of a Date object (from 0-59)	1	3
getMonth()	Returns the month from a Date object (from 0-11)	1	3
getSeconds()	Returns the seconds of a Date object (from 0-59)	1	3
getTime()	Returns the number of milliseconds since midnight Jan 1, 1970	1	3
getTimezoneOffset()	Returns the difference in minutes between local time and Greenwich Mean Time (GMT)	1	3
getUTCDate()	Returns the day of the month from a Date object according to universal time (from 1-31)	1	4
getUTCDay()	Returns the day of the week from a Date object according to universal time (from 0-6)	1	4
getUTCMonth()	Returns the month from a Date object according to universal time (from 0-11)	1	4

FF: Firefox, IE: Internet Explorer

METHOD	DESCRIPTION	FF	IE
getUTCFullYear()	Returns the four-digit year from a Date object according to universal time	1	4
getUTCHours()	Returns the hour of a Date object according to universal time (from 0-23)	1	4
getUTCMinutes()	Returns the minutes of a Date object according to universal time (from 0-59)	1	4
getUTCSeconds()	Returns the seconds of a Date object according to universal time (from 0-59)	1	4
getUTCMilliseconds()	Returns the milliseconds of a Date object according to universal time (from 0-999)	1	4
getYear()	Returns the year, as a two-digit or a three/four-digit number, depending on the browser. Use getFullYear() instead !!	1	3
parse()	Takes a date string and returns the number of milliseconds since midnight of January 1, 1970	1	3
setDate()	Sets the day of the month in a Date object (from 1-31)	1	3
setFullYear()	Sets the year in a Date object (four digits)	1	4
setHours()	Sets the hour in a Date object (from 0-23)	1	3
setMilliseconds()	Sets the milliseconds in a Date object (from 0-999)	1	4
setMinutes()	Set the minutes in a Date object (from 0-59)	1	3
setMonth()	Sets the month in a Date object (from 0-11)	1	3
setSeconds()	Sets the seconds in a Date object (from 0-59)	1	3
setTime()	Calculates a date and time by adding or subtracting a specified number of milliseconds to/from midnight January 1, 1970	1	3
setUTCDate()	Sets the day of the month in a Date object according to universal time (from 1-31)	1	4
setUTCMonth()	Sets the month in a Date object according to universal time (from 0-11)	1	4
setUTCFullYear()	Sets the year in a Date object according to universal time (four digits)	1	4
setUTCHours()	Sets the hour in a Date object according to universal time (from 0-23)	1	4
setUTCMinutes()	Set the minutes in a Date object according to universal time (from 0-59)	1	4
setUTCSeconds()	Set the seconds in a Date object according to universal time (from 0-59)	1	4
setUTCMilliseconds()	Sets the milliseconds in a Date object according to universal time (from 0-999)	1	4
setYear()	Sets the year in the Date object (two or four digits). Use setFullYear() instead !!	1	3
toDateString()	Returns the date portion of a Date object in readable form		
toGMTString()	Converts a Date object, according to Greenwich time, to a string. Use toUTCString() instead !!	1	3
toLocaleDateString()	Converts a Date object, according to local time, to a string and returns the date portion	1	4

METHOD	DESCRIPTION	FF	IE
toLocaleTimeString()	Converts a Date object, according to local time, to a string and returns the time portion	1	4
toLocaleString()	Converts a Date object, according to local time, to a string	1	3
toSource()	Represents the source code of an object	1	-
toString()	Converts a Date object to a string	1	4
toTimeString()	Returns the time portion of a Date object in readable form		
toUTCString()	Converts a Date object, according to universal time, to a string	1	4
UTC()	Takes a date and returns the number of milliseconds since midnight of January 1, 1970 according to universal time	1	3
valueOf()	Returns the primitive value of a Date object	1	4

FF: Firefox, IE: Internet Explorer

MATH OBJECT

The Math object allows you to perform mathematical tasks.

Syntax for using properties/methods of Math:

```
var pi_value=Math.PI; var sqrt_value=Math.sqrt(16);
```

Note: Math is not a constructor. All properties and methods of Math can be called by using Math as an object without creating it.

MATH OBJECT PROPERTIES

PROPERTY	DESCRIPTION	FF	IE
E	Returns Euler's constant (approx. 2.718)	1	3
LN2	Returns the natural logarithm of 2 (approx. 0.693)	1	3
LN10	Returns the natural logarithm of 10 (approx. 2.302)	1	3
LOG2E	Returns the base-2 logarithm of E (approx. 1.442)	1	3
LOG10E	Returns the base-10 logarithm of E (approx. 0.434)	1	3
PI	Returns PI (approx. 3.14159)	1	3
SQRT1_2	Returns the square root of 1/2 (approx. 0.707)	1	3
SQRT2	Returns the square root of 2 (approx. 1.414)	1	3

FF: Firefox, IE: Internet Explorer

MATH OBJECT METHODS

METHOD	DESCRIPTION	FF	IE
abs(x)	Returns the absolute value of a number	1	3
acos(x)	Returns the arccosine of a number	1	3
asin(x)	Returns the arcsine of a number	1	3
atan(x)	Returns the arctangent of x as a numeric value between -PI/2 and PI/2 radians	1	3
atan2(y,x)	Returns the angle theta of an (x,y) point as a numeric value between -PI and PI radians	1	3
ceil(x)	Returns the value of a number rounded upwards to the nearest integer	1	3
cos(x)	Returns the cosine of a number	1	3
exp(x)	Returns the value of Ex	1	3
floor(x)	Returns the value of a number rounded downwards to the nearest integer	1	3
log(x)	Returns the natural logarithm (base E) of a number	1	3
max(x,y)	Returns the number with the highest value of x and y	1	3
min(x,y)	Returns the number with the lowest value of x and y	1	3
pow(x,y)	Returns the value of x to the power of y	1	3
random()	Returns a random number between 0 and 1	1	3
round(x)	Rounds a number to the nearest integer	1	3
sin(x)	Returns the sine of a number	1	3
sqrt(x)	Returns the square root of a number	1	3
tan(x)	Returns the tangent of an angle	1	3
toSource()	Represents the source code of an object	1	-
valueOf()	Returns the primitive value of a Math object	1	4

FF: Firefox, IE: Internet Explorer

REGEXP OBJECT

The regular expression object describes a pattern of characters.

Syntax for creating a RegExp object:

`var txt=new RegExp(pattern,attributes);` or `var txt=/pattern/attributes;`

pattern specifies the pattern of the regular expression

attributes specifies global ("g"), case-insensitive ("i"), and multiline matches ("m")

REGEXP OBJECT PROPERTIES

PROPERTY	DESCRIPTION	FF	IE
global	Specifies if the "g" modifier is set	1	4
ignoreCase	Specifies if the "i" modifier is set	1	4
input	The string on which the pattern match is performed	1	4
lastIndex	An integer specifying the index at which to start the next match	1	4
lastMatch	The last matched characters	1	4
lastParen	The last matched parenthesized substring	1	4
leftContext	The substring in front of the characters most recently matched	1	4
multiline	Specifies if the "m" modifier is set	1	4
prototype	Allows you to add properties and methods to the object	1	4
rightContext	The substring after the characters most recently matched	1	4
source	The text used for pattern matching	1	4

REGEXP OBJECT METHODS

METHOD	DESCRIPTION	FF	IE
compile()	Change the regular expression	1	4
exec()	Search a string for a specified value. Returns the found value and remembers the position	1	4
test()	Search a string for a specified value. Returns true or false	1	4

FF: Firefox, IE: Internet Explorer

STRING OBJECT METHODS THAT SUPPORTS REGULAR EXPRESSIONS

METHOD	DESCRIPTION	FF	IE
search()	Search a string for a specified value. Returns the position of the value	1	4
match()	Search a string for a specified value. Returns an array of the found value(s)	1	4
replace()	Replace characters with other characters	1	4
split()	Split a string into an array of strings	1	4

REGEXP MODIFIERS

MODIFIER	DESCRIPTION	FF	IE
i	Perform case-insensitive matching	1	4
g	Perform a global match. Find all matches (do not stop after the first match)	1	4
gi	Perform a global case-insensitive match. Find all matches (do not stop after the first match)	1	4
m	Perform multiline matching	1	4

REGEXP MODIFIERS–POSITION MATCHING

MODIFIER	DESCRIPTION	FF	IE
^	Get a match at the beginning of a string	1	4
$	Get a match at the end of a string	1	4
\b	Word boundary. Get a match at the beginning or end of a word in the string	1	4
\B	Non-word boundary. Get a match when it is not at the beginning or end of a word in the string	1	4
?=	A positive look ahead. Get a match if a string is followed by a specific string	1	4
?!	A negative look ahead. Get a match if a string is not followed by a specific string	1	4

REGEXP MODIFIER–CHARACTER CLASSES

MODIFIER	DESCRIPTION	FF	IE
[xyz]	Find any character in the specified character set	1	4
[^xyz]	Find any character not in the specified character set	1	4
. (dot)	Find any character except newline or line terminator	1	4
\w	Find any alphanumeric character including the underscore	1	4
\W	Find any non-word character	1	4
\d	Find any single digit	1	4
\D	Find any non-digit	1	4
\s	Find any single space character	1	4
\S	Find any single non-space character	1	4

REGEXP MODIFIER—LITERALS

MODIFIER	DESCRIPTION	FF	IE
\0	Find a NULL character	1	4
\n	Find a new line character	1	4
\f	Find a form feed character	1	4
\r	Find a carriage return character	1	4
\t	Find a tab character	1	4
\v	Find a vertical tab character	1	4
\xxx	Find the ASCII character expressed by the octal number xxx	1	4
\xdd	Find the ASCII character expressed by the hex number dd	1	4
\uxxxx	Find the ASCII character expressed by the UNICODE xxxx	1	4

REGEXP MODIFIERS—REPETITION

MODIFIER	DESCRIPTION	FF	IE
{x}	Finds the exact (x) number of the regular expression grouped together	1	4
{x,}	Finds the exact (x) or more number of the regular expression grouped together	1	4
{x,y}	Finds between x and y number of the regular expression grouped together	1	4
?	Finds zero or one occurrence of the regular expression	1	4
*	Finds zero or more occurrences of the regular expression	1	4
+	Finds one or more occurrences of the regular expression	1	4

REGEXP MODIFIERS—GROUPING

MODIFIER	DESCRIPTION	FF	IE
( )	Finds the group of characters inside the parentheses and stores the matched string	1	4
(?:)	Finds the group of characters inside the parentheses but does not store the matched string	1	4
|	Combines clauses into one regular expression and then matches any of the individual clauses. Similar to "OR" statement	1	4

REGEXP MODIFIERS—BACK REFERENCE

MODIFIER	DESCRIPTION	FF	IE
( )\n	Back reference. Uses the stored matched string. i.e. from the ( ) modifier	1	4

FF: Firefox, IE: Internet Explorer

STRING OBJECT

The String object lets you work with text.

Syntax for creating a String object:

```
var myStr=new String(string);
```

STRING OBJECT PROPERTIES

PROPERTY	DESCRIPTION	FF	IE
constructor	A reference to the function that created the object	1	4
length	Returns the number of characters in a string	1	3
prototype	Allows you to add properties and methods to the object	1	4

STRING OBJECT METHODS

METHOD	DESCRIPTION	FF	IE
anchor()	Creates an HTML anchor	1	3
big()	Displays a string in a big font	1	3
blink()	Displays a blinking string	1	
bold()	Displays a string in bold	1	3
charAt()	Returns the character at a specified position	1	3
charCodeAt()	Returns the Unicode of the character at a specified position	1	4
concat()	Joins two or more strings	1	4
fixed()	Displays a string as teletype text	1	3
fontcolor()	Displays a string in a specified color	1	3
fontsize()	Displays a string in a specified size	1	3
fromCharCode()	Takes the specified Unicode values and returns a string	1	4
indexOf()	Returns the position of the first occurrence of a specified string value in a string	1	3
italics()	Displays a string in italic	1	3
lastIndexOf()	Returns the position of the last occurrence of a specified string value, searching backwards from the specified position in a string	1	3
link()	Displays a string as a hyperlink	1	3
match()	Searches for a specified value in a string	1	4
replace()	Replaces some characters with some other characters in a string	1	4

FF: Firefox, IE: Internet Explorer

METHOD	DESCRIPTION	FF	IE
search()	Searches a string for a specified value	1	4
slice()	Extracts a part of a string and returns the extracted part in a new string	1	4
small()	Displays a string in a small font	1	3
split()	Splits a string into an array of strings	1	4
strike()	Displays a string with a strikethrough	1	3
sub()	Displays a string as subscript	1	3
substr()	Extracts a specified number of characters in a string, from a start index	1	4
substring()	Extracts the characters in a string between two specified indices	1	3
sup()	Displays a string as superscript	1	3
toLowerCase()	Displays a string in lowercase letters	1	3
toUpperCase()	Displays a string in uppercase letters	1	3
toSource()	Represents the source code of an object		

FF: Firefox, IE: Internet Explorer

NUMBER OBJECT

The Number object is an object wrapper for primitive numeric values.

Syntax for creating a Number object:

```
var myNum=new Number(number);
```

Note: If the number parameter cannot be converted into a number, it returns NaN

NUMBER OBJECT PROPERTIES

PROPERTY	DESCRIPTION	FF	IE
constructor	Returns a reference to the Number function that created the object	1	4
MAX_VALUE	Returns the largest possible value in JavaScript	1	4
MIN_VALUE	Returns the smallest possible value in JavaScript	1	4
NaN	Represents "Not-a-number" value	1	4
NEGATIVE_INFINITY	Represents a value that is less than MIN_VALUE	1	4
POSITIVE_INFINITY	Represents a value that is greater than MAX_VALUE	1	4
prototype	Allows you to add properties and methods to the object	1	4

NUMBER OBJECT METHODS

METHOD	DESCRIPTION	FF	IE
toExponential()	Converts the value of the object into an exponential notation	1	5.5
toFixed()	Formats a number to the specified number of decimals	1	5.5
toLocaleString()			
toPrecision()	Converts a number into a number with a specified number of digits	1	5.5
toString()	Converts the Number object into a string	1	4
valueOf()	Returns the value of the Number object	1	4

FF: Firefox, IE: Internet Explorer

APPENDIX C

Document

DOCUMENT OBJECT

The Document object represents the entire HTML document and can be used to access all elements in a page. The Document object is part of the Window object and is accessed through the window.document property.

DOCUMENT OBJECT COLLECTIONS

COLLECTION	DESCRIPTION	IE	F	O	W3C
anchors[]	Returns a reference to all Anchor objects in the document	4	1	9	Yes
forms[]	Returns a reference to all Form objects in the document	4	1	9	Yes
images[]	Returns a reference to all Image objects in the document	4	1	9	Yes
links[]	Returns a reference to all Area and Link objects in the document	4	1	9	Yes

DOCUMENT OBJECT PROPERTIES

PROPERTY	DESCRIPTION	IE	F	O	W3C
body	Gives direct access to the <body> element				
cookie	Sets or returns all cookies associated with the current document	4	1	9	Yes
domain	Returns the domain name for the current document	4	1	9	Yes
lastModified	Returns the date and time a document was last modified	4	1	No	No
referrer	Returns the URL of the document that loaded the current document	4	1	9	Yes
title	Returns the title of the current document	4	1	9	Yes
URL	Returns the URL of the current document	4	1	9	Yes

IE: Internet Explorer, F: Firefox, O: Opera, W3C: World Wide Web Consortium (Internet Standard).

DOM METHODS–GETTERS AND SETTERS

GETTERS FOR DOCUMENT ELEMENTS

CODE	PURPOSE	NOTES
document.getElementById('id')	Gets the element with the ID 'id'	myElement=document. getElementById ('menu')
getElementByTagName('tagname')	Gets all the elements with the tag name 'tagname'	myLinks=getElementBy TagName('a')

GETTERS FOR ATTRIBUTES AND TEXT NODES

CODE	PURPOSE	NOTES
node.nodeName	Returns the name of the node (the element's name or #textNode)	
node.nodeValue	Returns the type of the node (1=element, 3=text)	
node.nodeType	Returns the type of the node (1=element, 3=text)	
node.getAttribute('attribute')	Gets the value of the attribute with the name 'attribute'	myPicAttribute=node. getAttribute('alt')

GETTERS FOR ADJACENT ELEMENTS

CODE	PURPOSE	NOTES
node.previousSibling	Gets the previous sibling of 'node'	
node.nextSibling	Gets the next sibling of 'node'	
node.nodeChildren	Creates an array of all child objects of 'node'	
node.firstChild	Gets the first child of 'node'	
node.lastChild	Gets the last child of 'node'	
node.parentNode	Gets the parent of 'node'	

SETTERS—CREATING, INSERTING AND DELETING ELEMENTS

CODE	PURPOSE	NOTES
`node.setAttribute('attribute', 'value')`	Sets the value of the attribute with the name 'attribute'	This method is unreliable in IE. It's safer in all cases to set the object directly with obj. property=value
`document.createElement('elementName')`	Creates a new element with the name 'element-Name'	
`document.createTextNode('Some text')`	Creates a new text node containing the text 'Some text'	
`newNode=node.cloneNode(boolean)`	Make clone of node in new node, including any child nodes if boolean=TRUE	
`node.appendChild(newNode)`	Appends newNode as last child of node	
`node.insertBefore(newNode, oldNode)`	Inserts newNode as a new child node of node before oldNode	
`node.removeChild(oldNode)`	Removes child oldNode from node	
`node.replaceChild(newNoode, oldNode)`	replaces child node newNode of node with node newNode	
`element.innerHTML`	Reads or writes all HTML within the element as a string, including all child elements	

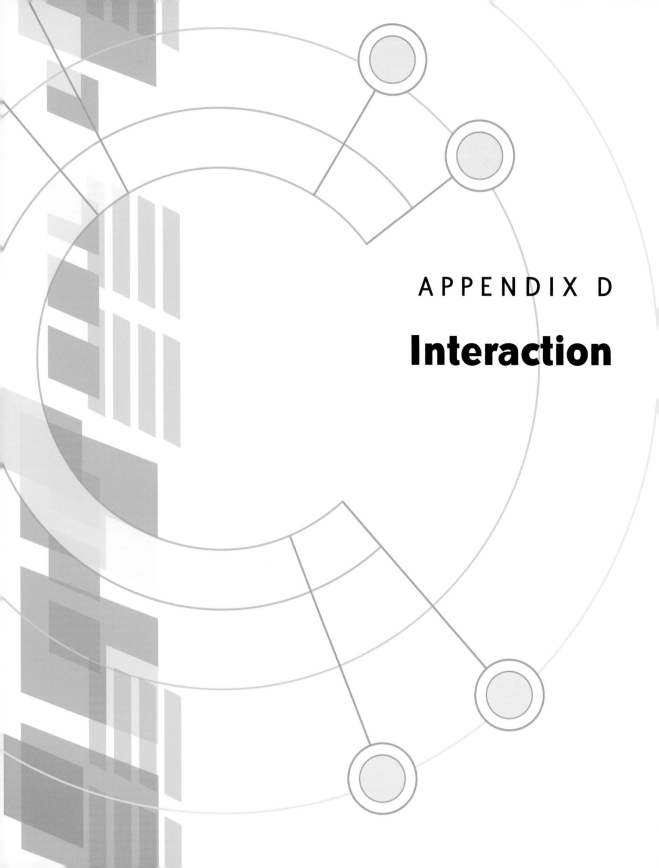

APPENDIX D

Interaction

HTML ASCII REFERENCE

ASCII is a 7-bit character set containing 128 characters. It contains the numbers from 0-9, the upper-case and lowercase English letters from A to Z, and some special characters. The character-sets used in modern computers, HTML, and Internet are all based on ASCII. The following table lists the 128 ASCII characters.

ASCII PRINTABLE CHARACTERS

ASCII CHARACTER	KEYCODE	DESCRIPTION
	32	space
!	33	exclamation mark
"	34	quotation mark
#	35	number sign
$	36	dollar sign
%	37	percent sign
&	38	ampersand
'	39	apostrophe
(	40	left parenthesis
)	41	right parenthesis
*	42	asterisk
+	43	plus sign
,	44	comma
-	45	hyphen
.	46	period
/	47	slash
0	48	digit 0
1	49	digit 1
2	50	digit 2
3	51	digit 3

ASCII CHARACTER	KEYCODE	DESCRIPTION
4	52	digit 4
5	53	digit 5
6	54	digit 6
7	55	digit 7
8	56	digit 8
9	57	digit 9
:	58	colon
;	59	semicolon
<	60	less-than
=	61	equals-to
>	62	greater-than
?	63	question mark
@	64	at sign
A	65	uppercase A
B	66	uppercase B
C	67	uppercase C
D	68	uppercase D
E	69	uppercase E
F	70	uppercase F
G	71	uppercase G
H	72	uppercase H
I	73	uppercase I
J	74	uppercase J
K	75	uppercase K
L	76	uppercase L
M	77	uppercase M
N	78	uppercase N
O	79	uppercase O
P	80	uppercase P
Q	81	uppercase Q

ASCII CHARACTER	KEYCODE	DESCRIPTION
R	82	uppercase R
S	83	uppercase S
T	84	uppercase T
U	85	uppercase U
V	86	uppercase V
W	87	uppercase W
X	88	uppercase X
Y	89	uppercase Y
Z	90	uppercase Z
[	91	left square bracket
\	92	backslash
]	93	right square bracket
^	94	caret
_	95	underscore
`	96	grave accent
a	97	lowercase a
b	98	lowercase b
c	99	lowercase c
d	100	lowercase d
e	101	lowercase e
f	102	lowercase f
g	103	lowercase g
h	104	lowercase h
i	105	lowercase i
j	106	lowercase j
k	107	lowercase k
l	108	lowercase l
m	109	lowercase m
n	110	lowercase n
o	111	lowercase o

ASCII CHARACTER	HTML ENTITY CODE	DESCRIPTION
p	112	lowercase p
q	113	lowercase q
r	114	lowercase r
s	115	lowercase s
t	116	lowercase t
u	117	lowercase u
v	118	lowercase v
w	119	lowercase w
x	120	lowercase x
y	121	lowercase y
z	122	lowercase z
{	123	left curly brace
|	124	vertical bar
}	125	right curly brace
~	126	tilde

JAVASCRIPT EVENT REFERENCE

Events are normally used in combination with functions, and the function will not be executed before the event occurs.

EVENT HANDLERS

New to HTML 4.0 was the ability to let HTML events trigger actions in the browser, like starting a JavaScript when a user clicks on an HTML element. Below is a list of the attributes that can be inserted into HTML tags to define event actions.

ATTRIBUTE	THE EVENT OCCURS WHEN...	FF	N	IE
onabort	Loading of an image is interrupted	1	3	4
onblur	An element loses focus	1	2	3
onchange	The user changes the content of a field	1	2	3
onclick	Mouse clicks an object	1	2	3
ondblclick	Mouse double-clicks an object	1	4	4
onerror	An error occurs when loading a document or an image	1	3	4
onfocus	An element gets focus	1	2	3
onkeydown	A keyboard key is pressed	1	4	3
onkeypress	A keyboard key is pressed or held down	1	4	3
onkeyup	A keyboard key is released	1	4	3
onload	A page or an image is finished loading	1	2	3
onmousedown	A mouse button is pressed	1	4	4
onmousemove	The mouse is moved	1	6	3
onmouseout	The mouse is moved off an element	1	4	4
onmouseover	The mouse is moved over an element	1	2	3
onmouseup	A mouse button is released	1	4	4
onreset	The reset button is clicked	1	3	4
onresize	A window or frame is resized	1	4	4
onselect	Text is selected	1	2	3
onsubmit	The submit button is clicked	1	2	3
onunload	The user exits the page	1	2	3

FF: Firefox, N: Netscape, IE: Internet Explorer

Index

  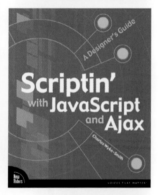